Plants & Animals

A special collection from the World of Wonder series

Plants & Animals

A special collection from the World of Wonder series

By Laurie Triefeldt

Quill Driver Books

Sanger, California

Copyright © 2008 by Laurie Triefeldt. All rights reserved. No part of this book may be reproduced in any form or by any electronic or mechanical means including information storage and retrieval systems without permission in writing from the publisher, except by a reviewer, who may quote brief passages in a review.

Printed in China

Published by Quill Driver Books/Word Dancer Press, Inc.
1254 Commerce Way
Sanger, California 93657
559-876-2170 • 1-800-497-4909 • FAX 559-876-2180

QuillDriverBooks.com
Info@QuillDriverBooks.com

Quill Driver Books' titles may be purchased in quantity at special discounts for educational, fund-raising, training, business, or promotional use. Please contact Special Markets, Quill Driver Books/Word Dancer Press, Inc., at the above address, toll-free at 1-800-497-4909, or by e-mail: Info@QuillDriverBooks.com

Quill Driver Books/Word Dancer Press, Inc. project cadre:
Doris Hall, Stephen Blake Mettee, Carlos Olivas

Quill Driver Books and colophon are trademarks of
Quill Driver Books/Word Dancer Press, Inc.

First printing

ISBN 1-884956-72-6 • 978-1884956-72-0

To order another copy of this book, please call 1-800-497-4909

Library of Congress Cataloging-in-Publication Data

Triefeldt, Laurie, 1960-
  World of wonder. Plants and animals / by Laurie Triefeldt.
    p. cm.
  ISBN-13: 978-1-884956-72-0 (hardcover)
  ISBN-10: 1-884956-72-6 (hardcover)
  1. Animals. 2. Plants. I. Title.
QL45.2.T75 2008
570—dc22

2007024896

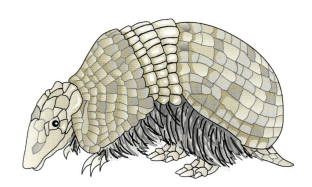

For Coco Bean

Contents

Animal Homes 1	Mythical Creatures 43
Anteaters, Armadillos, and Sloths 2	Night Creatures 44
Bats 3	Oceans 45
Bears 4	Night Hunters 49
Beetles 5	Pandas 50
Big Cats 6	Parrots 51
Biodiversity 7	Peguins 52
Bugs 8	The Rise of Mammals 53
Cactuses 9	Prehistoric Oceans 54
Camels 10	Primates 55
Hungry Plants 11	Prosimians 56
The Domestic Cat 12	Anthropoids 57
Conifers 13	Hominoids 58
Crocodiles 14	Rabbits and Hares 59
Deserts 15	Tropical Rainforest 60
Dinosaurs 16	Rats and Rodents 64
The Rise of Dinosaurs 17	Coral Reefs 65
The Jurassic Period 18	Reindeers 66
The Cretaceous Period 19	Salamanders 67
Dogs 20	Sargasso Sea 68
Dolphins 21	Scorpions 69
Dragons 22	Seals and Sea Lions 70
Earth Day 23	Seashells 71
Eggs 24	Life at the Seashore 72
Elephants 25	Sharks 73
Endangered Species 26	Shorebirds 74
The Florida Everglades 27	Snakes 75
Flightless Birds 28	Spiders 76
The Language of Flowers 29	Squirrels 77
Frogs and Toads 30	Swamp, Marsh, and Bog 78
The Galapagos Islands 31	Swans 79
Giraffes 32	Tigers 80
Grasslands 33	Trees 81
All About Groundhogs 34	Trout 82
Hippos 35	Turtles and Tortoises 83
Horses 36	Underfoot 84
Koalas 37	Venomous Animals 85
Lemurs 38	Vultures 86
Lions 39	Weeds & Wildflowers 87
Marsupials 40	Whales 88
Migration 41	Whaling 89
Mushrooms 42	Wolves 90
	Index 91

Burrowers

Animals that dig (burrow) holes to make a home are called burrowers. Some, like prairie dogs and ants, dig in the earth, making elaborate tunnels and rooms. Others, like the woodpecker burrow into trees. Ocean creatures, like the sea urchin, dig out homes in the sand.

Groundhogs are also known as woodchucks. Unlike their cousin the prairie dog, groundhogs prefer to live alone.

Groundhogs live two to four feet underground in **dens** or **burrows** that consist of several tunnels and rooms. They like to build summer dens near sunny open fields and where the food supply is plentiful. Winter dens are often near dry wooded areas. Sometimes they will dig a burrow under a barn or shed. You can spot a groundhog den by looking for the pile of dirt that often marks the main entrance.

An **ant colony** or city has many rooms and tunnels. Each chamber has a purpose, a room for eggs, a room for larvae and for pupae in cocoons. Some ants live in inside dead trees. Your house can also be a home for ants.

Trapdoor spiders There are about 20 species of trapdoor spiders. They live in burrows with trapdoor entrances. These spiders hunt at night, waiting for prey to approach.

Underwater houses

Many animals that live in the water also build homes there. The tropical "well-digger" jawfish digs a tunnel in the ocean floor and lines it with stones and pebbles. Many other fish build under water nests and some air breathing creatures like the water spider and the beaver prefer water homes.

Water spiders make silk nests underwater that they fill with air bubbles. The air-filled bell is anchored underwater by spider threads. Water spiders leave the nest only to catch food or get more air for the bell. They are native to Europe and Asia.

The stickleback is a freshwater fish that constructs a nest that looks like a lot like a bird's nest. The male secretes a glue-like substance which is used to cement leaves and roots into a nest.

ANIMAL HOMES

Real estate agents often quote the mantra "location, location, location" as the most important thing to consider when choosing a home. The saying holds true, even in the animal world. Where an animal lives can be very important to survival and (like people) they need homes that protect them from the elements and predators. Many animals are talented architects and build their homes, others borrow or share dwellings, some find homes in the natural habitat around them.

Garden spider's web
It is not unusual to spot an orb web in the garden or stretched across a pathway. Here is how those intricate webs get there.

| The spider spins a Y-shaped frame between two objects. | Air currents help the spider send threads over long distances. | More and more threads are added for strength. | The spider waits for its dinner to fly into the web. |

Weaverbird's nest
There are more than 125 species of weaverbirds. Most live in the grasslands and marshes of Africa. The male bird builds the nest and hopes to find a mate. If more than a week passes and the nest fails to attract a mate, the nest is abandoned and the male builds a new one. Nest building techniques improve with experience.

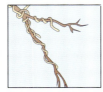

| The weaverbird chooses a strong forked branch as the nest foundation. | The building material is mostly blades of grass and or strips of palm fronds. | Resembling the weave of a basket, the nest takes shape. |

Soldier crabs excavates in the sand
Soldier crabs are named for their habit of moving in large groups at one time. They live in mangroves, beaches and estuaries. When disturbed they burrow into the sand.

   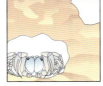

| Soldier crabs build sand houses with air bubbles. | Small bits of sand are pushed outward and upward. | As the crab works, a dome is created. | As the crab digs deeper, a ceiling is formed. |

Building a beaver lodge
Beavers will often work together as a family to build the perfect home. During construction of their ideal residence they will dig a temporary shelter under the bank of a pond or river. Beavers like to build in deep water. If the water is not deep enough, they will build a dam to raise the water level of their neighborhood before beginning working on the lodge.

| Beavers have very sharp chisel-shaped teeth, perfect for felling trees. The beaver gnaws the trees and branches into manageable sizes and floats or drags the material to a chosen building site. | Clumsy on land, the beaver lets the current of the water help carry his supplies. Working slowly, taking time to eat and relax, the beaver creates a tangle of debris and little by little a lodge begins to take shape. | Once the structure is three or four feet (0.9 to 1.2 m) high and ten or twelve feet (3 to 3.6 m) across, the beaver chews a tunnel through the mound of sticks, creating an underwater entrance. | When the beaver's tunnel is above water level he will excavate a feeding chamber and above that a sleeping chamber. The finished lodge is safe and weatherproof, perfect for raising a family. |

The elf owl is about 5½ inches long. It is one of the world's smallest owls. Found in desert lowlands and canyons, this nocturnal bird nests in woodpecker holes in the saguaro cactus as well as the cavities of oak and pine trees.

Living in trees

Everybody knows that birds build nests in trees. But did you know they also burrow into them? The elf owl carves its nest into cactuses and many woodpeckers make their homes inside tree trunks. The tropical hornbill literally walls herself into a tree trunk home while incubating her eggs. And not all bird nests are made of grasses. Some birds like the ovenbird of Central and South America build clay nests.

Birds are not the only animals that live in trees. Insects and many other animals take advantage of the shelter trees provide.

Squirrel drey

Squirrels generally build more than one nest, so that they can move easily if a nest is damaged or threatened. A summer nest is called a drey and is padded with leaves, grasses, chewed bark and other materials.

Raccoon

Many mammals use decaying trees for homes. Foxes, wolves, coyotes, raccoons, even bears will make dens in uprooted and dead trees.

Sculptors

Wasps have a talent for sculpting their houses. Many make paper nests from chewed-up wood. Others build nests from mud or live in burrows.

Mud daubers are a type of wasp that build long tube shaped nests out of clay or mud. The female wasp collects the mud and carries it to her building site.

Paper wasps make paper pulp by chewing wood and mixing it with saliva. The female wasp then builds a paper nest of tiny cells.

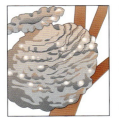

The potter wasp builds a clay nest that looks like a pot and fills it with food, then she lays an egg and seals the nest.

Giant anteater
Myrmecophaga tridactyla

Three-toed sloth
Bradypus tridactylus

Anteaters, armadillos and sloths are members of the Edentata group of animals. Edentates share an evolutionary connection of having few or no teeth. Endentata means "the toothless ones."

Anteaters, armadillos and sloths have very low metabolic rates and body temperatures, characteristic of the ancient Xenarthra order of animals.

Nine-banded armadillo
Dasypus novemcinctus

The nine-banded armadillo is the most common of armadillos, but the only one found in North America. Armadillos grow to about 2 feet (61 cm) long and weigh around 15 pounds (6.8 kg). One of the most amazing things about this species is that it almost always gives birth to identical quadruplets (four), either all male or all female.

Anteaters, armadillos & sloths

There are four species of anteaters. They are native to southern Mexico and northern South America.

The giant anteater (sometimes called the ant bear) is the largest of anteaters. It can grow to be more than 6 feet (1.8 m) in length, with tails measuring up to 3 feet (0.9 m) long. It is found in tropical Central and South America, but hunting and habitat loss has damaged populations and the species is threatened. It walks on the sides of its feet to protect sharp claws; the result is a strange, shuffling gait.

Silky anteater
Cyclopes didactylus

The silky anteater is about the size of a squirrel and grows to about 20 inches (50 cm) long. It has a prehensile tail that can wrap around tree limbs.

Anteaters are the only members of the scientific order Endentata to be completely toothless. As their name suggests, anteaters love to eat ants, but they also like termites and will sometimes eat soft fruit. They have long snouts and sticky tongues, perfect for trapping and devouring insects. They will feed and then move on, taking care not to destroy a nest that could feed them again later.

Anteaters are generally solitary creatures. The mother will give birth to one offspring a year and will carry the baby on her back.

Aardvarks, pangolins and echidnas can be confused with anteaters. Despite similarities, they are not related.

The giant anteater can flick its 2-foot-long (60 cm) tongue in and out 150 times per minute. One giant anteater can eat up to 30,000 insects in a day.

There are 20 species of armadillos. They can be found in South America and in some southern U.S. states.

Giant armadillo
Priodontes maximus

Armadillos are named for the Spanish word "armado," which means "one that is armed." This is because armadillos have hinged, bony plates that form strong, flexible bands which protect their bodies. This heavy skin should cause an armadillo to sink in water, but they have a special ability to blow up their intestines with air for added buoyancy — they can swim if they have to. Armadillos have long, sharp claws, ideal for digging and burrowing. They mainly eat insects, earthworms and spiders, but will eat plants and sometimes small vertibrates, like snakes.

Many species are nocturnal and only come out at night. They have poor eyesight, but an excellent sense of smell.

It is considered a pest by many landowners because its burrowing can damage crops and undermine buildings. But armadillos also benefit people by eating harmful insects and grubs. In South America, some people eat armadillos.

The three-banded armadillo is the only armadillo that rolls into a ball when threatened. Most armadillos will run away or dig a hole to hide in.

Three-banded armadillo
Tolypeutes matacus

There are five species of sloths. They are found in the tropical rainforests of Central and South America.

Hidden in the trees, the three-toed sloth can easily be mistaken for a branch. The animal moves so slowly as to be almost undetectable. It may take 30 seconds for it to move a leg just a few inches. Sloths even sneeze slowly!

Enlargement of a sloth hair showing corrugated ridges where algae grows.

Sloth moth
Bradipodicola hahneli

Algae, moths and other insects make a home in the rough coat of the sloth.

Two-toed sloth
Choloepus hoffmanni

Sloths are extremely slow-moving creatures that spend most of their lives hanging upside down. They move so slowly that most predators do not see them. Sloths live in the rainforest canopy and only come down to the ground to defecate (once every week or so). While on the ground, they are quite awkward and helpless. Sloths have almost no tails or ears and their noses are flat. Depending on the species, they have two or three toes on their front feet, with long, hooked claws that wrap around branches. Because they have spent so much of their evolutionary lives upside down, their hair grows in the opposite direction from other furry mammals.

Their shaggy, coarse hair is home to a plant and an insect. The plant is a microscopic algae that grows in the grooves of the sloth's corrugated hair. This gives the animal a greenish color and is an excellent camouflage against enemies. The insect is a tiny moth that weaves its way in and out of the fur, eating the algae.

Sloths feed on leaves, buds and young twigs. Their low metabolism (the process of turning food into energy) means they do not eat much compared to animals of a similar size.

BATS

The **hammer-headed bat** is a type of fruit bat.

Kinds of bats

Bats belong to the Chiroptera order. Chiroptera comes from the Greek words meaning "hand" and "wing." Scientists divide bats into two groups — megabats (megachiroptera) and microbats (microchiroptera). Megabats are also known as fruit or flying fox bats. Megabats generally have big eyes and excellent eyesight. Most do not use echolocation to find food. They rely on fruit and nectar for food. Because megabats are not found in the Americas, they are sometimes called Old World bats. Microbats are smaller and eat mostly insects. They have big ears, but small eyes and rely on echolocation to find food.

Home sweet home

Most bats like to live in dark places, like caves, tree or rock crevices and sometimes in buildings. Fruit bats like to live in trees, hanging from the branches. Where a bat lives is called a **roost**. They tend to live in large colonies of thousands or millions of bats. Bats are **nocturnal**, which means they sleep most of the day.

Winter solutions

Bats that live in colder climates will **hibernate** or **migrate** in winter. Many North American bats hibernate in caves, surviving on stored fat. Hibernation is a state of deep sleep. The bat's heart rate slows and its body temperature drops. Some bats migrate to warmer climates and plentiful food supplies. Tropical bats do not need to hibernate, because the climate is warm all year round, but they have been known to migrate in search of new food sources. Bats are strong, skilled flyers and with a good wind have been known to reach speeds of up to 60 mph.

Baby bats

Pregnant bats leave their regular roosts and join a special nursing colony, where they give birth and raise their young. They usually give birth once a year and generally have one baby at a time, but some, like the hoary and red bat can have as many as four babies at a time.

A baby bat is called a **pup**. Newborns are large compared with other mammal babies. They are born bald and with their eyes closed. Most bats nurse for about six to eight weeks before venturing into the outdoors for food. If a bat survives the challenges of growing up, it can live a long life. Some species live more than 30 years.

There are more than 900 species of bats, 40 of which live in North America. They are the only mammal that can fly. Bats come in many shapes and sizes. The largest, called the flying fox, has a wingspan of up to 5 feet, while the kitti's hog-nosed bat, native to Thailand is about the size of a bumble bee. Sometimes feared in Western cultures, the bat is a symbol of long life and happiness in Japan. Many bats provide a valuable service to people by eating large quantities of destructive insects.

Anatomy 101

Most bats have fur or hair and they come in a variety of colors. Some people think their bodies look very mouselike. Bats digest food more quickly than many animals. This helps them maintain an ideal flying weight.

A bat's hands are also its wings. Long fingers support strong and elastic wings. There is a claw on the thumb that is used for climbing, gripping and grooming.

Bats that eat insects and smaller animals often use their tail membrane to help catch and hold prey.

What do they eat?

Depending on the species, the bat diet can be very diverse. Seventy percent of bats prefer insects and can eat half their weight in mosquitoes and moths in one night. The tropics are home to a number of bats that eat plants, pollen and nectar. These vegan bats pollinate the plants and help new growth by spreading seeds in their **guano** (excrement). It is estimated that more than 500 plants depend on bats for pollination. Some bats eat fish, frogs, lizards, rodents and small birds.

There are three bat species that drink blood. The common vampire bat favors the blood of cattle and other domestic livestock, while the hairy-legged and white-winged vampires feed on the blood of birds.

Sound and seeing

Bats are not blind and many have excellent eyesight. Many bats (mostly insect eaters) use sound to find food. (This is why they have such big ears). The bat emits a high-pitched sound from the nose or mouth. As the sound bounces off objects, the bat is able to determine exactly where the object is, even when it is moving. This is called **echolocation**. (Some dolphins also use this method to find food.) Modern radar equipment is based on the same principle. Most of the sounds that bats make are so high that the human ear cannot hear them. Scientists who study bat sound use devices that can measure **ultrasounds**.

Sonic fishing

A fisher bat flies towards the water, emitting high-pitched sounds (see the solid line). When a fish breaks the surface, it reflects back the bat sound, creating an **echo**. Beeping again, the bat uses its curved talons to hook the fish. While biting into its prey the bat remains silent.

Bat wings are so thin that blood flowing through the veins can be sometimes be seen.

The knees of a bat face backwards, making walking difficult.

Bats ears are constantly twitching, even when the bat is sleeping.

Did you know: Bat guano (waste droppings) is a rich fertilizer, prized by farmers in many countries.

Funny faces

Bats have unusual faces. Many have odd noses, some long, others short, and some have extra folds of skin around the nostrils. Their ears can be quite strange, too, coming in a variety of shapes and sizes.

Flying foxes eat mostly fruit and live in Africa and Asia.

Vampire bats eat about 1 tablespoon of blood a day.

There are about 70 species of **horseshoe** bats. They live in groups and generally roost in caves.

Leaf-nosed bats have large ears and a "leaf" on their noses. The California leaf-nosed bat is currently listed as a candidate species on the list of threatened native wildlife in Arizona.

 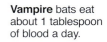

Slit-faced bats are also known as hollow-faced bats. They live in the tropics and are found in Africa and in Malaysia and Indonesia. They usually roost in caves, tree hollows and buildings.

Hoary bats are the largest in North America, with a wingspan of about 16 inches. They live alone in trees and migrate in winter.

Danger in the night

Hawks and owls are the main predators of bats. Snakes will also prey on bats. Opossums, raccoons and skunks will eat bats that have fallen to the ground.

Cooper's hawk

Saving the bat

Bat populations have suffered greatly at the hands of humans. Almost 40 percent of North American bats are threatened or endangered. Their roosts and natural habitats are destroyed to make way for new homes and buildings. Pesticides find their way into the food chain and they are poisoned. Some people kill bats because they think they are scary and dangerous, others because the bats eat their crops and are thought to be pests. And in some places, people eat fruit bats.

BEARS

There are seven species of bears, eight if you include the great panda: Big brown bears, American black bears, Asiatic black bears, polar bears, sun bears, sloth bears, spectacled bears and the great pandas. Zoologists argue over whether the panda belongs to the bear family, to its own unique family or the raccoon family. Recent research suggests that the giant panda is a member of the bear family.

Big brown bears
Big brown bears are found in the west of North America and parts of Asia and Europe. The **Alaskan brown bear** (also known as the Kodiak bear) is the largest of bears. The **grizzly bear** is found mostly in Alaska and western Canada. The **brown bear of Asia and Europe** was sometimes used in a vicious entertainment called bearbaiting, where the bear is tied up and forced to defend itself against dogs.

American black bears
The American black bear is common throughout forests of North America. The **island white bear**, or **Kermode's bear,** which is found along the coast of British Columbia, has white fur and claws. The **blue bear**, or **glacier bear,** lives in the mountains of southeastern Alaska and has fur that sometimes looks bluish.

Asiatic black bears
The Asiatic black bear is also known as the **Himalayan** or **moon bear**. It is slightly smaller than its American cousins. Asiatic black bear has a reputation for being very fierce and aggressive.

Giant panda
The giant panda lives in the mountains of Asia and is in great danger of extinction due to habitat loss.

Polar bears
Polar bears live in the North Pole, mostly in areas that border the Arctic Ocean. They are sometimes referred to as the **ice bear**, **sea bear**, **white bear** or **walking bear**. The Inuit people call the polar bear **nanook**, and have hunted it for centuries.

Sun bears
Sun bears, also called Malayan bears, are the smallest species of bear. Sun bears live in the Malay Peninsula, Borneo, Burma, Indochina, Sumatra and Thailand.

Sloth bears
The sloth bear is sometimes called the **Indian bear** because it lives in the jungles of India and Sri Lanka. It has also been nicknamed the **honey bear** because it likes honey so much. Unless they are in danger, sloth bears move very slowly.

Spectacled bears
The spectacled bear is the only bear found in the Southern Hemisphere and the only bear native to South America. It lives in the mountain forests of Bolivia, Colombia, Ecuador, Peru and Venezuela. It is named for the large light-colored circles of fur around its eyes, which look like glasses or spectacles. Hunting and habitat destruction has made this bear quite rare.

Sloth bear
Sloth bears hunt mostly at night and eat birds' eggs, grubs, insects, plants and honey. During the day, they sleep in shallow caves or under shrubs.

Spectacled bear
Spectacled bears feed mostly on plants, but they also eat fruit, nuts, honey, small animals and insects. They sometimes build treehouses or platforms, where they like to eat.

Sun bear
The fur of the sun bear is short and some people say it feels like velvet.

Giant panda
Pandas feed on bamboo and they need to eat a great deal of it — they eat as much as 85 pounds (39k) of bamboo shoots a day.

Polar bear
Polar bears feed mostly on seals, young walrus and fish. These bears can swim 3 to 6 miles (5 to 10 km) per hour. Polar bears travel extensively in search of food and have been known to travel 75 miles (120 km) a day.

Asiatic black bear
The Asiatic bear is sometimes hunted for its fur and bones.

Grizzly bear
Grizzlies have huge curved claws that are ideal for digging and as weapons. Grizzlies can reach speeds of up to 30 mph (48km), but they can't maintain that speed for very long.

American black bear
It is estimated that black bears outnumber brown bears in North America 10 to 1. Black bears are excellent tree climbers and when running, can reach speeds of up to 25 mph (40k).

Big and furry lifestyles
Bears are intelligent animals with a strong sense of curiosity and an amazing sense of smell. Bears are generally solitary animals that get together only to mate. When two bears do meet, they generally respond aggressively and often will fight savagely, sometimes to the death. Bears tolerate others only when food is very plentiful.

Dinner time
Bears have been classified as **carnivores** (animals that eat meat), but most bears will eat whatever is available. Only polar bears live on a mostly meat diet. Most bears also eat fruit, nuts, honey, grasses, leaves, insects and fish. Bears will travel long distances in search of food. An average bear's hunting ground is about 10 to 12 square miles (26-31 square kilometers). Polar bears have been found on iced drifts, more than 200 miles (320k) from land.

Napping the winter away
Many bears spend the winter in sleep. Scientists disagree on whether bears enter true hibernation or if they are just dozing. Black and brown bears that live in colder climates will find or build a den to sleep in for the winter. Tropical bears like the sun bear and sloth bear do not need to sleep in the winter. Polar bears live in a very cold place, but unless they are pregnant, remain active throughout the year.

Baby bears
American black and brown bears are born in January or February. A female usually has two cubs, but can have just one, or as many as four. Newborns are very tiny and weigh $1/2$ to 1 pound (0.23 to 0.5 k). A month later the cubs have fur and open their eyes. They leave the den in the spring and spend the summer playing and eating and by the fall a cub can easily have put on 40 pounds (18k). It generally takes one to two years for a cub to reach full maturity.

Caution and wisdom
Bears are very powerful and can move with dangerous speed and great agility. **Do not feed bears!** More and more often, bears are found at campsites, in back yards and at dumping grounds — places where people have left food. A female bear protecting her cubs can be especially aggressive.

Teddy bears
Teddy bears became popular in the early 1900s and there are several stories about their origin.

The English claim: The teddy bear is based on the nickname of King Edward VII.

The American version: In 1902, President Theodore Roosevelt refused to shoot a bear cub on a hunting trip. Stuffed bears (known as "Teddy's bears.") began to show up on store shelves.

The German tradition: Margarete Steiff showed her toy bears at a trade fair in 1903. Steiff bears are still collected today.

Shapes and sizes of bears
Average adult height and weight of species.

Alaskan brown bear
Length: 9 feet (2.7 m)
Weight: 500 pounds (230 k)

Polar bear
Length: 8 ft. (2.4m)
Weight: 1,000 lbs. (454k)

American black bear
Length: 5 ft. (1.5m)
Weight: 300 lbs. (140k)

Asiatic black bear
Length: 5 ft.(1.5m)
Weight: 250 lbs. (113k)

Sloth bear
Length: 5 ft. (1.5m)
Weight: 250 lbs. (113k)

Giant panda
Length: 5 ft. (1.5m)
Weight: 250 lbs. (113k)

Spectacled bear
Length: 5 ft. (1.5m)
Weight: 250 lbs. (113k)

Sun bear
Length: 3 ft. (1.5m)
Weight: 100 lbs. (45k)

Insects in armor
BEETLES

Cucumber beetle

There are more than 300,000 species of beetle. They come in all shapes and sizes and live just about everywhere.

All in the family
Beetles are insects and belong to the order of Coleoptera. Coleoptera is the largest of insect orders — about 40 percent of the world's insects are beetles.

Scientists (or zoologists) who study insects are called entomologists. Specialists who study only beetles are called coleopterists.

Coleoptera are distinguished by hard forewings and thin, folded hindwings. They range greatly in size and have mouth parts that enable them to chew.

Some kinds of beetles

Sweet potato weevil

Weevils (Curculionidae) are the largest family of beetles, consisting of more than 40,000 species. Also known as billbugs or snout beetles, weevils are considered a pest. Weevils have long **snouts** and are dull in color, except for the brightly colored tropical species.

Colorado potato beetle

Leaf beetles (Chrysomelidae) are another agricultural pest. Particularly, the Colorado potato beetle is well known for its destruction of potato crops. Some leaf beetles play dead when disturbed or threatened. There are at least 25,000 species in this beetle family.

Calosoma (ground beetle)

Ground beetles (Carabidae) are usually **nocturnal**, meaning they sleep during the day. If you turn over a rock, you just might discover one. Because ground beetles eat other insects, they are sometimes used for pest control. There are about 20,000 species.

Japanese beetle

Scarabs (Scarabaeidae) have clublike antennae. They are the beetles often depicted in ancient Egyptian art. **Dung** beetles and tumblebugs eat and reproduce in the waste of herbivores. June-bugs and Japanese beetles are garden pests that wreak havoc on plants by chewing large holes in leaves. There are more than 20,000 kinds of scarab beetles.

Predacious diving beetle

Click beetles (Elateridae) are also called **fire** beetles. Click beetles are known for the clicking sound they make.

Predacious diving beetles (Dytiscidae) live in fresh **water** and feed on snails, tadpoles and small fish.

Ladybug

Ladybugs (Coccinellidae) are also known as ladybirds and ladybeetles. Adults have round bodies and are often red, orange or yellow with black spots. Gardeners like ladybugs because they eat aphids and other insect pests.

Firefly

Fireflies (Lampyridae) are sometimes called lightning bugs, and there are about 1,900 species in the firefly family.

Species sampler

Nicrophornae Silphinae
Carrion beetles **Soldier beetle** **Frog beetle** **Eastern hercules**

Long-horned beetle **Leaf beetle** **Dung beetle** **Golden tortoise beetle (leaf beetle)** **Tiger beetle**

NOTE: Beetles shown are not drawn to scale

Anatomy 101
Like all insects, beetles have **six** legs and three body parts: the head, thorax and abdomen.

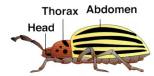
Head **Thorax** **Abdomen**

Most beetles have two pairs of wings — hard (often colorful) forewings called **elytra** and delicate, transparent hindwings that are kept folded under the forewings until needed for flight. (Most, but not all, beetles can fly.) Beetles use their antennae for touch and smell. Most beetles have excellent eyesight and can see color and motion. Although some beetles have long legs and others short legs, all have legs that consist of five segments with claws on the end.

Elytra

The elytra act like body armor for the beetle. Elytra have no veins and are opaque (not transparent).

Wing

Some beetles taste and hear with their feet.

The circle of life
Beetles have a complex life cycle in which they undergo a complete metamorphosis. Metamorphosis means "change of body form and appearance." When beetle eggs hatch, larvae (**grubs**) are born. The larvae grow and shed their skin (**molt**) several times before turning into a pupa. The pupa may appear dormant, but the insect's body is experiencing great changes inside. Muscles, nerves and tissue are dissolved and new ones are formed. When the change is complete, an adult beetle emerges.

Ladybug metamorphosis
The larva is born, after eating and molting for about a week, it changes into a pupa.

Day 6, Day 7, Day 21, Day 28
About 15 to 20 eggs are laid.
Day 1, Day 36, Day 35, Day 37

The pupa breaks open and an adult ladybug is born.

The good, the bad and the ugly

Beneficial beetles
Beetles play an important role in the environment. Like other insects, they provide an important source of food for many animals. Scarabs and some other types of beetles are pollinators, while dung beetles reuse the dung of herbivores, therefore removing millions of tons of waste.

Southern pine beetle

Bad beetles
Some beetles are considered pests because they feed on crops, trees or stored food.

Beastly beetles
The huge mandibles, or jaws, of the stag beetle are meant to intimidate predators.

Checkered beetle

Giant stag beetle

Fun things to do
You can test a beetle's sense of smell by building a maze. (Scarab beetles work best.) Construct the maze with tape and heavy bristol board or cardboard. The walls only need to be about half an inch high. Place your beetle at one end and some meat (dog or cat food works well) at the other end. Cover the maze with some clear plastic wrap and watch what happens!

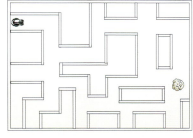

Pet beetles
You can learn a lot about insects by watching them. Beetles can be kept in a jar with some sand or soil at the bottom. Add layers of oatmeal or bran. Many beetles like mealworms. They may be hard to find, but add a layer of them if you can locate any. Supply moisture with a fresh piece of apple or carrot every day. A crumbled paper towel makes a good place for the beetle to hide under. Experiment with what they eat by giving them tiny bits of fruit, meat, cheese or bread. You should return your insects to the wild after a few days.

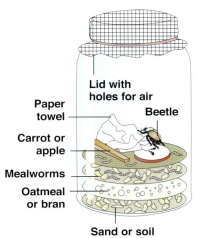
Lid with holes for air
Paper towel
Beetle
Carrot or apple
Mealworms
Oatmeal or bran
Sand or soil

Favorite feelers
Beetle antennae are as varied as the species itself. Below are some examples of beetle antennae.

Fastest animal on Earth

A cheetah's supple spine is the secret to its speed. Coiling and uncoiling like a spring, it catapults the cheetah forward. After creeping close to the prey, the cheetah springs out with its long and muscular hind legs. The cat inhales huge amounts of air, arching its back and pulling its feet together. Then, the spring-like spine stretches, shooting the legs to full extension. When the front legs touch the ground, the spine curls again, ready to propel the legs into another stride. Unlike slower animals, the cheetah's back legs push sequentially instead of together. This means that half the time, a running cheetah has all four feet off the ground at once. During a chase, a cheetah's long tail streams out behind, acting like a rudder to help it turn. The cheetah is the fastest land animal over short distances — running up to 70 mph, with an average chase of 560 feet lasting less than a minute. Often, the cat needs to rest after bringing down prey. The cheetah hunts in daylight, when other big cats are sleeping. Vultures and hyenas will often steal a cheetah's catch.

Big Cats
Powerful predators of family Felidae

Tiger
Length	7-10 feet
Weight	160-700 lbs.
Litter size	3-4 average
Life span	Up to 15 years
Status	Critically endangered

Jaguar
Length	5-7 feet
Weight	150-260 lbs.
Litter size	1-4 average
Life span	12-16 years
Status	Near threatened

The Jaguar inspires respect and fear. Its name means "a beast that kills its prey with one bound." The cat was chosen as a central theme in myth, legend and religion in Latin America. It is the largest cat in the Western hemisphere, and for indigenous peoples symbolized immense power. Dominant in the forest, it uses strength and cunning to overcome prey, by climbing, swimming and navigating easily. Most big cats kill with a throat or neck bite, but the jaguar bites the skull between the ears. Like other big cats, they hunt by following trails until encountering prey. They then stalk and rush, or wait in ambush, leaping on the unsuspecting. Jaguars swim well and during the hottest part of the day, will lie partly submerged in water. One myth says the cat's spotted coat was made when the jaguar dabbed mud on its body with its paws. Like leopards, **melanistic** or black jaguars are common.

Tigers are the largest felines. Hunting alone, the tiger will stalk its prey. Tigers live in the forests and grasslands of Asia. They can range from tropical areas in the Far East to the Arctic Ocean, roaming the snowbound forests in Siberia. Siberian tigers are the largest tigers, up to 10 feet in length and weighing more than 700 pounds.

Snow Leopard
Length	7 feet
Weight	85-165 lbs.
Litter size	2-3 average
Life span	15-18 years
Status	Endangered

A gray and white dappled coat allows the Snow Leopard to blend into its mountain habitat. Oily, dense, wooly fur protects it from harsh weather. Hunting wild sheep and goats, it is agile, and an excellent leaper. Moving along ridges, bluffs, and cliffs, it follows migrating prey.

Snow leopards are rare and are in decline because their fur is in demand. Sometimes Asian medical practitioners use the snow leopards' bones, more now because the preferred tiger bones are scarce.

Cheetah
Length	4-5 feet
Weight	86-143 lbs.
Litter size	3-5 average
Life span	2-14 years
Status/Asian	Critically endangered
Status/	Vulnerable

Adult cheetahs are solitary hunters. They do not have the muscle power to drag large prey like the leopard. Despite this disadvantage, the cheetah has a skill no other cat has: Speed.

Incredible speed gives it the advantage when chasing prey on open land. It also makes up for the lack of canine teeth which allow other cats to bring down large animals. When a cheetah takes prey, it eats where it killed.

Puma
Length	7-9 feet
Weight	135-160 lbs.
Litter size	2-3 average
Life span	Up to 15 years
Status/Florida	Endangered

Technically a little cat, this large animal has a number of names, including cougar, mountain lion, panther, and catamount (cat of the mountains). Habitat ranges from mountains to deserts. There are claims of vertical jumps up to 15 feet, aided by a thick tail to balance. When hunting, this solitary cat moves through its range until hearing prey. Creeping as close as possible, it charges, bounding and killing. It can snap an elk's neck with one pull and can sprint as fast as 40 mph, but has little stamina. It must catch its prey in a few bounds or give up.

Leopard
Length	5-7 feet	Life span	12-17 years
Weight	60-200 lbs.	Status	Various
Litter size	1-4 average		

Grace, stealth and power define the leopard. This patient feline stalker will slink from patch to patch, creeping close to prey, then burst out to snare it. After a kill, it moves up a tree with the carcass in tow, pulling it 20-30 feet high. Some are **melanistic** – producing a black fur background and even darker spots. This condition has inspired the name "black panther."

Lion
Length	5-7 feet
Weight	330-500 lbs.
Litter size	3-4 average
Life span	15-20 years
Status/Asiatic	Endangered
Status/Others	Vulnerable

Lionesses kill more often than male lions, catching most of the prey. They also establish the range and stability of the pride. Usually, a pride is a closed group of related adult females, who stay together for life. They hunt together with coordinated tactics. Cubs are protected and raised communally, nursed by any lioness with milk. Males of the pride force transient males and grown male cubs out. During a hunt, the pride forms a V-shape. Some charge, forcing victims into the waiting jaws of the other lions. After the kill, the pride gorges, then sleeps for hours.

BIODIVERSITY
Variety is the spice of life

Biological diversity, or biodiversity, is all about the huge variety of life and environments on Earth and the unique relationships between them. Biodiversity is vital to the survival of our planet. How we manage and protect the biodiversity of Earth impacts the health of the planet and, ultimately, the health of people.

Pacific dogwood
North America

Pohutukawa
New Zealand

It is easy to overlook another important benefit of biodiversity — its beauty.

THE TREE OF LIFE

Biodiversity is not just about the number and variety of **species** inhabiting the Earth. It is also concerned with where the species live — environments and **ecosystems**, such as rain forests, oceans, wetlands and deserts. **Genetic** diversity is another level of biodiversity. It looks at the world of genetics within all living organisms. These three levels of biodiversity — genes, species and ecosystems — are interlocked and each can influence another. If one level is damaged, the effects can spread through other levels. Scientists have identified about **1.75 million species**. About a million of these are insects. But there are probably millions upon millions more species yet to be discovered.

- **Mollusks:** Includes oysters, mussels, clams, snails, slugs, limpets, squids, cuttlefish and octopuses **4%**
- **Chordates:** Includes all mammals, birds, amphibians, reptiles and vertebrate fish **3%**
- **Viruses:** Parasitic, self-replicating, nucleic acid entities **1%**
- **Nematodes:** Round, tapered, thin worms (not segmented) **1%**
- **Bacteria:** Refers to simple, unicellular organisms **1%**
- **Other 7%**
- **YOU ARE HERE!** (Somewhere)
- **Arthropods:** Includes crustaceans, insects, centipedes, millipedes and spiders **61%**
- **Land plants:** Includes mosses, ferns and seed plants **15%**
- **Protoctists:** Neither animals, plants, fungi or prokaryotes. Comprised of eukaryotic microorganisms **5%**
- **Fungi:** Includes mildew, molds, mushrooms, plant rusts and slime molds **4%**

Before 1800, the **North American Passenger Pigeon** numbered in the billions. But habitat loss and over hunting caused its extinction. The last pigeon died in 1914.

Historical range of the passenger pigeon

There are more than **6 billion people** on Earth, and this number grows by 90 million every year.

It is estimated that 3 species become extinct every hour.

Efforts to conserve genes, species and habitats have slowed, not stopped, the loss of biodiversity.

BIG BENEFITS

The health and diversity of genes, species and ecosystems have a huge impact on the lives of people. We depend on the complex web of nature for our health, environment and economies.

Plants take carbon dioxide out of the air and put oxygen into it. Plants, trees, animals and micro-organisms act like **filters** to keep soil and water clean. In North America alone, insects pollinate crops worth $6 billion to $12 billion. Humans cultivate or harvest more than 7,000 species of wild plants. More than two-thirds of prescription **drugs** in the U.S. are made with the chemicals from plants and fungi. More than 4 billion people around the world use plants to make traditional medicines. All the things you need and use every day come from raw materials made possible by the Earth's diversity.

In the U.S., nearly 4,500 species are threatened with extinction. (Forty-three kinds of birds and 39 species of mammals are already extinct.) In Canada, 487 plant and animal species are threatened. (Thirteen species have become extinct.)

Half of the planet's **rain forests** no longer exist. Logging and agriculture are largely responsible. Rain forests are special because at least 50% (maybe more) of the world's biodiversity exists in these wet, tropical habitats.

The Nile perch, released into Lake Victoria in Africa for food and sports fishing, has been a disaster. The perch is well on its way to eating all of the native species.

SAD, BUT TRUE

As human population continues to grow and the demand for land and natural resources increases, the stresses on nature also grow. Habitat loss, over-harvesting, climate change, pollution and the introduction of non-native species to new areas are resulting in the extinction and endangerment of many species. It is estimated that extinctions are occurring 100 to 1,000 times faster than they would naturally (without damaging human activities).

The Alliance for Zero Extinction (AZE) has identified 595 global sites that represent the last refuge of one or more of the most highly endangered species. These are the world's most threatened **hot spots**. The pie chart below shows a breakdown of critically threatened species by taxonomy.

Countries with the most AZE sites

Mexico	63	Cuba	18
Colombia	48	United States	18
Brazil	39	Venezuela	18
Peru	31	India	16
Indonesia	29	Madagascar	18
China	23	Honduras	14
Ecuador	19	Philippines	11
Australia	18	Guatemala	9

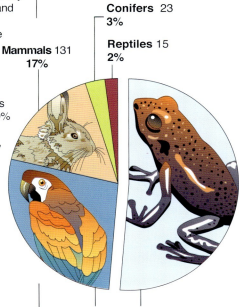

- **Conifers** 23 — **3%**
- **Reptiles** 15 — **2%**
- **Mammals** 131 — **17%**
- **Birds** 217 — **27%**
- **Amphibians** 408 — **51%**

Of the 950,000 species of insects, almost half are beetles.

MAKE A DIFFERENCE

If we want to save and preserve the Earth's biodiversity, we have to change how we think about the world around us. It's easy to get involved and join a group or community dedicated to saving our planet. Let's try to **restore** damaged habitats, **reduce** pollution, **respect** endangered-species laws and **conserve** our natural resources.

A typical insect has three parts to its body and three pairs of legs. Insects do not have backbones. They are supported by a sort of skeleton on the outside of their bodies.

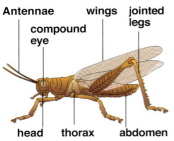

Insects have developed a variety of mouth parts. They have adapted for chewing, sucking, piercing and sucking and lapping.

Butterflies and moths

Butterflies and moths are amazing in their variety of size, shape and color. They are known as Lepidoptera, from the Greek words for scale and wing, because their wings are covered with thousands of overlapping scales. There are approximately 170,000 species of Lepidoptera in the world. About one-tenth of these are butterflies and the rest are moths.

Butterfly antennae

Moth antennae are pointed at the ends, not knobbed like a butterfly's.

Butterflies have a long, hollow tube called a proboscis which they use to sip nectar. When the proboscis is not being used, it stays coiled.

In less than a month the monarch goes through four stages of life: egg, caterpillar, pupa and adult. These changes are known as metamorphosis.

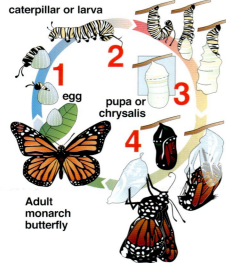

caterpillar or larva
1
egg
2
pupa or chrysalis
3
4
Adult monarch butterfly

The adult monarch feeds on the nectar of flowers, its favorite being the milkweed. Monarchs are the only insects that fly south for the winter. Some travel almost 2,000 miles before reaching their destination.

BUGS

The word bug can be used to describe any creepy crawler, but "true bugs" are a specific species. Insects make up the largest group of animals in the world. More than 900,000 species have been identified and it is likely that many more will be discovered. Insects have been classified into 25 groups. The beetle order alone includes 250,000 species.

Flies

Flies and their relatives **Diptera** have small antennae, large eyes, two wings and sucking mouth parts. There are so many types of flies in the world that scientists have trouble keeping track of them. It is estimated that there are up to 100,000.

Common housefly

A fly finds food by scent and tastes with its feet. Digestive juices are spread on the food, then dabbed up with a spongelike mouth.

Mosquitoes

These pests have been the bane of man for centuries. Adult females live 30 days or more; the male lives only 7-10 days. Both females and males drink nectar, but only females bite and drink blood. Drinking blood is required in order to lay eggs. The mosquito finds its victim, or host, by sensing the warm moist air around the body.

In the center of the proboscis are two very slender tubes. Saliva flows through one tube into the bite. Blood is sucked into the mouth through the other.

Bees, wasps and ants

Hymenoptera are mostly social insects that live in colonies. They often have two pairs of thin, transparent wings and are the only type of insects with stingers.

The cells are used to store honey and pollen. The bees make honey from nectar and pollen. They eat the honey in winter.

Honey bees make wax and shape it into **honeycombs**.

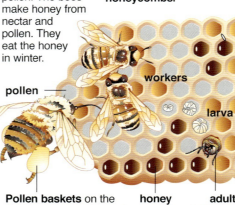

Pollen baskets on the hind legs are made up of many short, stiff hairs.

Ants

There are more than 10,000 kinds of ants. Ants eat both plants and animals and are famous for their ability to carry 50 times their body weight. An ant colony or city has many rooms and tunnels. Some ants live in the ground, others inside dead trees. Your house can also be home to ants.

Ants use their antennae to taste, smell, touch and hear.

Ants eat by putting chewed food in a pouch where the liquid is squeezed out and swallowed. They spit out the solid leftovers. The queen is the only ant that lays eggs. Worker ants look after the queen and feed her.

Ant city

Wasps

Wasps eat mainly spiders, insects and other small animals. Many make paper nests from chewed up wood; others build their nests from mud or live in burrows.

Hornets, like all wasps, are generally peaceful, but they are easily excited near their nests and will attack an enemy that gets too close. Thousands of hornets can live in one huge nest.

Yellow jacket

Cicada killers are very large, solitary wasps. They attack and use **cicadas** (the large insects that buzz loudly from treetops) as food for their larvae.

Cicada killer

Cicada

Grasshoppers

Grasshoppers, **roaches** and their relatives **Orthoptera** have chewing mouth parts and live on land. They have leathery forewings and folded fanlike hindwings (some lack wings).

Roach

Grasshopper

Lice

Anaplura are small, flat, wingless parasites with piercing and sucking mouth parts. Their legs have claws that cling to a warmblooded host.

Not insects

Many creepy crawling animals are confused with insects. **Spiders** have only two body divisions and eight legs. **Crustaceans** mostly live in water and have at least 10 legs. **Centipedes** and **millipedes** have many segments to their bodies; centipedes have long antennae and millipedes have short antennae.

Keeping bugs

You can learn a lot about insects by watching them. Beetles can be kept in a jar with a little sand or soil at the bottom. Experiment with what they eat by giving them tiny bits of fruit, meat, cheese or bread. Stick insects make good pets, and some people keep ant farms. You should return your insects to the wild after a few days.

Dragonflies

(Odonata) have long slender bodies with two pairs of long, equal-sized wings.

Beetles

Coleoptera have hard forewings and thin, folded hindwings. They range in size from small to large and have chewing mouth parts.

Fireflies or lightning bugs are not really flies or bugs, but beetles.

Water scavenger beetles feed on decaying matter at the bottom of ponds and rivers.

Japanese beetles are garden pests that wreak havoc on plants by chewing large holes in leaves.

Ladybugs are also known as ladybirds. Gardeners love these beetles because they eat aphids, which damage garden plants.

What are cacti?

Cactus plants (pl. cactuses or cacti) belong to a larger group of plants called succulents. Succulents have undergone adaptations in order to live in arid regions of the world, and can be found — from British Columbia to Patagonia — in deserts, coastal regions, jungles, mountains and prairies.

It is thought that cacti evolved from small, leafy jungle trees. Fossils of cacti are rare because arid climates are poor regions for fossil formation.

Cacti growth forms
Cacti grow in one of 10 basic shapes.

- Columnar Stout
- Columnar Reclining
- Columnar Stout, branching above
- Columnar Stout, branching at the base
- Globular Cylindric
- Globular Spherical
- Segmented Flat stems
- Hanging Segmented leaf cactus
- Leaf cactus

CACTUSES
REMARKABLE SURVIVORS OF ARID REGIONS

Northern Range — North America — Desert — Central America — South America — Southern Range

Surviving extremes

Cacti can survive extremes of heat and cold. Time has modified their typical leafy plant shapes. Cacti evolved thick stems, which they use to conserve water. Photosynthesis takes place in the stems instead of leaves. Cacti also have **spines**, hairs, spikes or bristles. These highly modified leaves provide protection for the fleshy plant. They also shade and cool the plant.

Cacti collect water in a variety of ways. Absorbing roots lie just below the soil surface and spread over a wide area to take advantage of light rains. Often, spines angle toward the ground and act as drip-tips for fog, dew and rain, which the roots then collect. Most cacti have water-storage tissue with sturdy walls that prevent the plant from collapsing in severe dryness.

To slow evaporation, the **stomata**, or air passages, of most cacti are sunken below the surface of the plant, reducing water-vapor loss by up to 70 percent. Stomata can close completely in high heat, preventing air and water vapor from escaping.

The downside of these adaptations is that most cacti grow very slowly. They are unable to compete with faster-growing leafy plants in a moist environment. Many flower sparsely or rarely, or don't reproduce as quickly as other plants. Some are so specialized that dwindling **habitats** threaten their survival.

Thorny issues
Cactus spines have evolved into a remarkable variety of shapes, colors and sizes. Here's a look at the shapes of most cactus spines:

- Needle-like and protruding
- Radial spines with no central spike
- Radial spines with central spike
- Conical spines
- Stout spines with curved center spine
- Bristly, hair-like spines
- Comb-like spines
- Flexible, flat spines
- Stout, banded central spine
- Radial with hooked center spine

The **prickly pear** (left) is of the genus Opuntia. It has many pads that look like pancakes. The plant has sweet, edible red fruit that is often collected and sold in produce markets.

Cacti of the genus Echinocactus are barrel-shaped and grow very slowly. Some have stout spines that are very attractive in color. The one at right is the **horse crippler cactus**. Its spines are very hard and can injure a horse if stepped on.

Cacti of the genus Mammilaria (below) are small; the largest are no more than 4 inches (10.16 cm) wide. They are usually called **pincushion** or **thimble** cacti. Their flowers are brilliantly colored, and often bloom in a ring at the top.

The Christmas cactus flowers in early winter. Plant breeders have cultivated it to have different flower colors.

This **Christmas cactus** (above) is of the genus Zygocactus. These cacti are epiphytic (they grow on tree branches and other plants) and are leaf-type, with jointed stems.

Saguaro are one of the largest cacti, reaching up to 60 feet (18 m) high. They are members of the genus Cereus. All Cereus are columnar, ribbed and tall. The fruit of the saguaro is used by the Tohono O'odham Indians to make a heavy syrup.

Classifying cacti

Using a method of classification called the International Code of Botanical Nomenclature, scientists who study plants (**botanists**) name cacti according to rules, which include:

1. There is only one correct, valid name for a plant type.
2. If two species are recognized where formerly only one was recognized, the original name only applies to one of the two species.
3. The earliest published name of a plant has priority over any name given later.
4. Every plant name is tied to a particular specimen, which a botanist designates typical of what he thinks is a new species.

How cacti are grouped
There is much disagreement over the classification of plants and animals. According to most scientists, cacti are classified as follows (this list does not include smaller groupings):

Kingdom	Plants
Division	Magnoliophyta "Covered seeds"
Class	Dicotyledonae "Two seed leaves"
Order	Caryophyllales "Thorny, fleshy stemmed plants"
Family	Cactaceae "The cactus"

Cactus habitats

Cacti grow in the following types of arid regions:

True deserts
Cacti in these areas grow in very dry climates, with irregular rainfall of less than 3.9 inches (100 cm) per year. Soil is typically high in rock, low in humus (decomposed animal and plant matter) and lacks fertility.

Desert grasslands
These areas typically border true deserts. Sparse vegetation may accompany cacti, depending on elevation. Well-drained soil and higher humus content make these regions different from true deserts.

Chaparrals
Low areas of almost continuous bushes, small trees and shrubs cover deeper soil in the chaparral. Usually, these areas receive higher rainfall during the winter and have drier summers.

Sub-tropical forests
These are the humid, warm regions of Central and South America. Shade, higher rainfall and fertile soils mark these regions.

Camels
The "Ships of the Desert"

Camel basics

Camels are cud-chewing mammals of the family Camelidae. They belong to the order Artiodactyla. About 10 million years ago a common camel ancestor, the camelid, migrated to Asia from north America, where they became extinct about 2 million years ago. Some also travelled south, becoming llamas, alpaca and guanaco, which did not develop humps, but are camel relatives. Research has shown that in the embryonic stage, dromedary camels have a small second hump that does not develop further. It is thought that the camelid probably looked like today's wild Bactrian camels.

Camels are herbivores and eat grass, leaves, and grains. They can drink up to 32 gallons (120 liters) of water at one time. Today, there are two distinct species:

- **Camelus dromedarius** lives in North Africa and the Middle East. Also called Dromedaries, or Arabian camels, all are domesticated – beginning about 5,000 years ago. Today, there are no wild Camelus dromedarius.

- **Camelus bactrianus** lives in eastern Asia. Nearly all of the Bactrian camels alive today are domesticated. In 2002, a small, wild, migratory herd of about 950 animals in northwest China and Mongolia were placed on the critically endangered species list. They have been classified as **Camelus bactrianus ferus** and are genetically different from the domesticated Bactrians.

Camels can survive on very little or no water for long periods of time. They can eat salty vegetation as well as thorny plants living in the desert. Their urine is highly concentrated. After finding water, camels can drink enormous quantities. They can endure temperature extremes, both hot and cold, and heat is quickly lost because all of the camel's fat is located in the hump on the back.

Camels were once hugely important to the economics of the Arabian, Gobi and Saharan deserts. The "Silk Road" was travelled by way of camels, and great numbers of explorers, merchants and their goods relied on camels for transport. Until recent times, camels were used in caravans, as transportation, and for meat and milk. Camel wool was used for clothes, and their manure was used for fuel after being dried. The camel was a status symbol and form of wealth. Today, reliance on the camel has diminished, and even its meat is considered less appealing than lamb or beef. Camel herds have been greatly reduced in Arabia, except in Saudi Arabia and the United Arab Emirates, where they are animals of leisure and raised as a hobby. In large areas of the Sahara, and across north Africa, the camel is still a vital necessity for human survival.

Dromedaries

Camelus dromedarius, or Arabian camel, has a single hump and short hair. They reach about 6.5 feet (2 meters) high and 9.75 feet (3 meters) long and can weigh up to 1600 pounds (725 kg.)

They are believed to have been domesticated in Arabia between 4000 and 2000 BC.

Arabian camels have two toes on each foot and thick sole pads – which protect the foot when crossing hot desert sands. Camels can close their nostrils against flying sand, and their eyes are protected by long eyelashes. Arabian camels use both legs on one side of the body in parallel motion when running. With a rider, they can maintain a rate of 8 or 9 miles per hour for several hours. A food reserve of fatty tissue is carried in the form of a hump on the back.

Bactrian Camels

Native to the steppes of eastern Asia, the Bactrian camel has two humps on its back. Bactrian camels are over 7 feet (2 meters) tall and weigh more than 1600 pounds (725 kg.)

Like the dromedary, they can survive desert heat and sand and have wide, padded feet and thick leathery pads on their knees and chest. Their ears are lined with protective hairs, and they have bushy eyebrows plus two rows of very long eyelashes. Thick fur and under wool keep them warm at night and protect their skin against daytime heat. They are stocky and hardy and range from northern Iran to Tibet. When loaded with cargo they move at about 2.5 miles an hour.

It is thought that Bactrians were domesticated around 2500 BC, in the northern near east. Wild herds were described by Nikolai Przhevalsky, a Russian geographer and explorer, during the late 19th century.

Some scientists believe that the Bactrian camel can be divided into different subspecies. A wild herd living within a part of the Gashun Gobi region of the Gobi Desert is different from domesticated herds behaviorally and genetically. There are possibly three genetic groups different from domesticated camels, but, with few wild camels to study, it is uncertain what natural diversity within the camel population would have been. Another difference in this subspecies is the ability to drink and metabolize slushy saltwater. Domesticated camels will not drink salt water.

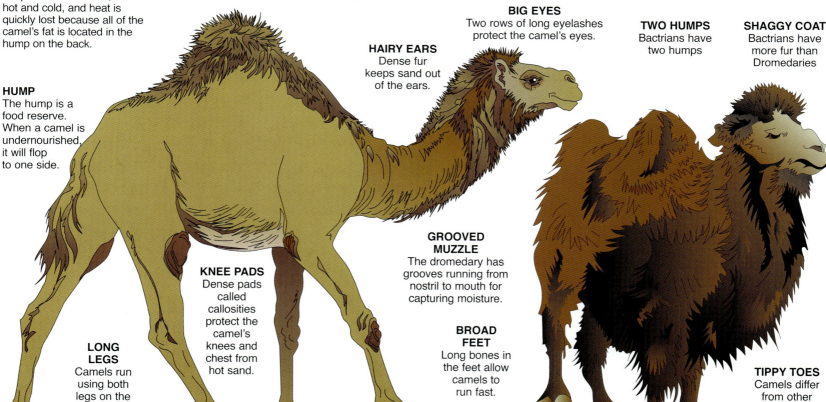

HUMP The hump is a food reserve. When a camel is undernourished, it will flop to one side.

LONG LEGS Camels run using both legs on the same side of the body

KNEE PADS Dense pads called callosities protect the camel's knees and chest from hot sand.

HAIRY EARS Dense fur keeps sand out of the ears.

BIG EYES Two rows of long eyelashes protect the camel's eyes.

GROOVED MUZZLE The dromedary has grooves running from nostril to mouth for capturing moisture.

BROAD FEET Long bones in the feet allow camels to run fast.

TWO HUMPS Bactrians have two humps

SHAGGY COAT Bactrians have more fur than Dromedaries

TIPPY TOES Camels differ from other ungulates in that they stand on the next-to-last joints of the toes.

HUNGRY plants
Carnivores in the bog, marsh and swamp

The basics
Carnivorous plants are rare plants that grow worldwide. They live in bogs, marshes and swamps and have the same needs as all plants – sunlight, nutrients and water. They make food by photosynthesis. But carnivorous plants differ in one aspect: their habitat does not provide them with enough **nitrogen**, a soil and airborne nutrient essential for growth. This group of plants has adapted to the deficiency by evolving ways to trap, kill and digest small insects and animals and then absorb nitrogen from their bodies.

Carnivorous plants fall into two categories: **active** or **passive trappers**. The active trappers have moving parts that hold an insect as it is killed and digested. Passive trappers do not move, but have equally lethal methods of preventing an insect from escape.

Carnivorous groups
Carnivorous plants are grouped into 7 **genera** (groups of like plants or animals). Here's how scientists have organized them:

GENUS	COMMON NAME
Dionaea	Venus' flytrap
Drosera	Sundews
Cephalotus	West Australian pitcher plant
Nepenthes	Tropical pitcher plants
Sarracenia	American pitcher plants
Pinguicula	Butterworts
Utricularia	Bladderworts

How the Venus' Flytrap captures and digests an insect meal

Step one An insect is attracted to the sweet-smelling liquid on the flytrap leaf, having no suspicion of its fate.

Step two The insect brushes against two of the **trigger hairs** on the inside of the leaf. It snaps shut, capturing the insect.

Step three When the insect stops wiggling, the closed leaf oozes a special fluid that begins to breakdown the body.

Step four After 8 to 10 days, the soft parts of the insect dissolve into the fluid, which is absorbed back into the leaf.

Step five The leaf reopens, and the undigested, hard fly parts fall away. Each trap can work only three times.

Step six After its third meal, the leaf turns brown, then black. Later, it dies, and a new leaf sprouts from the plant.

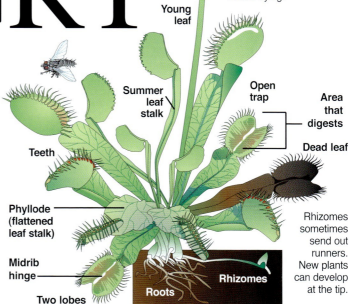

Closed trap Each trap is red on the inside and secretes a sweet nectar. It can consume three meals before dying.

Rhizomes sometimes send out runners. New plants can develop at the tip.

Venus' flytrap
The well-known Venus' flytrap lives in bogs in North Carolina. It grows from a special root system called a **rhizome**, and clusters of leaves form low to the ground. In spring, flower stalks and special traps grow from the plant to enable it to capture insects. Two trigger hairs must be touched before traps can spring shut around an unwary insect. It only takes about two-fifths of a second for them to close.

Passive trappers

Butterworts
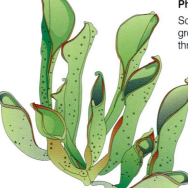

Butterworts grow in marshes, bogs or swamps. Most have thick, fleshy, pale green leaves that grow in a cluster. Flowers rise above the cluster on thin stems, in spring or early summer. The leaves are about half an inch long and have two kinds of **glands**. The first kind produces a sticky, oily liquid that feels buttery. A musty odor attracts insects to it. When the insects arrive and touch the leaf, they are held fast by the sticky liquid. The edges of the leaf then roll upward, forming a bowl-like shape. Then the second set of glands secrete the digestive enzymes into the bowl, killing the insect and digesting its nutrients. After a few days, the dried-up remains of the insect fall away from the now-flattened leaf.

Pitcher plants
Pitcher plants come in many sizes and shapes. They have special leaves that form hollow tubes or jug-like structures capable of holding rainwater. These special leaves are the traps. Most have clever features that **imprison** insects until they become exhausted and fall into the water in the base of the jug-like leaf. There they drown, and enzymes are secreted into the rainwater to digest them.

Scientists divide the tropical pitcher plants into two groups: **highland** (3,000-10,000 feet) and **lowland** (0-3,000 feet) depending on what elevation they grow at.

Trumpet pitchers The hood is an insect lure and also a rain roof. Flowers are produced on a separate stalk. Trumpets can reach up to 3 feet tall in some species.

Phial pitcher Some tropical pitchers grow on vines that wind through trees.

Marsh pitcher The simplest pitcher plant. It produces sweet-smelling nectar. The tubes are set at an angle, preventing rainwater from overfilling the pitchers.

Active trappers

Waterwheels
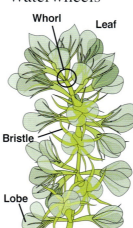

Waterwheels are **aquatic** plants found in Australia, Africa, Europe, India and Japan. The plant is small and it floats in still ponds and swamps just below the water's surface. It measures 4 to 12 inches long and has tiny, transparent leaves. Along the thin stem, leaf whorls are arranged like the spokes of a bicycle wheel. The **whorls** have eight bunches of leaves each.

The trapping mechanism is the leaf. Each one is about a quarter of an inch long, and can trap only tiny water insects, larvae or microscopic **plankton**. The leaves have two **lobes**, trigger hairs inside the lobes, and bristles. When food enters the trap, the lobes snap shut.

Bladderworts
Bladderworts are found all around the world in quiet swamps, bogs and ponds. Like waterwheels, they lack roots, and they produce long flower stalks that rise above the surface of the water. The bladderwort traps insects in tiny air sacs, or **bladders**. Each bladder is about a fifth of an inch long. At the loose end are trigger hairs arranged around a tiny trapdoor. The trapdoor opens inward. To capture an insect, the bladder uses **suction** – an unsuspecting insect brushes a trigger hair, causing the bladder to expand, the trapdoor to open, and water and insect are sucked in. Digestive **enzymes** immediately set to work.

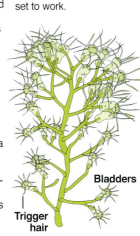

Sundews
Spatulate-leaf sundew Sticky hairs cover the leaf.

Thread-leaf sundew Leaves can move

Round-leaf sundew

The sundews are found in Europe, Australia, and the United States. The leaves are varied in shape, but each is covered in hairs. Each hair carries a glistening drop of glue-like liquid that shimmers to entice insects. Once an insect lands, it becomes entangled in the hairs. Often the whole leaf will wrap around the insect to engulf it. Then the hairs secret digestive juices.

The domestic cat

All cats, from big to small, and wild to tame, belong to the animal family Felidae. The domestic cat has become a popular pet around the world. With a reputation for being aloof and mysterious, cats are pretty and playful companions.

Ancestors

Cats are descended from a carnivorous, weasel-like animal called **Miacis** that lived about 50 million years ago. This animal was also the ancestor of dogs, bears, raccoons, civets, weasels and skunks.

Miacis
Paleocene period
(65 million to 55 million years ago)

The first cats appeared about 10 million years after the Miacis. (That's ten or twenty million years before the dog.) There were two early branches of cat: hoplophoneus and dinictis. The saber-toothed tiger was a member of the hoplophoneus group, which died out about 12,000 years ago. The dinictis branch of the family is more adaptable than its cousin and is the closer ancestor to today's domestic cat.

Domestication

Exactly when and where cats were first tamed and domesticated is unknown.

Cats served a useful purpose in ancient times by killing a variety of pests, such as rodents, insects and snakes. By about 1500 B.C., cats had become **sacred** to the Egyptians and to harm one was punishable by **death**. The Egyptian goddess of love and fertility **Bast** (or Bastet) was represented as a woman with the head of a cat. Archeologists have discovered huge Egyptian cat cemeteries with thousands of cat **mummies**. Many cat mummies were accompanied by mummified rats and mice, so that the cat could hunt in the next world.

It is believed that Greek and Phoenician traders brought cats to Europe and the Middle East around 1000 B.C. In Rome, the cat became a symbol of **liberty** and was thought of as a guardian spirit.

During the Middle Ages in Europe, cats were linked with **witchcraft** and became a symbol of evil. Hundreds of cats were killed during this time. This may have contributed to the spread of the plague or Black Death in the mid-14th century which killed millions of people and was carried by rat fleas.

Cats regained their status as cute, but deadly, rodent exterminators in the 17th century. The domestic cat arrived in North America with explorers and colonists.

Anatomy 101: Inside and out

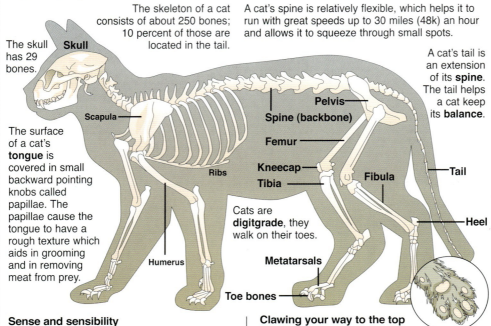

The skeleton of a cat consists of about 250 bones; 10 percent of those are located in the tail.

A cat's spine is relatively flexible, which helps it to run with great speeds up to 30 miles (48k) an hour and allows it to squeeze through small spots.

The skull has 29 bones.

A cat's tail is an extension of its **spine**. The tail helps a cat keep its **balance**.

The surface of a cat's **tongue** is covered in small backward pointing knobs called papillae. The papillae cause the tongue to have a rough texture which aids in grooming and in removing meat from prey.

Cats are **digitgrade**, they walk on their toes.

Sense and sensibility

A cat's senses are developed for **hunting**. Their highly developed sense of smell is not as powerful as a dog's, but much better than a human's. Cats can hear over long distances and at a much higher frequency (65kHz) than humans (22kHz). Cats don't see as well as people, but their eyesight is attuned to catching movement and adapting to dim light. A cat's whiskers serve as a sort of antennae.

Night eyes

Cats have a layer of cells behind their retina called the **tapetum**. These reflector cells mirror small quantities of light, allowing a cat to see in very dim light. The pupils of a cat's eyes close to tiny slits in bright sunlight and open wide in the dark.

Clawing your way to the top

Cats have **retractable** claws. When not in use the claw is pulled in and held under the skin by ligaments. Retracting the claws helps the cat keep them sharp. One reason that cats scratch stationary objects is to maintain and sharpen their claws.

Wall painting in Egypt depicts a man and his cat hunting birds.

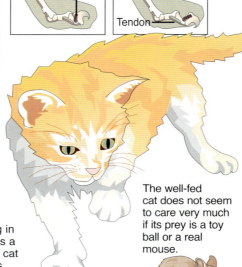

The well-fed cat does not seem to care very much if its prey is a toy ball or a real mouse.

Why does he do that?

Even though it has long been tamed, the domestic cat still has many of the basic instincts of its wild cousins. Cats born in the wild or abandoned will revert back to a wild state and are called feral cats. The life of a feral cat is generally very short, because domestic cats are not ideally suited to life on their own any more.

Why do cats purr? Purring is caused by air vibrating in the larynx (voice box) in a space called the glottis. Cats purr mostly when they are happy, but they also purr when sick or in pain. It may be that purring when they are sick is a way for the cat to comfort itself.

Why do cats rub up against people? When a cat rubs against people and inanimate objects it releases scents that mark the spot and the person as its own and part of its territory.

Why do cats hunt and stalk? When cats hunt, stalk and play with toys or prey they are responding to a basic instinct. Domestic cats, like their wild cousins, are born to be predators.

Why do cats arch and fluff up their fur? When a cat is frightened or angry it will arch its back and its fur will bristle. This makes the cat look bigger and more intimidating and may serve to scare away another animal.

Why do cats get so active at night? Cats are excellent hunters and their acute night eyesight makes evening hunting more productive.

Getting older

Cat's age	Human equivalent
6 months	10 years
8 months	13 years
1 year	15 years
2 years	24 years
4 years	32 years
6 years	40 years
8 years	48 years
10 years	56 years
12 years	64 years
14 years	72 years
16 years	80 years
18 years	88 years
20 years	96 years
21 years	100 years

11th or 12th century, bronze, Islamic incense burner in the shape of a cat.

Name that breed: Test your knowledge

Below are some pictures of different breeds. Can you identify the breed? A book on cat breeds from the library might help you, and so may the hints under each picture.

1. Most popular of long haired cat breeds.
2. This cat has short, wavy hair.
3. Most popular of the short haired cats.
4. Its short, bluish-gray fur is unique.
5. Intelligent and ancient breed from Turkey.

6. This muscular cat has golden eyes.
7. This kitty might look good in a kilt.
8. This cat has a bushy fox-like tail.
9. This large cat looks a little bit like a raccoon.
10. Blue eyed beauty with white paws from Burma.

Scoring

Give yourself 1 point for every cat identified correctly.

- 1-2 You need to improve your cat breed identification skills
- 3-5 You're pretty good at this
- 6-8 Very impressive
- 9-10 Awesome! AA++

Answers

1. Persian
2. Devon Rex
3. Siamese
4. Russian Blue
5. Turkish Angora
6. Burmese
7. Scottish Fold
8. Somali
9. Maine Coon
10. Birman

Conifers

Plant basics

Scientists who study and classify plants are called **botanists.** One way they classify plants is into two categories: **vascular** and **nonvascular.** The nonvascular plants do not have specialized tissues that transport water and nutrients between parts of the plant. Some nonvascular plants are algae and mosses. The vascular plants have special transport systems within their tissues. They include most of the land plants. Among the **terrestrial** (land) plants there are three groups that can be organized based upon how they reproduce:

Ferns The simplest group of vascular land plants.

Gymnosperms are vascular plants with simple seed-producing structures, the most familiar being cones. They do not flower.

Angiosperms are complex flowering plants that produce seeds enclosed within an ovary.

What about the conifers?

Conifers are sometimes called **evergreens,** because most have adapted to their climate by holding on to their needles throughout the year. But some evergreens like the larch and the dawn redwood shed their needles in winter.

California: land of the Giants

Biggest trees

The **sequoia** grows to be the biggest conifer. Living at elevations of 6,500 feet, it is one of the fastest growing trees in the world, with bark as thick as 4 feet. Sequoias have survived for 2,000 to 3,000 years. Some of the largest ones are 35 feet in diameter and up to 300 feet in height.

One tree in California has been named "General Sherman" and is the world's largest tree. Measuring 274.9 feet, its diameter around the base is 102.6 feet. The total volume of the trunk is 52,508 cubic feet. A branch that fell in 1978 had a diameter of over 6 feet and a length of 140 feet. That branch alone was larger than any tree growing in the United States east of the Cascade mountain range.

Tallest trees

The **coast redwood** is another type of sequoia tree. They grow up to 1 to 2 feet per year, and live in a narrow strip of land along the California and Oregon coast. Many grow to be more than 300 feet tall. They can also be as old as 4000 years.

Oldest trees

California is also the home of the world's oldest trees. **Dendrochronology** is the study of annual tree rings. Dendrochronologists have estimated that some of the **bristlecone pines** in California are between 4,000 and 5,000 years old.

Grand fir

This tree grows primarily in British Columbia, western Washington and Oregon, and in the Rocky Mountains. Firs have smooth, leathery needles, unlike the sharp, spiky ones of the spruces. Fir cones grow upward from the branch, and the tree holds them until the scales peel off and blow away in the wind.

Monterey cypress

The cypress, along with juniper and cedar trees, have tiny, overlapping scales instead of the more familiar needles of the pines, firs and spruces. In junipers, they are also spiky. The cones of all cypresses have 6 to 12 thick, disc-like scales.

Young cones are green and compact.

Yew

The yew is more primitive than other conifers in that it produces berries rather than cones. The berries, which are poisonous, resemble small olives, as each berry contains a single seed. Like the ginko, the yew has separate-sex trees, producing either male or female flowers.

Morinda spruce

This tree is native to the Western Himalayas. It grows to be more than 30 feet tall and has the largest needles of any spruce.

Uses for conifers

There are very few gymnosperms that have not been used by people. Some of the trees that grow in the tropics produce edible nuts that are eaten by local people. The Western red cedar filled most of the needs of Pacific Northwest Coast peoples. Conifers have been used for shelter, fuel, papermaking and clothing. Today, they provide softwood lumber and wood pulp for the 14 major timber producers in North America. Most of it comes from just a few species planted over millions of acres of managed forests.

Monkey puzzle

This tree, also called the Chile pine, has been on the Earth since the dinosaurs. It grows on the border between Chile and Argentina, and in public gardens all over the world. The tree has unusual overlapping scales and forms a dense canopy. The name came from a Victorian plant collector who commented, "Well, it would puzzle a monkey to climb that."

Old cones are brittle and brown.

Cones

Cones are the seed-bearing parts of a conifer. They are male or female and both types usually grow on the same plant.

Cross-section of stone pine cone

Scale Two seeds form inside each scale.

Reproduction

1. Airborne pollen floats from male to female cones.

Male cones — **Pollen** — **Female cones**

Scale — **Egg**

Ovule

2. Pollen enters ovules. The ovules then develop into seeds.

3. Scale begins to grow.

Embryonic tree

4. Each scale forms two winged seeds. Some cones hold their seeds for many years.

Two seeds per scale

Needles and scales

The needles or scales of conifers, which differ from the leaves of the broadleaf plants, have parallel veins and a waxy covering called a **cuticle** that conserves moisture.

The pines all have long needles that grow in clusters of two, three or five.

Scotch pine

Monterey pine

Arolla pine

Gallery of North American conifers

Eastern red cedar — Eastern half of United States, Southern Ontario — 40 to 50 feet

Balsam fir — Eastern Canada, Northern United States — 40 to 60 feet

Northern white cedar — Southeastern Canada, North eastern United States — 30 to 50 feet

Eastern larch — North America — 40 to 60 feet

Douglas fir — U.S. and Canadian Pacific coast — 180 to 250 feet

Loblolly pine — Southeastern U.S. into Texas — 90 to 100 feet

Monterey cypress — Monterey County, California — 60 to 80 feet

Black spruce — Canada, Northeastern United States — 30 to 50 feet

CROCODILES

Crocodiles are a member of the **reptile** order *Crocodilia*, which also includes alligators, gharials and caimans. Crocodilians are close relatives of ancient **dinosaurs**. Years of being hunted by man brought many of these creatures to the brink of extinction. Due to conservation efforts some species have recovered, but others remain seriously endangered. About 20 species of crocodilians exist today.

All in the family

The word "reptile" is from the Latin repere, which means "to crawl."

Reptiles are divided into four groups; one of these is the crocodilians. Scientists have divided the crocodilian family into three subgroups: crocodiles; alligators and caimans; and gharials.

American alligator
Alligator mississippiensis
Range: Southeastern United States
Size: Up to 18 feet (5.5 m)

American crocodile
Crocodylus acutus
Range: Southeastern United States, Southern Mexico, Central America and northern South America
Size: Averages 12 feet (3.5 m)

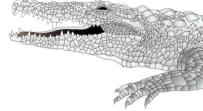

Gharial
Gavialis gangeticus
Range: Northern India
Size: Up to 23 feet (7 m)

Nile crocodile
Crocodilus niloticus
Range: Africa
Size: up to 16.5 feet (5 m)

Spectacled Caiman
Caiman crocodilus
Range: Venezuela to South Amazon basin
Size: 5 to 6.5 feet (1.5 to 2 m)

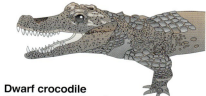

Dwarf crocodile
Osteolaemus tetraspis
Range: West Africa, south of the Sahara
Size: Up to 5 feet (1.5 m)

Crocodiles have excellent night vision due to a reflective layer of cells called the **tapetum**. These reflector cells mirror even small quantities of light.

The phrase "crocodile tears" is used to describe someone who is faking sadness or remorse. A crocodile does not weep over the victim it just ate, but crocodiles do produce tears to help lubricate and clean their eyes. Tears are especially apparent when a crocodile has been out of the water for a while and the eyes start to dry out. While under water, a protective membrane serves as an extra eyelid. The membrane can interefere with a crocodile's focus, so they rely heavily on hearing underwater.

Which is which?
The easiest way to tell an alligator from a crocodile is to look at its **nose**. Alligators have a wide, U-shaped snout. Crocodiles have a longer, pointed V-shaped nose.

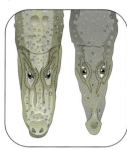

Alligator   Crocodile

Spinal cord · Lung · Intestines · Kidney · Cloaca · Stomach · Liver · Heart

Most reptiles (lizards, snakes and turtles) have three-chambered hearts, but crocodiles have a four-chambered heart (like birds and mammals).

Crocodiles can crawl along on their bellies or raise themselves off the ground in a high walk. They are capable of moving quite quickly and can travel considerable distances by land.

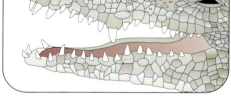

Crocodiles have **60 to 70 teeth**, which they lose and grow back continually.

Crocodiles have five toes on their front feet, but only four toes on their back feet. Webbing on the feet between their toes helps crocodiles move quickly through water and walk more easily in mud.

Interesting facts

Crocodilians share many characteristics and lifestyles. Social animals, they live in warm (tropical) climates in freshwater marshes, rivers, lakes and swamps (only the saltwater crocodile lives in salt water). Strong swimmers, these **carnivores** (meat eaters) spend much of their time in water, but they are born on land and have lungs, not gills. Some crocodilians can stay underwater for up to 30 minutes if they have to, but a typical dive is about 15 minutes. Crocodilians are vertebrates (animals with backbones). Because they are reptiles, they are cold-blooded; their body temperature changes with that of their environment.

Dinner time

Crocodilians are designed to be superior hunters, and many will eat just about anything they can catch, including people. Their teeth are ideal for grabbing and crushing prey, but not for chewing. Instead of chewing, crocodilians rip their food apart or swallow it whole. Crocodilians have very high levels of acid in their stomach to help them digest every part of an animal — even the bones. And they store more than half of the energy supplied by a meal as fat in their tails, backs and abdomens. Because they can store so much energy, it is possible for a large crocodilian to go up to two years without a meal.

Excellent parents

Like most reptiles, crocodilians lay **eggs**. Crocodilian mothers build nests and lay one clutch of eggs a year. A clutch may consist of 15 to 80 eggs (depending on the species). The mother fiercely guards her nest, while the male stays nearby to assist her, but he will not get too close to the nest for fear of being attacked himself. (Some species dig holes in the ground, others combine mud, leaves and branches and build above ground.) The sex of the babies is determined by the **temperature** of the eggs during the first few weeks. If the nest is below 86 F (30 C), all are female; above 93 F (34 C), all are male. Temperatures in between will produce both sexes. Some mothers will help break the eggs by gently chewing on them. Some crocodilian parents will protect their young until they are old enough to look after themselves (about 3 months), while other crocodilian parents provide no further care for their offspring once the young hatch.

Alligator eggs and incubation

Day 1

Day 38

Day 52

Day 65

An alligator may lay 50 to 60 eggs in a nest as large as 10 feet wide and 3 to 6 feet deep.

The eggs are incubated by the heat of the sun and decaying plant matter. The sex of the babies is determined by the temperature of the eggs during the first few weeks.

Baby alligators use a special egg tooth to break out of their shells.

Deserts

What is a desert?

Deserts are arid regions that occur on every continent. They cover about one-fifth of the Earth's land surface. Most desert regions are near the equator, where the sun's rays strike the strongest. Deserts usually have these things:

- They receive less than 10 inches of precipitation per year.
- Most have hot temperatures for part of the year.
- More moisture is lost through evaporation than is received as rainfall.
- Desert plants and animals have adapted for surviving their harsh environment.

Types of desert

- **Polar deserts** are arid because any moisture is either frozen or evaporated by harsh winds.
- **Cold winter deserts** lie between 35 and 50 degrees latitude and are hot in the summer and freezing in winter. They lie inland, where ocean moisture cannot reach them, or in the rain shadow of a mountain.
- **Subtropical deserts** straddle the Tropic of Cancer or Tropic of Capricorn about 23 degrees latitude in either direction.
- **Coastal deserts** are dry and cold at night because of the nearby ocean currents. Fog forms over the land, but years can pass between rain showers.

Spadefoot toads can burrow deep into desert soil while it is wet from spring rains. Females lay eggs in rain puddles, and the tadpoles grow quickly, before the dry season. In the dry season, the toads remain in their moist burrows for months.

Dune formation

Only about one-fourth of the world's deserts are covered by sand. The rest are a mixture of other types of features, including rock, gravel, dried clay or salt.

Sand dunes can travel hundreds of feet per year, gradually covering non-desert areas. This process, called desertification, also occurs when land is suffering from drought or agricultural misuse. Normal dune formation begins with saltation, a process where wind causes grains of sand to fly into the air. When the sand grains hit the ground, it causes more grains to launch into the wind.

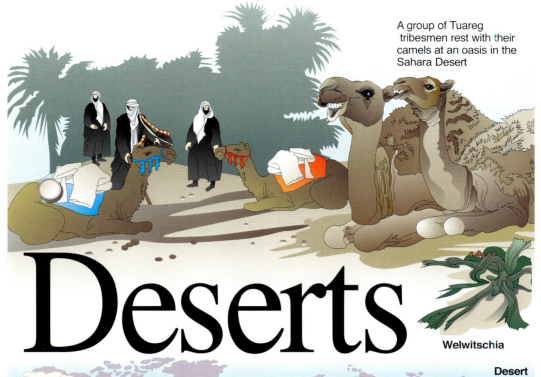

A group of Tuareg tribesmen rest with their camels at an oasis in the Sahara Desert

Welwitschia

Desert lynx

World deserts

Though all deserts have the obvious characteristics of sand, temperature and aridity in common, each desert is a unique ecosystem with specific plants and animals found only there. Here are some facts of note about some of the world's desert regions:

Sahara desert

The Sahara is the world's largest desert and covers the top third of the African continent. It stretches 3,100 miles across and 1,200 miles from North to South. Sahara means "desert" in Arabic, and many experts consider its neighbor, the Arabian desert, to be a continuation of the Sahara. An oasis is formed when water seeps up from underground, forming islands of green. Many nomadic tribes wander the Sahara, trading goods and camels at small settlements around the oases. Tuareg tribesmen live as traders, and are famous for their indigo-colored cloth. They have long been important traders of salt, carrying it by caravan from salt pits in Bilma, Niger, throughout the Sahara.

Turkestan desert

This region in central Asia is composed of two separate deserts called the Kara-Kum (black sand) and Kyzul-Kum (red sand). The region is extremely dry and in winter, cold Siberian and Arctic winds can reduce the temperature to minus 44°F. Total precipitation is less than 4 inches per year. Because of human settlement, many native animals have been forced out of the region by herdsmen, including carnivores, like the caracal or desert lynx.

Namib desert

The Namib desert is blanketed in fog every day from the Atlantic Ocean. It rains less than an inch per year there, so the fog is the main source of water for all of the creatures who live in the Namib. Many very unusual plants like the welwitschia live there. It can live to be 2,000 years old, and absorbs moisture from fog through its leathery, strap-like leaves.

Adaptation is the key to desert survival

Desert plants have developed special features to survive searing heat, harsh winds, cold nights and lack of water. Most have dense root systems that may extend for many feet to tap whatever water is available.

Desert animals tolerate temperature extremes and lack of water. In order to survive the quest for food and survival, many desert animals have evolved in a variety of ways to cope with their harsh environment.

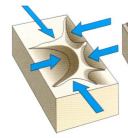

To conserve water **cactuses** have evolved fleshy, thick stems covered in protective spines.

Kangaroo rats do not need to drink. They are able to make water inside their bodies from the seeds they eat.

Antelope jackrabbits have evolved long legs to help them run quickly above the hot desert sand. Their long ears are full of tiny blood vessels that are cooled by the air – a kind of air conditioning for the blood.

Star

Star dunes are formed by converging winds from many directions. The arms radiate from a central ridge.

Longitudinal

Longitudinal dunes form troughs that carve deeply into the floor of the desert. Crests form as the wind changes direction.

Parabolic

Parabolic dunes form with horns facing the wind, usually because vegetation anchors the horns and sand builds behind them.

Transverse

Transverse dunes are formed by winds that sweep sand into ripples perpendicular to the wind. They are gently sloped on the windward side.

Seif

Seif dunes are wobbly ridges caused by shifts in the wind direction.

Barchan

Barchan dunes are crescent shaped and form in constant winds from one direction. The horns face away from the wind and are caused by sand moving rapidly.

DINOSAURS

Dinosaur basics

Dinosaurs were large reptiles that dominated the land during the Mesozoic ("middle-life") era of geologic time. They evolved as a result of mass extinctions at the end of the Permian period, about 248 million years ago.

The name "dinosaur" means "terrible lizard." It was given to these animals by Richard Owen, a British anatomist (a scientist who studies the anatomy of animals) in 1842. Many prehistoric animals are mistakenly grouped with dinosaurs by novices.

Here's what makes a dinosaur a dinosaur:

▶ **All dinosaurs lived** during the Mesozoic era, between 227 million and 65 million years ago.

▶ **All dinosaurs were** reptiles that lived on land. Most did not swim or fly.

▶ **All dinosaurs were** members of a group of reptiles called the **archosaurs** ("ruling reptiles"), which included crocodiles, flying reptiles and thecodonts, a primitive form of reptile.

Dinosaurs evolved from a common ancestor into two main groups, about 220 million years ago. It is thought that birds, who survived the catastrophic extinctions at the end of the Mesozoic era, are their modern relatives.

This type of relational diagram is called a **cladogram**.

Changing Earth: The Mesozoic era

The study of **plate tectonics** allows **geologists** (scientists who study the Earth's land and rocks) to track the movement of Earth's continents over time.

Here's a peek at what our planet probably looked like during the Age of Reptiles:

The **Triassic** period began with the continents joined in one great land mass, called **Pangea**. Toward the late Triassic period, there was upheaval and violent geologic activity. Very slowly, the continents began to separate.

The **Jurassic** period was mild weather-wise, and no polar ice caps meant higher sea levels. Marine life forms were widespread and abundant.

During the **Cretaceous** period, land masses separated and moved considerably, looking more like the modern map.

How fossils are formed and found

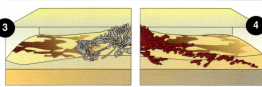

1. An animal dies. Fossils form best if the carcass is covered quickly with sediment — water and mud.

2. The flesh rots away, and the bones are slowly covered with layered sediment.

3. Permineralization occurs if some or all of the original material remains, but has been strengthened by minerals that were dissolved in the water that had soaked into the bony structure.

4. Petrification occurs if water that contained minerals soaks into the pores of the bony structure, entirely replacing them with minerals.

5. **Weathering**, Earth movements and/or erosion, cause the fossil to become exposed.

A look at hips

Since the 19th century, dinosaurs have been grouped into two distinct types based upon the structure of their hipbones.

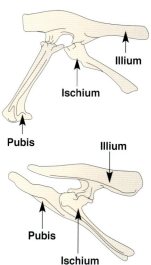

Saurischian ("lizard-hipped") dinosaurs had hipbones arranged so that the upper bone (illium) made firm contact with the backbone. The two lower bones (pubis and ischium) pointed forward and backward, providing a large area for the attachment of the huge leg muscles. Some lizard-hipped dinosaurs were plant eaters, others were meat eaters.

Ornithischian ("bird-hipped") dinosaurs had hipbones arranged with the pubis and ischium pointing backward, much like modern birds. All bird-hipped dinosaurs were plant-eaters.

Making a dinosaur: From field to museum

An incredible amount of work is required to obtain a fossil and transport it back to a museum for preparation and display. After locating a suitable site, scientists search for bone shards or promising rock formations. The chances of finding an intact animal are rare; often, a few bones or a skull are all that remain of an animal in the rock.

Once a fossil is chosen to be excavated, a team of scientists and technicians must painstakingly expose each bone or fragment and remove it from the surrounding rock. Small hand tools, picks, dental tools and bristle brushes aid the diggers.

Each bone is numbered, photographed and catalogued onsite. Then they are carefully wrapped, crated and shipped back to a laboratory for cleaning, study and preparation.

Dinosaur hunters

The study of dinosaurs is not limited to palaeontologists. Geologists, anatomists, evolutionists, oceanographers and zoologists contribute to our knowledge.

Richard Owen (1804–1892) As the first superintendent of the British Museum of Natural History, he reviewed fossil reptiles and named them after the Greek words deinos and sauros, or "terrible lizards."

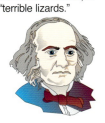

Gideon Mantell (1790–1852) A family doctor living in Sussex, England. Mantell published a description of an animal he named Iguanodon, after its living relatives.

Edward Drinker Cope (1840–1897) was an American naturalist who specialized in mammal and dinosaur fossils. His collection is part of the American Museum of Natural History in New York.

Edwin Colbert (1905–2001) excavated the famous Ghost Ranch site in New Mexico. An abundance of Coelophysis skeletons (carnivores from the late Triassic period) were found there.

Stephen Jay Gould (1941–2002) developed the evolutionary theory called "Punctuated Equilibrium." It states that most evolution occurs in short bursts, interspersed with long periods of stasis.

The rise of dinosaurs

The Triassic period marked the beginning of a time of recovery for life on Earth. Mass extinctions at the end of the previous period — the Permian — were brought about by all-time low sea levels, global climate changes, and low oxygen levels in the atmosphere and water.

Extinction brought major developments in the surviving land animals, including the emergence of ruling reptiles, called the **archosaurs**, which dominated the land.

Habitats diversified, and land plant life adapted significantly. Life in the sea also began to flourish again, and bony fish, corals and mollusks formed Earth's first primitive reef systems.

Eudimorphodon
(YOU-die-MORF-o-dahn)
Wingspan: About 2.5 feet (.75 m)

Flying reptiles, or pterosaurs, evolved about 70 million years before the first-known birds. Eudimorphodon is the earliest-known, and had very sharp, pointed teeth, probably to help it catch fish.

Most of the animals on this page never shared the same habitat or lived at the same time, but they are shown in scale with each other.

Placerias
(pluh-SEHR-ree-uhs)
Length: About 11.5 ft (3.5 m)

A hippopotamus-like, herding **therapsid**, or mammal-like reptile, it was not a dinosaur. Placerias ate roots, ferns, moss and other low-lying plants.

Plateosaurus
(PLAT-ee-oh-sore-uhs)
Length: About 26 feet (8 m)

Did you know?
- The name **Triassic** refers to the threefold division of rocks of this age that were found in Germany.
- Scientists agree there was a worldwide disaster that occurred about 200 million years ago, toward the end of the Triassic period. Some scientists believe the geological evidence points to a meteor impact, which coincides with a mass extinction that eliminated half the major groups of life and allowed the small surviving dinosaurs to evolve and diversify during the Jurassic period.
- Spiral-shelled mollusks called **Ammonites** evolved rapidly in the Triassic. The distinct forms of their changing shells are used as **index**, or **indicator, fossils** to aid scientists in dating the surrounding rock strata.

Coelophysis
(seel-OH-fie-sis)
Length: About 10 feet (3 m)

The best skeletal remains were discovered in 1947 by Edwin Colbert at Ghost Ranch, N.M. Several hundred animals were jumbled together in a mass grave. Phytosaurs, fish, clams and crayfish were also found at the site, providing a snapshot of the Triassic ecosystem.

Euparkeria
(eew-PARK-er-ee-ya)
Length: About 2 feet (.6 m)

Euparkeria is a close relative of the archosaurs. Its body form is unusual for reptiles of the time, in that the hind limbs are longer than the fore limbs. Scientists believe it is a sister group to all other Archosauria, or is part of the lineage leading to dinosaurs.

← Going back in time

APPROXIMATE PLACEMENT OF THESE REPTILES AND DINOSAURS ON THE GEOLOGIC TIMESCALE

The Scythian Epoch	The Middle Triassic Epoch	The Late Triassic Epoch
248 to 241 million years ago	241 to 227 million years ago	227 to 205 million years ago

Euparkeria — Early Triassic — South Africa

Placerias — Late Triassic — N. America
Coelophysis — Late Triassic — N. America
Plateosaurus — Late Triassic — Western Europe
Eudimorphodon — Late Triassic — Italy

The Jurassic Period

The Jurassic period began with a worldwide disaster that wiped out many forms of life. Small dinosaurs, crocodiles and mammal-like reptiles survived the change, but many large reptiles became extinct. Plant life was also affected. Conifers and thick-leaved evergreens called cycads grew along the shores of shallow lakes. The **ginkgo** tree, which still survives in modern times, evolved during this period. Moist environments became more common, but generally the climate was dry. The skies were full of flying reptiles, and the first birds evolved from the dinosaurs.

Stegosaurus
(STEG-oh-SORE-us)
Length: About 30 feet (9 m)
The largest-known plated dinosaur, this herbivore had a very small skull and brain for such a large animal. It also had rows of tall, bony plates running along its back. While scientists disagree about their use, they may have helped release body heat.

Apatosaurus
(ah-PAT-oh-SORE-us)
Length: About 70 feet (21 m)
This giant herbivore (plant-eater) was called brontosaurus until 1978, when scientists re-evaluated the skeleton. This giant dinosaur weighed as much as five adult elephants and used its tail for balance.

Allosaurus
(AL-oh-SARE-us)
Length: About 35 feet (10.5 m)
This gigantic carnivore (meat-eater) was the largest predator of the Late Jurassic period. Allosaurus had bony, rough ridges above the eye sockets. It fed on large game like the Apatosaurus, and hunted anything it could trap and kill. Allosaurs may also have been scavengers, feeding on dead or dying animals.

Archaeopteryx
(AR-kee-OP-ter-iks)
Length: About 1.5 feet (.45 m)
Archaeopteryx occupies a special place in evolutionary history — as a link between reptiles and birds. Fossils show it had a wishbone, clawed fingers on its wings, a long tail with a bony core (similar to that of small dinosaurs) and feather-like structures on the wings and tail.

Scutellosaurus
(skoo-TEL-o-SAWR-us)
Length: About 4 feet (1.2 m)
This small bird-hipped dinosaur had hundreds of small, armored, bony plates on its back. It could walk on two or four legs and probably sprinted on its back legs to evade predators.

Did you know?

- Drought was a constant threat during the Jurassic period.
- Because of plate collisions and the opening of new ocean basins, there is no ocean floor in the present-day basins that is older than Jurassic age.
- The Jurassic had an abundance of cycads (left). The plants were widespread over the entire Earth, along with conifers.
- Mammals were still rare during this period, and were small, nocturnal insect eaters.

← Going back in time

APPROXIMATE PLACEMENT OF THESE DINOSAURS ON THE GEOLOGIC TIMESCALE

The Lias Epoch (Early Jurassic)
205 to 180 million years ago

The Dogger Epoch (Middle Jurassic)
180 to 159 million years ago

The Malm Epoch (Late Jurassic)
159 to 144 million years ago

Scutellosaurus
Early Jurassic
N. America

Stegosaurus
Late Jurassic
N. America

Archaeopteryx
Late Jurassic
Europe

Allosaurus
Late Jurassic
N. America

Apatosaurus
Late Jurassic
N. America

The Cretaceous Period

The name **Cretaceous** comes from the Latin word for chalk. Millions of fossilized marine organisms and shells are found in chalky deposits in rock dating back to this period. Massive floods invaded the land, and as the oceans swelled, North America was divided by a shallow sea. Geologic activity pushed the Rocky Mountains upward, and sediments from the mountains washed eastward onto plains, where a vast number of dinosaurs roamed. Dinosaurs flourished and diversified into more species than ever before. Though scientists disagree, most say the climate during this time began to change from humid and very warm to cooler and drier.

At the end of the Cretaceous, an inexplicable event brought about a great extinction. On land, the dinosaurs died out, survived by most of the plant life and newly evolving smaller mammals. A smaller fraction of the marine animals and plants survived the event.

Pteranodon
(TERR-an-O-donn)
Wingspan: 23 feet (7 m)
This flying reptile probably was a glider. Its relatively large eyes may have helped it search for fish.

Triceratops
(try-SERRA-tops) **Length:** About 30 feet (9 m)
These massive herbivores had a bony neck frill. They were one of the last of the dinosaurs to evolve, and one of the most numerous. They traveled in small groups or herds.

Oviraptor
(OH-vih-RAP-tor)
Length: About 6 feet (1.8 m)
The earliest fossil of an oviraptor was found near a nest containing what were thought to be the eggs of Protoceratops. Up until a few years ago, scientists thought the ovirapto was an "egg thief," but then proved that the eggs were her own.

Deinonychus
(die-NON-i-kus)
Length: About 8 feet (2.5 m)
This predator was fast, agile and intelligent. It was believed to be a pack hunter, using the enlarged "terrible claw" on the second toe of each foot to disembowel its prey.

Tyrannosaurus rex
(tie-RAN-oh-SORE-us-REX)
Length: About 46 feet (14 m)
Perhaps the most well-known of all dinosaurs, the Tyrannosaurus rex was an awesome predator that could have weighed up to 8 tons. It was armed with fangs measuring up to 6 inches long and had a bite force that could have easily ripped through a car roof. The function of its tiny, two-fingered hands remains a mystery. It is lilkely that the Tyrannosaurus rex both hunted and scavenged.

Did you know?
- Sea level was high throughout much of the Cretaceous period. At its maximum height, only about 18 percent of the Earth's surface remained uncovered by water, as compared to approximately 28 percent today.
- Carnivorous dinosaurs developed many kinds of advanced teeth and claws during the Cretaceous period.
- Many new types of plants devolped during this time, including figs, magnolias, poplars, willows, sycamores and herbs. With the advent of many new plant types, insects also diversified.

← Going back in time

APPROXIMATE PLACEMENT OF THESE DINOSAURS ON THE GEOLOGIC TIMESCALE

The Neocomian Epoch (Early Cretaceous) 144 to 127 million years ago	The Gallic Epoch (Middle Cretaceous) 127 to 90 million years ago	The Senonian Epoch (Late Cretaceous) 90 to 65 million years ago
Deinonychus Early Cretaceous N. America		Pteranodon Late Cretaceous Europe / Oviraptor Late Cretaceous Asia / Tyrannosaurus rex Late Cretaceous N. America / Triceratops Late Cretaceous N. America

DOGS

They have been human companions for 10,000 years, maybe longer, but through the centuries the domestic dog has not lost its charm.

Way back when

Dogs are thought to be the descendants of a carnivorous, weasel-like animal called the **Miacis** that lived about 50 million years ago. The Miacis had five toes and was probably a good climber.

Miacis
(Paleocene period: 65 million to 55 million years ago)

The **Cynodictis** evolved 20 million years ago. This animal had some doglike characteristics.

Cynodictis
(Eocene period: 55 million to 38 million years ago)

About 10 million years ago a creature evolved called the **Tomarctus**. Tomarctus resembled a wolf and is the ancestor of all members of the dog family.

Tomarctus
Miocene period
(25 million to 5 million years ago)

Archeologists have discovered evidence that people and dogs have lived together for at least 10,000 years. This makes dogs the **oldest** known domesticated animal. The **saluki** is considered the oldest of the present-day breeds. The saluki probably originated in the Middle East around 5000 B.C. By 1500 B.C., Egyptian art depicts a variety of dog breeds that resemble mastiffs and hunting dogs.

Mexican pottery dog from the Colima culture A.D. 300

Dogs can hear high-pitched sounds that humans cannot, and, some dogs like the bloodhound can track a 4-day-old scent. Dogs see the world in shades of gray and blue.

Anatomy 101: Inside and out

Dogs come in many shapes and sizes, but they all share basic physical characteristics. A dog's skeleton has about 320 bones (this number varies depending on how many bones are in the tail).

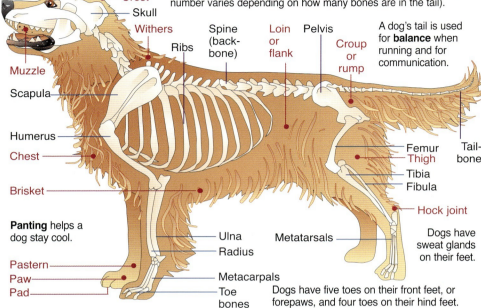

A dog's tail is used for **balance** when running and for communication.

Dogs have sweat glands on their feet.

Dogs have five toes on their front feet, or forepaws, and four toes on their hind feet.

Panting helps a dog stay cool.

Impeccable breeding

Dogs have been bred for many practical reasons: hunting, herding, guarding and even keeping humans warm. Toy dogs in ancient China were carried in wide sleeves to help keep a person's hands warm. It was not until the establishment of the first kennel clubs in Europe that breed histories and pedigrees were recorded.

Today there are more than 400 kinds of **purebred** dogs. A purebred is a dog whose **sire** and **dam** (father and mother) are of the same breed and whose ancestors were also purebred, dating back to the establishment of the breed. **Mixed-breed** dogs are also known as **mutts** or **mongrels**. These dogs have parents of different breeds or are of mixed breeding themselves.

Working for a living

Sporting dogs are also called gundogs because they are bred to assist hunters. Pointers, setters, retrievers and spaniels are sporting dogs. **Hounds** are also hunting dogs. Beagles, basset hounds and bloodhounds rely on scent to hunt and are also known as scent hounds. **Working dogs** have been bred to perform a particular job. Siberian huskies pull sleds, Newfoundlands are well-suited to rescue work. **Terriers** specialize in hunting rodents and small animals. **Toy dogs** are mostly bred as companions and to compete at dog shows. **Utility** or **nonsporting dogs** are generally larger breeds; the poodle originally specialized in retrieving ducks for French hunters. The collie and German shepherd are **herding dogs**.

Name that breed: Test your knowledge

Below are some pictures of different breeds. Can you identify the breed? You get bonus points if you can name the AKC classification, too. A book on dog breeds from the library might help you.

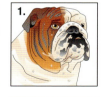

Famous canines

Laika — The first dog in space, aboard the Soviet satellite Sputnik 2 in 1957.

Lassie — A line of popular collies in movies and in television. The first Lassie starred in the 1943 movie Lassie Come Home.

Le Diable — A French dog trained to smuggle items across the border. His owners dyed his hair different colors to confuse the guards.

Rin Tin Tin — Famous German shepherd movie star. "Rinty" was in many movies before his death in 1932.

Saur or Suening — This dog was put on the throne of Norway for three years by an angry king in the 11th century.

What are we talking about?

Bitch — A female dog.
Breed — A kind of dog with consistent traits.
Kennel — A place where dogs are bred and boarded.
License — Permission by a government agency allowing you to keep a dog; a fee is usually required.
Neuter — A surgery that prevents male dogs from impregnating female dogs.
Pedigree — A list of the dog's ancestors.
Registration papers — Proof that a purebred and its parents are on record at a dog registry (kennel club).
Spay — A surgery that prevents female dogs from getting pregnant.

Egyptian jackal statue A.D. 300

Pet dog from a Greek vase (c. 380–360 B.C.)

Ancient Roman guard dog

Scoring

Give yourself 1 point for every dog identified correctly and another point for each correct classification.

1–5 You need to improve your dog breed identification skills
5–10 You're pretty good at this
10–15 Very impressive work
15–20 Awesome! A++

Answers
1. English bulldog (Utility)
2. Bloodhound (Hound)
3. Border collie (Working)
4. Bull terrier (Terrier)
5. Dalmatian (Utility)
6. Irish setter (Sporting)
7. Saluki (Hound)
8. Skye terrier (Terrier)
9. Pomeranian (Toy)
10. English springer spaniel (Sporting)

Big and small: dog sizes

Dogs come in many sizes, from the Chihuahua (world's smallest dog) to the larger breeds like the heavyset St. Bernard or the tall Irish wolfhound. This chart shows the average weight and shoulder height for several breeds.

Chihuahua
1–6 pounds
(0.5–3 kg)
5 inches
(13 cm)

English cocker spaniel
26–34 pounds
(12–15 kg)
16 inches
(41 cm)

Collie
50–75 pounds (23–34 kg)
22–26 inches (56–66 cm)

St. Bernard
140–200 pounds (64–90 kg)
26–30 inches (66–76 cm)

Irish wolfhound
126–145 pounds (57–66 kg)
32–34 inches (81–86 cm)

DOLPHINS

By definition
Dolphins are not fish. They are aquatic **mammals**. Closely related to **whales** and porpoises, they belong to a group of mammals called cetaceans (sih-TAY-shunz). Dolphins breathe air and feed their young **milk**. They are also warmblooded, which means they maintain a relatively consistent body temperature regardless of the temperature of their surroundings.

The word dolphin is used to describe two kinds of cetaceans: Marine dolphins and river dolphins. There are 32 species of marine dolphin and five species of river dolphin.

All in the family
Kingdom	Animalia
Phylum	Chordata
Subphylum	Vertebrata
Class	Mammalia
Order	Cetacea
Family (marine)	Delphinidae
Family (river)	Platanistidae

Fresh air
Dolphins breathe air through a nostril called a blowhole. While it is underwater, the blowhole is sealed with a special muscle. Most dolphins surface to breathe every 30 or 60 seconds.

Speaking dolphin
Dolphins communicate in a variety of ways. Short **clicking** sounds and high-pitched squeals and whistles are often combined (scientists call these combinations phonations). Squeals sometimes express excitement, or they can signal an alarm. Clicking is also used for echolocation and helps the dolphin find food and friends. The clicks are created in nasal sacs behind the melon, an organ made of special fatty tissues that focus sound into a beam (like a flashlight). When the sound hits an object, sound waves bounce back. By listening to this echo, a dolphin can locate objects.

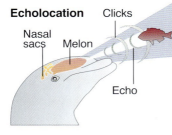

Echolocation — Clicks, Nasal sacs, Melon, Echo

A family affair
Most of what we know about dolphin behavior comes from observing animals in captivity.

Dolphins are extremely social and prefer to live in large groups, or **pods**. A pod of dolphins will hunt and play together for many years. They also protect the young, sick and injured within the group. By using their backs and flippers, pod members will sometimes help an injured or ill dolphin breathe by keeping it near the surface.

A male dolphin is called a **bull**, a female is a cow and a baby is called a calf.

Dolphins have captured the imagination and friendship of people for thousands of years. There are many ancient myths and legends about dolphins. Native Americans and Australian aborigines believed the dolphin was a messenger of the gods. Killing a dolphin in ancient Greece was a crime punishable by **death**. But we have not always been kind to this highly intelligent animal, and many species are threatened or on the verge of extinction.

Movies, television shows, aquariums and zoos have made the orca and the bottle-nosed dolphin the most popular and well-known of dolphins. The orca, or killer whale, is known for its friendliness and ability to learn clever tricks.

Orcas live in pods of three to 25 and can be found in oceans all over the world. They are fast swimmers and can reach speeds up to 30 mph (48 kph).

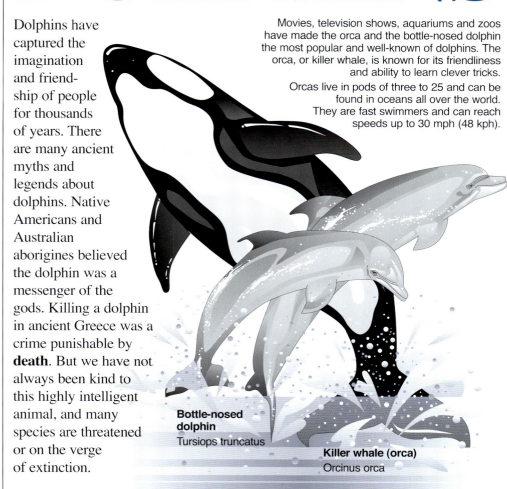

Bottle-nosed dolphin — Tursiops truncatus
Killer whale (orca) — Orcinus orca

These dolphins are in big trouble
This list shows some of the rarest and most threatened dolphins.

Species	Distribution	Estimated Pop.	Note
Baiji dolphin	Yangtze River, China	less than 100	Will probably become extinct
Bhulan dolphin	Indus River, Pakistan	less than 500	Population continues to diminish
Hector's dolphin	Coast of New Zealand	less than 4,000	Rarest marine dolphin
Susu dolphin	Rivers of India	4,000 to 6,000	Population continues to diminish

Anatomy 101

The brain of a bottle-nosed dolphin is slightly larger than a human brain. Tests have shown that cetaceans are very adaptable and that they use sophisticated problem-solving skills.

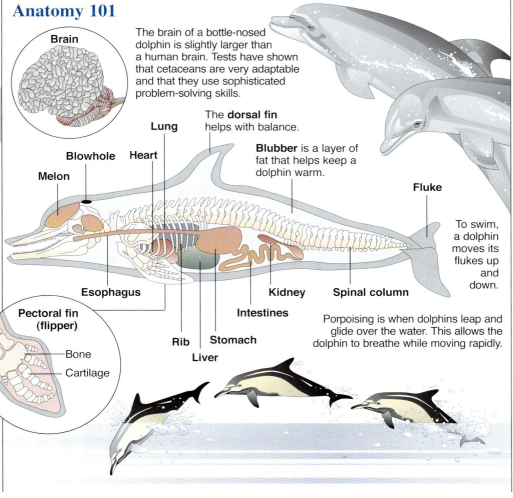

The **dorsal fin** helps with balance.

Blubber is a layer of fat that helps keep a dolphin warm.

To swim, a dolphin moves its flukes up and down.

Porpoising is when dolphins leap and glide over the water. This allows the dolphin to breathe while moving rapidly.

Labels: Brain, Lung, Blowhole, Heart, Melon, Esophagus, Pectoral fin (flipper), Bone, Cartilage, Rib, Stomach, Liver, Intestines, Kidney, Spinal column, Fluke

Marine dolphins
Dolphins range in size from 4 ft. (1.2 m) to 30 ft. (9 m) long and weigh from 100 pounds (45 kg) to 10 short tons (9 metric tons). They come in a variety of colors and markings.

NOTE: Illustrations are not to scale.

Indo-Pacific humpbacked
Sousa chinensis

Common dolphin
Delphinus delphis

Striped dolphin
Stenella coeruleoalba

Long-finned pilot whale
Globicephala melaena

Killer whale (orca)
Orcinus orca

Bottle-nosed dolphin
Tursiops truncatus

Risso's dolphin
Grampus griseus

River dolphins
River dolphins live in fresh water or brackish (slightly salty) water. They are found in the warm rivers and lakes of Asia and South America. All species of river dolphins are threatened due to habitat destruction by humans.

The five species
Baiji (Chinese river, Yangtze river or whitefin dolphin)
Boto (Amazon river dolphin)
Franciscana (La Plata river)
Susu (Ganges river dolphin)
Bhulan (Indus river dolphin)

Franciscana (La Plata river)
Pontoporia blainvillei

Baiji (Yangtze river)
Lipotes vexillifer

Bhulan (Indus river)
Platanista minor

DRAGONS

Okay, so they don't exist, but these giants of legend and folklore are still pretty cool.

Goin, Grabak, Gravitnir and Grafvolud (Norway) are the serpents living under the ash tree Yggdrasil, the "Tree of Life."

What is a dragon?
Today many people think of dragons as large, green, four-legged, winged reptiles with long necks and tails who breathe fire and hoard treasure. But historically and culturally, dragons have come in many forms. They could be any fantastic type of mythical monster. Snakes and dragons are almost interchangeable in some cultures. Serpentine dragons appear to be giant snakes, with snake-like behaviors. Sometimes the same word is used for both snake and/or dragon. To Polynesians, Mo'o (or Moko) means lizard. In a myth, Moko could be a dragon, or a tiny lizard.

Is it a dragon?
Dragons often possess similar traits. Some themes recur in myths or legends from different lands. To students of mythology, creatures that share the following traits or themes are thought of as dragons. A creature may not display all or even most of them, but will still be a dragon.

Traits many dragons share:
- Reptilian appearance
- Breathes or spits poison or fire
- Lives in or is associated with water
- Influences storms, rain and wind
- Can fly (even without having wings)
- Guards treasure, knowledge or another resource, and will fight to the death to protect it
- Displays magical or supernatural powers when alive; remains will have power even if the dragon is dead

Uncommon dragon traits:
- Bird-like appearance
- Roundels (circular panels) on the wings or body
- Ability to transform into another animal or human
- Holds a powerful position (god, or servant to one)

True or false?
Western dragons are evil; Eastern dragons are good. Not true! Eastern dragons can wreak havoc and cause massive destruction, usually by storm, sea or sky.

Dragons must have legs and wings. Wrong again! Many European myths describe dragons without limbs, such as wyrms, or the Jormungandr, the Midgard Serpent in Norse mythology.

Dragons must be intelligent. False. Although there are dragons who speak in riddles, this behavior is not true to them all. Taniwha (New Zealand) show maximum strength but minimal brain power.

Mythological dragons are large. Contrary to popular belief, tiny dragon spirits appear in some European household folk tales.

Leviathan (Israel) is a Biblical water creature which defies the power and skill of humans. His back is a row of shield-like scales and his eyes glow as bright as the rising sun.

Fafnir (Germany) began life as a dwarf. Rewarded with gold from the gods, he hid his hoard, guarding it day and night. Greed turned him into a dragon.

Chi Lung Wang (China) is one of many dragon kings. Associated with fire-fighting, he is invoked to help with the water pumps that extinguish the flames.

Quetzalcoatl (Central America) is the Aztec god of civilization. He is a feathered serpent and is sometimes shown swallowing his own tail.

Vitra (India) is a serpent-dragon who absorbed all the cosmic waters and then wrapped himself around a mountain to rest. The rain-god Indra killed Vitra with thunderbolts, releasing the waters.

Lernean Hydra (Greek) was a serpent with many heads. She lived in swampy waters near the town of Lerna. As soon as one of her heads was cut off, two more grew in its place.

Tiamat (Babylonia), a representation of the saltwater ocean, is the mother of all things and bore the gods of Babylon.

Hotu-Puku (New Zealand) ate many travelers. War parties were sent to find the missing. They hung a noose, with one man acting as bait. As Hotu-Puku put his head into the noose, it was pulled tightly until he died. He was cut open, and the missing bodies were found inside.

Earth Day

Our world

Earth is a unique place that supports a myriad of life forms. As human populations around the world continue to grow, it becomes more and more clear how important it is for people to protect the planet by using its resources wisely.

Earth Day has been very successful in making people aware of how rare and special the Earth's plants and creatures are. It has played an important role in bringing environmental issues to the forefront, helping many nations gain the support needed to change environmental laws and protect endangered habitats and animals.

An idea

In 1962 Senator Gaylord Nelson, the founder of Earth Day, began to think about the dismal state of the environment and its unimportance to U.S. politicians. He decided to to discuss his environmental ideas with the administration and to persuade President Kennedy to go on a national conservation tour. As a result of this meeting, the president began a 5-day, 11-state conservation tour in September of 1963. The tour did not succeed in putting environmental issues on the national political agenda, but it was the beginning of an idea that would eventually become Earth Day.

After the tour, Nelson continued to speak on environmental issues. Evidence of environmental degradation was appearing across the United States and the world. Although the politicians didn't take much of an interest, the people did.

In the summer of 1969, Nelson decided to organize a grassroots protest over what was happening to the planet.

At a Seattle conference in September 1969, Nelson announced plans for a nationwide demonstration on behalf of the environment. He invited everyone to participate in the event, which was scheduled for the following spring.

The immense response to Earth Day led to the need for a national headquarters. In January 1970, John Gardner, founder of Common Cause, provided office space. Four months later, on April 22, 1970, the first Earth Day was held. An estimated 20 million people took part.

President Kennedy and Gaylord Nelson.

"Earth Day worked because of the spontaneous response at the grassroots level. We had neither the time nor resources to organize 20 million demonstrators and the thousands of schools and local communities that participated. That was the remarkable thing about Earth Day. It organized itself."
— Gaylord Nelson

Sharing the planet

You can participate on Earth Day in a number of ways. Any action taken to care for our planet helps. Here are some ways to start:

Follow the three R's every day: **Reduce** the amount of waste you produce, **reuse** whatever you can, and **recycle** whatever you can't.

Keep informed of the latest actions being taken regarding the environment.

Ride public transportation one day or more per week.

Don't buy products with excessive packaging.

Fix dripping faucets.

Turn off lights when you are not using them.

Don't run the dishwasher unless it's full.

Contact direct-mail sources and request that your name be removed from mailing lists to reduce unwanted mail.

Plant drought-resistant plants in your yard.

Adopt a park and pick up trash when you visit it.

Buy shade-grown coffee to reduce dependence on slash-and-burn farming.

Start a compost pile.

Lower the thermostat.

Give up a few fast-food meals every month.

Ride a bike on local trips to reduce car use.

Wear natural fibers instead of synthetics.

Use a fan instead of air conditioning one day a week.

Don't indiscriminately use insecticides.

Try sand instead of salt to de-ice the pavement.

Encourage employers to provide clearly marked recycle containers.

Buy organic items.

Eat a non-meat meal once per week.

Use biodegradable products when possible.

Use recycled paper products.

Plant a tree.

Buy used furniture.

Plant a garden.

Join a wildlife organization

Use the National Parks system for vacations.

Carpool.

Support local farms and farmers' markets.

Achievements

➤ The Clean Air Act of 1970 was passed.

➤ Seven "Dirty Dozen" Congressmen — designated by the Earth Day organizers — were defeated in the 1970 elections.

➤ The military was forced to halt the use of mutagenic defoliants in the war in Southeast Asia.

➤ The Environmental Protection Agency was established.

➤ The Federal Occupational Health and Safety Act was passed by a coalition of labor and environmental groups.

➤ Within three years, the Clean Water, Endangered Species, and Resource Conservation and Recovery Acts were passed.

EGGS

Almost all animals make eggs in order to reproduce. Most mammals keep the egg inside the mother's body until the young are ready to be born. But many creatures — birds, most reptiles, insects and fish — lay their eggs. This page focuses mostly on the eggs that animals lay.

What is an egg?

All eggs start as tiny **cells** that, if fertilized, will grow into baby animals. When birds, snakes, turtles and insects mate, the eggs are fertilized inside the female. But most toads, frogs and fish fertilize their eggs **outside** the mother. Eggs come in many sizes, shapes and colors. Some have hard shells; others have soft shells. Birds lay just a few eggs each year, while an **oyster** can produce more than 500 million eggs in a year.

Anatomy 101

The **germinal disc**, or nucleus, is the part of an egg that becomes an animal. The rest of the egg serves as food and protection for the embryo.

Parts of a chicken egg

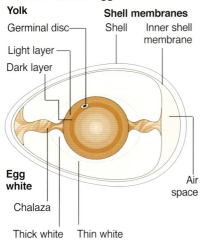

- Yolk
  - Germinal disc
  - Light layer
  - Dark layer
- Shell membranes
  - Shell
  - Inner shell membrane
- Egg white
  - Chalaza
  - Thick white
  - Thin white
- Air space

Kinds of eggs

The egg examples below are drawn to scale and are slightly smaller than actual size.

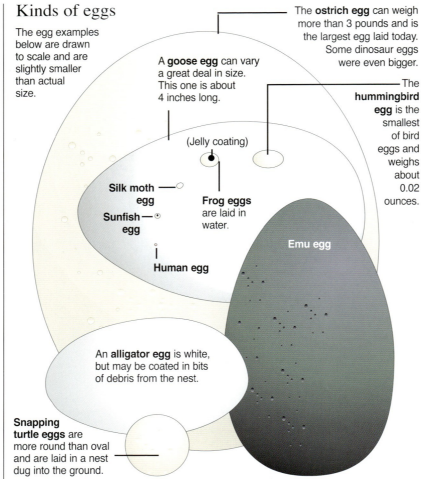

- The **ostrich egg** can weigh more than 3 pounds and is the largest egg laid today. Some dinosaur eggs were even bigger.
- A **goose egg** can vary a great deal in size. This one is about 4 inches long.
- The **hummingbird egg** is the smallest of bird eggs and weighs about 0.02 ounces.
- (Jelly coating)
- **Silk moth egg**
- **Sunfish egg**
- **Frog eggs** are laid in water.
- **Human egg**
- **Emu egg**
- An **alligator egg** is white, but may be coated in bits of debris from the nest.
- **Snapping turtle eggs** are more round than oval and are laid in a nest dug into the ground.

Chicken egg development

An egg begins as a cell called an **ovum**. Yolk particles form around the ovum until the yolk is the size of a fully formed egg. The yolk travels through a long tube called the **oviduct**. On its way, layers of **albumen** (protein nutrients) form, followed by shell membranes. The final shell is formed in the uterus. It takes more than 24 hours for the yolk to move through the oviduct and turn into an egg ready to lay.

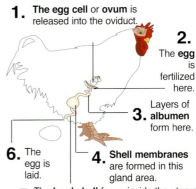

1. The **egg cell** or **ovum** is released into the oviduct.
2. The **egg** is fertilized here.
3. Layers of **albumen** form here.
4. **Shell membranes** are formed in this gland area.
5. The **hard shell** forms inside the uterus and colors develop on the shell.
6. The egg is laid.

A newly laid egg must be kept warm (**incubated**) if it is going to grow into a chicken. If the egg gets too cold the chick will die.

Day 1 The embryo begins to develop.
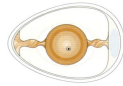

Day 3 The embryo has a head, a **heart** and a tail. The yolk develops blood vessels to feed the embryo.
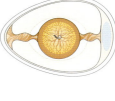

Day 7 A sac of water called the amnion forms around the embryo. Wings and legs begin to develop.
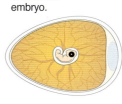

Day 12 Pimples where the feathers will grow are visible. A beak forms and a waste sac shares the space.

Day 20 One more day before the chick will hatch. A special egg tooth on the beak will help the chick break out of the shell.

Day 21 The first crack or break in the shell is called a **pip**. The chick uses all of its strength to break out of the shell and is born wet and tired.

The chick rests and warms up close to its mother and within a few hours it is dry and covered in a fluffy yellow down.

Insects

Insects lay a lot of eggs. Many of these hatch into larvae (caterpillars or grubs), which have another stage of development (growing inside a cocoon, pupa or chrysalis) before emerging as an adult.

- **Day 1** Lady bugs lay about 15 to 20 eggs.
- **Day 6**
- **Day 7** The eggs change color shortly before they hatch.
- **Day 21** The larva is born without wings; after eating for about a week it changes into a pupa.
- **Day 28**
- **Day 35** The pupa case breaks open and an adult ladybug is born.
- **Day 36**
- **Day 37** After about 24 hours, the ladybug changes color from yellow to red.

Fish

Different species of fish have a variety of ways to lay their eggs. Most fish eggs are fertilized in the water after they are laid, but some species, including sharks and rays, fertilize the eggs inside the mother.

- **Day 14** The rainbow trout can lay more than 1,000 eggs a year. Two weeks after they are laid, little fish bodies can be seen.
- **Day 25** About three weeks later, the baby trout (or alevin) emerges.
- **Day 28**
- **Day 84** The young trout (parr) develops black stripes. It takes two years for the trout to reach full maturity.

Frogs

Amphibians live part of their lives as water animals and part as land animals. Frogs, toads, newts and salamanders are amphibians. Most of these animals lay round, jelly-coated eggs. Some are laid one at a time; others are laid in string clusters.

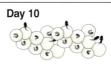 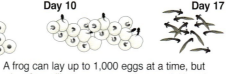 

- **Day 1**
- **Day 10** A frog can lay up to 1,000 eggs at a time, but only a few will manage to survive to adulthood. Most are eaten by predators.
- **Day 17**
- **Day 43** In six to eight weeks, the tadpoles develop back legs.
- **Day 53** In the span of about a month, the tadpole grows front legs and its tail begins to shrink.

It takes three years for a frog to reach full maturity and be able to lay eggs.

Alligator

Unlike many reptiles, alligators and crocodiles are excellent mothers. They carefully dig nests and remain nearby while the eggs incubate. Also, they often help out when it is time for the babies to hatch.

- **Day 1** An alligator may lay 50 to 60 eggs in a nest as large as 10 feet wide and 3 to 6 feet deep.
- **Day 38**
- **Day 52**
- **Day 65** The eggs are incubated by the heat of the sun and decaying plant matter. The sex of the babies depends on the temperature of the eggs during the first few weeks.

The baby alligator uses a special egg tooth to break out of the shell.

ELEPHANTS

The largest and heaviest land mammal in the world, the elephant is very smart and very strong. And with a life span of about 70 years, they live longer than any other land mammals (with the exception of humans).

African elephant

The African elephant (Loxodonta Africana) is the largest animal living on land. The largest is the bush elephant, which lives south of the Sahara. Forest elephants are found in Central and Western Africa. Males are larger than females, and a bush elephant can be 11 feet tall (3.4 m) and weigh up to 14,000 lbs. (6,300 kg) These animals have four or five toes on their front feet and three toes on their back feet. Both males and females have tusks. Wild populations are estimated at 400,000 to 600,000.

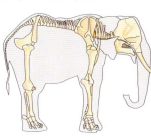

- African bush elephant
- African forest elephant

Asian elephant

The Asian or Indian elephant (elephas maximus) is smaller than its African cousin. A bull stands 9 to 10 feet (2.7 to 3.2 m) tall and weighs up to 11,000 lbs. (5,000 kg). The female is smaller than the male and has very small tusks or none at all. An Asian elephant has five toes on its front feet, and four toes on its back feet. This animal is listed as endangered, with wild populations estimated at 35,000 to 50,000. The Asian elephant has been domesticated by man and to this day is captured and trained to carry heavy loads. At one time it was even used in warfare.

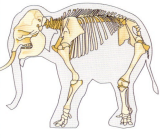

- Asian Elephant

Tusks are actually incisors, or front teeth. Tusks never stop growing.

African elephant

The easiest way to tell an African elephant from an Asian one is to look at their ears. African elephants have much larger ears. One way elephants keep cool is to flap their ears. They also take dust and mud baths or go swimming.

Asian elephant

Some elephants greet each other by intertwining trunks (like shaking hands).

Elephants breathe and smell with their trunks. African elephants have two finger-like lips on the end of their trunk; Asian elephants have just one of these extensions.

An elephant skull would be very heavy if it did not have small holes or pockets of air. Elephants chew by moving the jaw from side to side in a grinding motion.

The ridges on the African elephant's molar are lozenge- (diamond) shaped, and its scientific name loxodonta africana means lozenge teeth. The Asian elephant's molar has sharp ridges that cut the food when chewing.

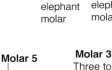

African elephant molar / Asian elephant molar

The toe bones of an elephant sit on a soft pad of fat that acts as a shock absorber and allows the animal to move very quietly, despite its size. The sole of the foot has thick skin with deep cracks and grooves for traction.

Fatty cushion

In its lifetime, an elephant has six sets of four molars (two on the top and two on the bottom). Over time, as old molars wear down, the new (larger) molars move from the back to the front.

Molar 6 is the last and largest molar; it appears when the elephant is about 40 years old.

Molar 5

Molar 4 shows what a worn-down molar looks like

Molar 3 Three to nine years

Molar 2 Appears at 18 months

Molar 1 Newborn

Elephants are still killed for their ivory tusks.

On the move

Elephants walk at about 3 to 6 miles (5 to 10 k) an hour but can double that speed when on the march and reach up to 25 miles (40 k) when frightened.

Musth

For several weeks in a year, adult males experience musth (pronounced muhst). High levels of the hormone testosterone cause unpredictable and aggressive behavior. During musth, the elephant oozes a thick, smelly, black fluid from a gland on the side of its head (between the eye and the ear).

Ancient ancestors

Fossil evidence suggests that elephants are descendants of the **moeritherium**, a mammal that lived 45 million years ago.

Food for thought

Elephants are **herbivores** and survive on many kinds of grass, leaves, fruits, roots and tree branches. Adult elephants spend 16 to 18 hours of every day eating. They can consume up to 330 lbs. (150 kg) of vegetation and drink up to 40 gallons (160 l) of water a day.

Elephants can travel more than 50 miles a day foraging for food and water. Migration routes are never too far from water, because an elephant can live for only about three days without it.

Wild elephants can live to 60 or 70 years of age. If it avoids being hunted and does not die from disease, it will die of old age in the form of starvation. Its final set of molars wears down to nothing, and the animal can no longer eat.

Family life

Elephants form tight-knit family groups, or **herds**. A herd generally consists of 10 to 12 related females and their offspring. The herd is led by a **matriarch** (the oldest and usually the largest female). This dominant female decides when to eat, rest or migrate.

Young males are forced to leave the herd when they reach maturity (age 10-16). Adult males often lead solitary lives or gather in small groups with other males. A lone male elephant is called a **rogue**.

Sensitive souls

Elephants can cry, play and even laugh. They also grieve when a calf is stillborn or a family member dies.

When a **calf** (baby elephant) cries, the entire family responds with caresses and soft, reassuring sounds. Elephants will lift or support an injured or ill herd member. And they have been known to rescue family members from natural disasters and man-made traps.

Moeritherium / Palaeomastodon / Dinotherium / Trilophodon / Mastodon / Woolly mammoth

Did you know?

- An elephant's heart is five times larger than a human heart.
- An elephant's trunk has more than 100,000 muscles.
- Elephants can't jump.
- Some elephants cry (with tears) when frustrated.
- The Asian elephant is more closely related to the ancient mammoth than to the African elephant.
- Elephants will rest their heavy trunks on their tusks.
- Humans can hear only a third of elephant sounds.
- An elephant never stops growing, so the larger an elephant is, the older it is.

The skin of an elephant can be up to 1½ inches (3 cm) thick in some places on its head and back, but is paper thin around the mouth. Elephants use touch as a form of communication, and their skin is not tough and leathery, but soft and sensitive.

BIRDS
78 endangered, 175 threatened, 10 candidates for listing

American peregrine falcon
Falco peregrinus anatum

Kirtland's warbler
Dendroica kirtlandii

Bald eagle
Haliaeetus leucocephalus

Hawaiian honeycreeper
Oreomystis mana

California condor
Gymnogyps californianus

ENDANGERED SPECIES
of the United States

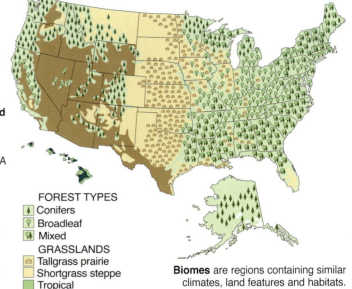

Extinction has been a part of the Earth's natural history since the beginning of life. It is estimated by scientists that as many as 99 percent of all the species that have ever existed on Earth are no longer around. Many factors may contribute to extinction, but it is generally accepted that changes to a creature's **habitat** are the greatest threat to its survival.

Mass extinctions (when many different groups of unrelated animal species die out) have occurred about five times during prehistoric eras. Usually these events take thousands of years before the last of a species dies. The most well-known mass extinction happened around 63 million years ago, when an unknown event triggered the end of the dinosaurs and large reptiles.

Each time a mass extinction has occurred, the planet has recovered due to a balance existing in nature. In order for a new life form to establish itself, it seems another must be lost.

Many scientists believe the Earth is undergoing a mass extinction now. As the human population continues to grow, more demands are placed on the Earth's **natural resources**. These demands for more food, water, farmland, living space and fuel cause humans to encroach further and further into wild spaces, forcing the plants and animals who have lived there to either adapt or die. Most of today's extinctions are taking place at an alarming rate. Since the discovery of North America in 1492, more than 60 species of vertebrates have died out – many within the past 100 years. Ten percent of all vertebrate species in the United States are in danger of being wiped out.

The U.S. passed the **Endangered Species Act** (ESA) in 1973. The powerful law makes any activity that reduces the survival chance of a listed species illegal. The ESA is currently protecting more than 1,200 plants and animals. For some, like the California condor or the black-footed ferret, which survive only in zoos and **captive breeding programs**, the outlook is grim. But others, like the bald eagle and gray wolf, have benefited from protection and are beginning to make a comeback.

Extinction is a normal part of the cycle of life. But man's role in the loss of many animals and plants might be halted.

FOREST TYPES
- Conifers
- Broadleaf
- Mixed

GRASSLANDS
- Tallgrass prairie
- Shortgrass steppe
- Tropical

DESERT
PERMANENT ICE
TROPICAL RAINFOREST

Biomes are regions containing similar climates, land features and habitats. Human development alters the appearance and natural systems within a biome. This map shows the biomes existing prior to modern development.

MAMMALS
63 endangered, 9 threatened, 11 candidates for listing

Bighorn sheep
Ovis canadensis

Ozark big eared bat
Corynorhinus townsendiingens

Canada lynx
Lynx canadensis

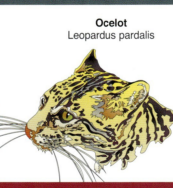
Ocelot
Leopardus pardalis

Gray wolf Canis lupus

Black-footed ferret
Mustela nigripes

FISH
69 endangered, 44 threatened, 11 candidates

Chinook salmon
Oncorhynchus tshawytscha

Shortnose sturgeon
Acipenser brevirostrum

REPTILES
14 endangered, 22 threatened, 5 candidates

Desert tortoise
Gopherus agassizii

Atlantic loggerhead
Caretta caretta

American alligator
Alligator mississippiensis

INVERTEBRATES
204 endangered, 75 threatened, 112 candidates

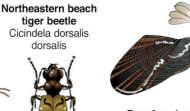
Northeastern beach tiger beetle
Cicindela dorsalis dorsalis

Mitchell's marsh satyr
Neonympha mitchellii mitchellii

Dwarf wedge mussel
Alasmidonta heterodon

California fresh-water shrimp
Syncaris pacifica

AMPHIBIANS
10 endangered, 8 threatened, 8 candidates

Arroyo toad
Bufo microscaphus californicus

California tiger salamander
Ambystoma californiense

California red-legged frog
Rana aurora draytonii

Wyoming toad
Bufo hemiophrys baxteri

The Florida Everglades

A fragile ecosystem

In 1906, Florida began to drain the Everglades to create farmland. Developers built canals to provide drinking water to ever-growing communities. The growth of agriculture and the demand for fresh water continues to threaten the Everglades and the rare and diverse plant and animal species it supports.

The Everglades is a slow-moving river full of **sawgrass**, (hence the area's nickname "River of Grass"). Sawgrass is named for its rough, saw-like leaf blades. Sometimes called Everglades river grass, it's not a grass at all, but a sedge. Sedges have triangular stems; true grasses have round stems. Sawgrass typically grows to about 9 ft.(2.75 m) tall.

Sawgrass
Cladium jamaicense

Zebra longwing
Heliconius charitonius

The park

The Everglades National Park was established in 1947 in order to conserve and protect one of the rarest subtropical regions of North America. The park covers about one-fifth of the original Everglades (more than 1.5 million acres, or 600,000 hectares).

Coastline: 137 miles (220 km)
Sawgrass and freshwater marsh: 572,200 acres (228,880 hectares)
Mangrove forests: 230,100 acres (92,040 hectares)
Birds: More than 400 species
Mammals: 25 species
Amphibians and reptiles: 60 species
Fish: 125 species
Trees: More than 120 species
Seed-bearing plants: More than 1,000 species
Endangered species: 14

Florida panther
Felis concolor coryi

The **Florida panther** is perhaps the rarest of Everglade animals. It is estimated that there are only 30 to 50 left in the wild. It has been on the endangered list since 1967. A subspecies of the mountain lion, the panther was a victim of 200 years of intense hunting and habitat loss.

Liguus tree snail
Liguus fasciatus

Mangroves are critical to the swamp ecosystem. There are three kinds of mangrove in the Everglades: red, black and white. Mangroves prevent soil erosion and build up the coastline.

Great blue heron
Ardea herodias

White pelican
Pelecanus onocrotalus

The Everglades are home to 16 species of wading birds. Wading bird populations have dropped 90 percent over the past century due to plume hunting (now illegal) and draining of the wetlands. The nesting populations in the southern Everglades dropped from an estimated 300,000 birds in the 1930s to between 10,000 and 15,000 in the 1990s.

The easiest way to tell an alligator from a crocodile is to look at their noses. Alligators have a wide, U-shaped snout. Crocodiles have a longer, pointed V-shaped nose.

Alligator   Crocodile

Alligators play a vital role in the survival of the Everglades. During the dry season (December through April), alligators dig holes that become pools of water. Plants thrive in "gator holes" and many animals depend on these mini marshes for food, shelter and water.

Alligators are carnivorous (meat eaters); they feed on crabs, crayfish, frogs, fish, snails, turtles, snakes, birds, raccoons, otters, deer and other alligators.

Florida is the only place in the world where alligators and crocodiles share the same habitat.

Red mangrove
Rhizophora mangle

Cypress tree knees

Bald cypress trees love water and have thick supportive bases to help them stay upright in muddy soils. The roots grow distinctive extensions called "knees," which poke up out of the water.

Roseate spoonbill
Ajaia ajaja

Green turtle
Chelonia mydas

There are 30 species of freshwater fish native to the Everglades. Fish are an important part of the food chain, providing food for larger fish, wading birds and alligators.

Least killifish
Heterandria formosa

Mosquitofish
Gambusia holbrooki

Florida Gar
Lepisosteus platyrhincus

The green turtle has been on the endangered/threatened list since 1978, but populations have not recovered. Female turtles return to the same beaches year after year to lay their eggs. There are few nesting areas left in North America, but Florida supports a large feeding population.

The **West Indian manatee** (or **sea cow**) lives in slow-moving rivers and coastal waters and grazes on seagrasses and aquatic plants. This animal eats 10 to 15 percent of its body weight a day, and when you weigh 1,000 pounds, that is a lot of food. Manatees grow to 8 to 15 feet (2.4 to 4.6 m) long. The manatee is endangered, and the Florida population is estimated to be about 2,000. Boat propellers are the biggest danger to this gentle giant.

West Indian Manatee
Trichechus manatus

Flightless birds

Several groups of birds have lost the ability to fly and have adapted to life on land.

Birds live all over the world and have ancestors related to ancient reptiles. The earliest known bird fossil dates back to more than 140 million years ago. Some **zoologists** (scientists who study animals) believe birds are modern-day dinosaurs with a few differences. The major difference is that birds have feathers or plumes that cover the body instead of scales. Birds also have evolved forelimbs that enable them to fly. But the hind limbs of most birds are covered with scales and claws, like their reptilian ancestors. Birds also have an extension to the sternum (breastbone) called a **keel**. This rounded bone connects to strong muscles that power the wings for lift and flight.

Some flightless birds are called **ratites**. Ratite is the Latin word for raft. These birds have a raft-like, flattened keel. Some ratites have strong, muscular legs — good for running away quickly from predators.

Another group of birds that do not fly are **penguins**. These marine birds have stiff flippers and an upright posture. Their short legs are placed far back on the body, so they waddle and cannot lean forward without falling over. Penguins appear to move slowly on land but can actually move as fast as humans. They are, however, more spectacular as swimmers.

One type of parrot, the **kakapo** of New Zealand, is the only nocturnal parrot in the world. It cannot fly, but will use its weak wings to glide to the ground from tree limbs.

The **tinamous**, a group of chicken-sized game birds from South America, are grouped with the ratites by some scientists. They are capable of weak flight, but spend most of their time on the ground. They live in the grasslands and plateaus near the Andes Mountains.

Many **ornithologists** (scientists who study birds) disagree on how to classify birds. New discoveries and theories continue to challenge the way we have traditionally grouped animals.

Kakapo
This bird's name means "night parrot" in the Maori language. Once plentiful, fewer than 70 now remain.
Habitat: Rainforests and grasslands of New Zealand.
Physical features: Weighs up to 8 pounds. About 2 feet long, with males larger than females.

Cassowary
The second largest bird in the world. Endangered due to loss of habitat. Lives about 40 to 50 years.
Habitat: Rainforests and swampy forests in Australia and New Guinea.
Physical features: Nearly 5 feet tall, it weighs up to 130 pounds. Females are more brightly colored and larger than males.

Rhea
Also called the **nandu**, this is the largest bird in the Americas. A fast runner, the rhea runs with its neck almost horizontal to the ground.
Habitat: Forests in South America.
Physical features: Grows up to 5 feet tall. Males and females are the same color, but the base of the male's neck is black.

Ostrich
The world's largest, heaviest bird, and also the fastest running — up to 43 mph. The ostrich kicks to protect itself.
Habitat: Dry savannas and deserts in Africa. Ostriches get water from the plants they eat.
Physical features: The ostrich can grow up to 9 feet tall, and weighs up to 345 pounds.

Emu
The third-largest bird in the world. Emus can run at speeds up to 30 mph.
Habitat: Grassland, savannas, and bush in Australia.
Physical features: 6 feet tall and about 110 pounds.

Tinamou
The tinamou is thought to be related to the rhea. They are very weak flyers with undeveloped keels.
Habitat: Forest, woodland and brush in Mexico and Central and South America.
Physical features: 8 to 21 inches.

Penguin
The penguin lacks flight feathers and has flipper-like paddles instead of wings. Some migrate vast distances in icy Antarctic waters, following fish and plankton. They form large colonies.
Habitat: Antarctic and southern oceans and shorelines.
Physical features: From 1 foot to 3 feet tall.

Emperor penguin

World distribution
All flightless birds live in the Southern Hemisphere. Most live in harsh or impenetrable habitats.

- Penguins
- Cassowaries
- Ostriches
- Emus
- Tinamous
- Rheas
- Kiwi and kakapo

Kiwi
This nocturnal bird is the national emblem of New Zealand. It lives about 40 years and is in danger of extinction.
Habitat: Forests, scrub, swamps, grasslands and farmlands.
Physical features: 18 to 33 inches long and about a foot tall, with females larger than males.

the language of flowers

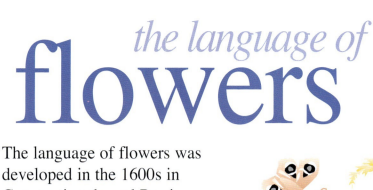

The language of flowers was developed in the 1600s in Constantinople and Persia. **Flowers** are symbolic of love blooming, but also of love waning and each flower has its own special meaning. The **red rose** was said to be the favorite flower of **Venus**, the goddess of love. Red is symbolic of strong emotions, yellow of jealousy. The **forget-me-not** represents true love. How you combine a bouquet can say quite a lot.

Flower lore and legend

Acacia - Secret love; elegance; friendship; hope
Acorn - Nordic symbol of life and immortality
Allspice - Compassion
Almond Blossom - Hope
Aloe - Grief
Alyssum - Beyond beauty
Ambrosia - Love returned
Amaranth - Fidelity
Amaryllis - Pride; timidity; splendid beauty
Apple blossom - Preference; good fortune
Arbor Vitae - Friendship
Arbutus - I love only you.
Aster - Love; daintiness
Azalea - Fragile passion, temperance, Chinese symbol of womanhood
Bachelor's Buttons - Celibacy; hope in love
Baby's Breath - Happiness; pure in heart
Basil - Best wishes; love
Bay Leaf - Strength
Begonia - Beware
Bird Of Paradise - Magnificence
Bluebell - Humility
Bouquet of withered flowers - Rejected love
Buttercup - Cheerfulness; childishness; riches
Cactus - Endurance; warmth; grandeur
Calendula - Joy
Camellia (in general) - Admiration; perfection;
Camellia (Pink) - Longing

Camellia (Red) - You're a flame in my heart.
Camellia (White) - You're adorable.
Carnation (in general) - Affection; fascination
Carnation (pink) - I'll never forget you.
Carnation (purple) - Capriciousness; whimsical
Carnation (red) - My heart aches for you; admiration
Carnation (solid color) - Yes
Carnation (striped) - No
Carnation (white) - Sweet and lovely; pure love
Carnation (yellow) - Rejection
Cattail - Peace; prosperity
Cedar - I live for thee
Chamomile - Patience
Chrysanthemum (in general) - Cheerfulness; You're a wonderful friend
Chrysanthemum (red) - I love you.
Chrysanthemum (white) - Truth
Clover - Good luck
Columbine - Folly
Cornflower - Delicacy
Coriander - Lust
Crocus - Cheerfulness; joy
Cyclamen - Goodbye
Daffodil - Respect; regard; unrequited love; deceit
Dahlia - Good taste
Daisy - Innocence; loyal love; purity; faith; cheer

Dandelion - Wishes come true; faithfulness
Delphinium - Airy
Dogwood - Durability
Eucalyptus - Protection
Fennel - Strength
Fern - Sincerity
Fir - Time
Flax - Fate
Forget-me-not - True love; memories; forget me not
Forsythia - Anticipation
Foxglove - Insincerity
Fuchsia - Good taste
Gardenia - You're lovely; secret love; refinement; joy
Geranium (Oak leafed) - Friendship
Gladiolus - Love at first sight; generosity
Grass - Submission; utility
Heather (lavender) - Admiration; solitude
Heather (pink) - Good luck
Heather (white) - Protection; wishes come true; good luck
Hibiscus - Delicate beauty
Holly - Good will; defense; domestic happiness
Hollyhock - Ambition
Honeysuckle - Devoted affection; sweet disposition
Hyacinth (general) - Rashness, sorrow, flower dedicated to Apollo
Hyacinth (blue) - Constancy
Hyacinth (purple) - I'm sorry

Hyacinth (white) - Loveliness
Hydrangea - Thanks; heartlessness
Iris - Faith; wisdom; valor
Ivy - Fidelity; friendship
Jasmine - Amiability; wealth; grace; elegance
Jonquil - Love me; affection returned; desire
Juniper - Protection
Larkspur (pink) - Fickleness
Laurel (mountain) - Ambition
Lavender - Devotion
Lemon - Zest
Lemon Balm - Brings love
Lilac - First love
Lily (general) - Purity
Lily (calla) - Beauty
Lily (day) - Coquetry
Lily (orange) - Hatred
Lily (tiger) - Wealth; pride
Lily (white) - Purity
Lily (yellow) - False; gay
Lily of the valley - Humility; perferct purity
Magnolia - Sweetness
Marigold - Grief; jealousy
Mimosa - Sensitivity
Mint - Protection
Marjoram (sweet) - Joy and happiness
Mistletoe - Kiss me; sacred plant of India, magic plant of the Druids

Monkshood - Beware
Moss - Maternal love; charity
Myrtle - Love; Hebrew emblem of marriage
Narcissus - Egotism
Nasturtium - Conquest; maternal love; charity
Oleander - Caution
Orange - Generosity
Orange Blossom - Wisdom; eternal love
Orchid - Love; beauty
Orchid (Cattleya) - Charm
Palm leaves - Victory
Pansy - Thoughts; love
Peony - Shame; anger
Peppermint - Warmth
Petunia - Anger
Phlox - Agreement
Pine - Hope; pity
Poppy (general) - Eternal sleep; imagination
Poppy (red) - Pleasure
Poppy (white) - Consolation; sleep
Poppy (yellow) - Wealth; success
Primrose - Early youth; young love
Queen Anne's Lace - Fantasy
Rose (red) - Love
Rose (white) - Eternal love; innocence; heavenly; secrecy and silence
Rose (pink) - Perfect happiness; believe me.

Rose (yellow) - Friendship; jealousy
Rose (single, full bloom) I love you; I still love you.
Sage - Wisdom; long life; domestic virtue
Snapdragon - No; deception; presumption
Spearmint - Warmth
Spiderflower - Let's elope
Strawberry - Perfection
Sunflower - Loyalty; haughtiness
Sweet Basil - Good luck
Sweet pea - Goodbye; thank you
Sweet William - Perfection; gallantry
Thyme - Courage
Tulip (general) - Fame; charity; declaration of love;
Tulip (red) - Believe me; declaration of love
Tulip (yellow) - Hopeless love
Violet - Modesty
Violet (blue) - Watchfulness; faithfulness; I'll always be true
Violet (white) - Let's take a chance on happiness
Water Lily - Purity of heart
Wistaria - I cling to you
Yarrow - Health; healing
Zinnia - Friendship
Zinnia (red) - Constancy
Zinnia (white) - Goodness

FROGS & TOADS
All about tailless amphibians

Although frogs have managed to survive for more than 350 million years, they are now beginning to disappear. Scientists are studying frogs and toads with renewed interest, because deformities and mass extinctions are being discovered worldwide and at an alarming rate.

It is suspected that pesticides and pollution are the cause of these extinctions. Because the frog drinks and breathes through its skin, it is sensitive to environmental changes. Frogs are considered an **indicator species** that can signal to scientists that a **biome** is out of balance. Frogs and toads live worldwide, and are an important group of animals because they eat many kinds of harmful insects. They are also an important food source for birds, fish and small predators. Efforts to study and perhaps halt the decline in populations are underway throughout the world. Perhaps it's not too late.

Frogs and toads undergo metamorphosis, meaning change of body form and appearance.

Masses of eggs are called **spawn**. Spawn must be surrounded by water to survive. During mating, some females can lay up to 20,000 eggs. Some species produce egg clumps that are big and blobby; other species' can look like long ribbons. Some lay single, separated eggs.

The embryo
Life begins when the fertilized cells begin to divide. The yolk divides into two, then four, then eight and so on, until the yolk elongates. At this point, the twitching embryo is called a tadpole. They will hatch out in about 6 days, after consuming most of the nutrients in the yolk.

The young tadpole
Tadpoles have two missions in life: Eat as much food as possible, and avoid being eaten. When newly hatched, gills are external, and the mouth and tail are small and weak.

Half and half
From six to nine weeks, the tadpole grows longer, stronger and more frog-like. The head region becomes distinct, and the eye larger. Limbs begin to break through the body wall, and the diet changes to include dead insects and small animals.

Fully formed
From nine to 16 weeks, the tadpole looks like a miniature frog, except it still has a tail. Gradually, the tail is absorbed into the body. Frogs and toads are eating machines — a single toad can consume more than 9,000 non-beneficial insects in one summer. Farmers greatly benefit from natural pest control, when toads take up residence on their land.

Bustin' out: At about six weeks, visible bulges along the body appear. Hind legs form first.

Mini me: Like frogs, with a tail, the tadpoles hang out at the edge of the pond, and gulp air at the surface.

A froglet greets the world: Young frogs hop out of the pond after absorbing the tail, usually after 12 to 16 weeks.

Frog or toad?
Frogs and toads are **amphibians**, which means "double life." Amphibians must live and breed in or near water to survive. Amphibians are divided into four **orders** by **herpetologists** (the scientists who study them): anurids (frogs and toads), apodans (worm-like caecaelians), trachystomata (sirens), and caudata (salamanders and newts).

All amphibians undergo **metamorphosis,** and though they were the first animals on Earth to give up life in the water, they must remain near it to develop. Eggs are laid in water, and a moist jelly surrounds the developing embryo. Some species are totally aquatic. Others live in treetops, some deep underground. All breathe through the skin, and are **ectothermic** (coldblooded).

Tailless amphibians are called anurids. All anurids are frogs. Some frogs are toads. Here's how they differ:

FROG	TOAD
Smooth, moist skin	Dry, bumpy skin
Long, strong hind limbs	Short hind legs
Moves by leaping or swimming	Moves by hopping
Lives in or near water	Lives in damp places, sometimes far from water

Sum of its parts
Frogs and toads are similar in body shape, but many adaptations exist from species to species. Here are the body basics – features that help to identify them:

JAVAN FLYING FROG
Sacral hump, Lateral fold, Ear, Muzzle, Eye, Heel, Back, Vocal sac, Femur, Belly, Tibia, Tarsus, Foot, Toe, Web, Finger, Adhesive disc

Gallery of frogs and toads

Dendrobates Poison dart frogs live in South America. Their skin is highly toxic.

American toad This nocturnal animal can sometimes be found in suburban yards.

Arroyo toad A beautiful, but critically endangered toad from Southern California.

Red-legged frog This famous frog was immortalized in Mark Twain's "Jumping Frog of Calaveras County."

Wyoming toad Another critically endangered toad, the Wyoming toad is a scarce sub-species of the Canadian toad.

Surinam toad One of the weirdest toads in the world, the female broods her eggs in small dimples that form on her spongy back.

Goliath frog The biggest in the world, the African giants can grow to 15.5 inches!

Leopard frog Once common subjects in high-school dissections, the Leopard frog is now on the endangered species list.

Golden Dart frog Another South American poison frog. Its color warns predators.

Paradoxical frog Strange pointed and elongated fingers have evolved due to an extra bone in the fingers. Tadpoles are larger than the adults.

Spadefoot toad Spadefoots are champion diggers, and have specially formed hind legs to help them burrow.

Marine iguanas and **Sally Lightfoot crabs** bask in the sun on partially submerged volcanic rocks

THE GALÁPAGOS ISLANDS

The Galápagos Islands, officially known as the Archipiélago de Colón, is a cluster of volcanic islands, islets and rocks located just under the equator, about 600 miles west of Ecuador in South America. The oldest of the islands are about 4 million years old. The youngest are still in the process of being formed, because the Galápagos Islands are in one of the most active **volcanic** areas in the world.

92° W
- Culpepper
- Wenman

MILES 0 — 75

- Pinta
- Roca Redonde
- Marchena
- Genovesa
- 90° W
- Equator
- San Salvador
- Baltra
- Fernandina
- Santa Cruz
- Isabela
- Santa Fe
- San Cristobal
- Santa Maria
- Española
- **Charles Darwin Research Station**

"Lonesome George"

Discovered by accident
The islands were discovered by chance in 1535, during a voyage to Peru by Fray Tomas de Berlanga, the Bishop of Panama. His ship was swept off course to the islands by strong currents. In his account of the adventure, he named the islands Las Encantadas ("The Enchanted").

Pirates and brigands
After the bishop's visit, the islands became a refuge for English pirates and privateers preying on the Spanish Armada. Based on the bishop's writings and sailors' descriptions of the thousands of large galápagos (**tortoises**) found there, the islands were mapped in 1574 as the "Insulae de los Galopegos." Later, the islands attracted new kinds of sailors: whale- and seal-hunters, who also hunted the islands' giant tortoises. Each island had its own unique variety of tortoises. Because tortoises could survive for up to a year with no food or water, they were used as food for sailors, resulting in the extinction of several species. Today, most of the survivors are critically endangered. The Pinta island tortoise is survived by a single male, named "Lonesome George," who lives at the Charles Darwin Research Station in Santa Cruz.

Modern Galápagos
Today, the Galápagos Islands are part of **Ecuador**. About 97 percent of the islands are classified as a national park. The remaining area is inhabited by about 17,000 people.

The islands are operated by the Galápagos National Park Service and the Charles Darwin Research Station. The park service provides rangers and guides, and is responsible for overseeing tourists. The research station conducts scientfific research and conservation programs.

Brief History

1485 The Chimu from northern Peru (ruled by the Incas) first visit the islands.

1535 Fray Tomas de Berlanga, the Bishop of Panama, is credited with the official discovery of the Galápagos Islands.

1593 – 1710 The islands become a favorite hide-out for pirates.

1793 – 1870 Exploitation of the Galápagos ecosystems brings the tortoise, fur seals and sperm whales to near-extinction.

1835 The HMS Beagle visits the islands. Charles Darwin observes similarities and differences in the plants and animals there. He concludes that, in order to survive, flora and fauna would gradually evolve based on environmental conditions.

1832 Ecuador takes official possession of the islands, renaming them Archipiélago del Ecuador.

1859 After 20 years of research, Darwin publishes The Origin of Species.

1892 Galápagos is officially named "Archipiélago de Colón" in honor of Christopher Columbus' discovery of the Americas 400 years earlier.

1959 On the 100th anniversary of the publication of Darwin's Origin of Species, the islands become Ecuador's first National Park. The Charles Darwin Research Station is established to assist in preservation of the islands.

1978 The islands are declared a World Heritage site by UNESCO underlining their universal value to mankind.

Scientific discoveries

Charles Darwin was the first to make a scientific study of the Galápagos Islands in 1835. A young student just out of university, he served as a naturalist in the around-the-world scientific and geographical voyage on board the HMS Beagle. He had previously spent four years exploring geology and wildlife in South America. Later in his life, Darwin maintained that the islands were the source of his ideas and research. Today, the Galápagos Islands are more closely associated with Darwin than any other visitor in the islands' history.

Dawin's research and theories
There are 13 species of finch native to the Galápagos Islands. Each has a specifically shaped beak. Darwin's study focused on the link between the beak shapes and the birds' feeding habits. His research resulted in the Theory of Evolution, in which he explained how changes in a plant or animal's characteristics might have occurred through natural selection. In this process, the plants or animals that can adapt their characteristics best to their environment are the ones most likely to survive. Darwin's ideas helped explain the basic similarities — or unity — among all living organisms because they evolved from common ancestors. Darwin's theories were contested in his time, and disputes continue today.

4 of Darwin's finches

Seed eater

Vegetation eater

Cactus eater

Insect eater

Island weather

Ocean currents determine the weather of the Galápagos Islands. Normally, from June to December, a cold current rises from the south. Near the sea, this creates a cool, moist fog called a garúa, but inland it is dry. In December, winds blow with less force, and the ocean is calm. Currents then change, surrounding the islands in the warm **Panama** current from the north. The Panama currents create a weather pattern of hot sunny mornings followed by clouds and occasional showers in the afternoons.

In the arid (dry) areas of the islands, it is common to see cacti that grow taller than a person. This one is opuntia. Red fruits follow yellow flowers in spring.

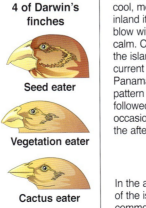

Many kinds of birds visit the islands. This is an **oystercatcher**, a shore bird that feeds on shellfish.

Gentle giants of the Savanna
GIRAFFES

Giraffes are native to Africa. The map shows where they can be found. Giraffe populations have declined greatly due to hunting and habitat loss. Today, most live in national parks or preserves.

A giraffe's prehensile tongue can be up to 21 inches (53 c) long.

Giraffes are herbivores (vegetarians) and feed mainly on leaves, fruit and twigs of trees found on the plains of central and south Africa. Acacia trees are their favorite food.

The tallest of all animals, giraffes have fascinated people since ancient times. Maybe this is because every thing about this animal is long — its legs, its neck, its bones, even its tongue!

What is in a name?
The word giraffe is from the Arabic word zirafah, which means the tallest of all. The ancient Romans called giraffes "camel leopards" which is how they got their scientific name — Giraffa camelopardalis.

All in the family
Male giraffes are called bulls and females are called cows. The female can have babies as young as 5 years old. She usually only has one at a time or, very rarely, twins.

It takes 14 to 15 months for a baby giraffe to grow inside its mother. This is called the **gestation** period. Baby giraffes are called **calves** and are 6 ft. tall when born. They can stand shortly after birth and may grow up to an inch every day. Young giraffes are defenseless and mothers stay near to protect them. Sometimes other mothers in the group will babysit, giving mom a break.

Did you know?
- Giraffes live about 25 years in the wild.
- Giraffes can go without water for up to two weeks. (They get much of the water they need from the plants they eat.)
- A full grown male giraffe can eat up to 72 lbs. (32 k) of leaves a day.
- Giraffes are nonterritorial, social animals that gather in loose herds of as few as six or as many as 40. (They do not form complex social groups.)
- Giraffes are quiet, but not mute. They make grunts, moans and short flutelike noises.
- Giraffes are **ruminant** animals. This means that they chew their **cud**, which is food that has been sent to the stomach and then returned to the mouth to be chewed again.

When the first giraffe arrived in Paris in 1827, the animal was so popular that women did their hair up high in a "giraffe" style.

Seeing spots
A giraffe's spots can range in color from light brown to dark brown on a white or cream colored background. The spots are very individual and like the fingerprints of people, no two giraffes have exactly the same pattern. All giraffes belong to the same species, but there are several subspecies that have different kinds of spots. **Reticulated** giraffes have an even pattern of spots on their coats. **Blotched** giraffes have spots that are irregular in size and shape.

Reticulated   **Blotched**

Defenses
Giraffes do not have many enemies. Humans and lions are their main enemies. Young giraffes also fall victim to leopards, hyenas and crocodiles. Giraffes have three basic ways to defend themselves.
- Their color and pattern camouflages them when they are near trees so that predators do not see them.
- Their long necks give them an almost bird's-eye view of the terrain so that they can usually see trouble coming. For this reason giraffes have been nicknamed the watchtowers of the Savanna.
- If they are attacked, giraffes use their powerful legs and hard hoofs to stun or kill predators.

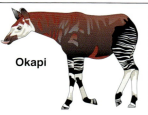

Okapi

The closest living relative of the giraffe is the **okapi**. The okapi lives in the dense forests of central Africa. Okapis stand about 6 ft. (1.8 m) tall and have stripes like a zebra on their legs. They have short knobby horns like the giraffe.

The average adult male is about 17 ft. (5.2 m) tall and weighs 2,600 lbs. (1,200 k).

Females are somewhat smaller, averaging about 14 ft. (4.3 m) tall.

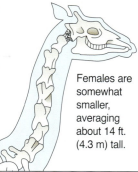

Giraffes walk by moving both legs on one side of the body forward.

Giraffes have strong legs and hoofs that can deliver a killing blow if needed. They can't run far, but they can run fast — reaching speeds of up to 35 mph (56 k).

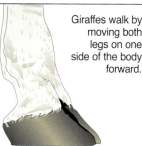

In order to drink or to eat something on the ground a giraffe spreads its front legs wide apart and bends its neck down.

Oxpeckers or tick birds eat ticks, insects and other parasites found on many animals, including giraffes. This helps keep the animals clean and disease free.

Grasslands

General properties of the world's grasslands

Grasslands are one of the Earth's major **biomes**. Biomes are geographical areas that support specific plant and animal communities. Grasslands can be found on every continent except Antarctica and make up about 27 percent of the Earth's vegetation. How grasslands form and develop depends on environmental factors like temperature, soil type, rainfall and humidity. The grasses themselves are divided into three types based on their height:

Tallgrass – 4.5 to 9 feet tall
Midgrass – 1.5 to 4.5 feet tall
Shortgrass – 0.5 to 1.5 feet tall

Generally, tallgrass habitats form on moist soil, and shortgrass habitats form on drier soil. Natural grasslands can form only where less moisture falls on the land than evaporates from it, and they can be thought of as transitional habitats between wet forests and deserts.

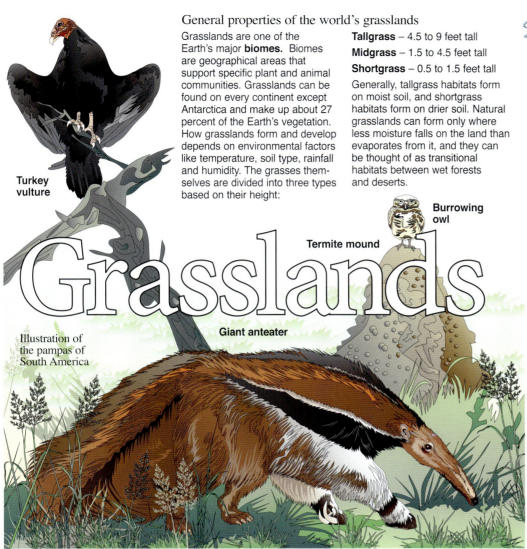

Turkey vulture

Illustration of the pampas of South America

Termite mound

Burrowing owl

Giant anteater

Six kinds of grasses

Grazing, pasture and forage grasses provide food for livestock and other animals. In winter dried grasses are turned into **hay** and **straw**. Orchard, smooth brome and timothy are examples of grazing grasses.

Turfgrasses are used for lawns and recreation areas. Kentucky bluegrass prefers cooler climates, while **bermuda** grass likes warmer temperatures.

Ornamental grasses are used to decorate gardens and parks. They come in a variety of colors.

Cereals are a vital food crop. Sometimes called grains, these grasses help feed people and domestic animals. **Wheat, rice, corn** and **oats** are examples of cereal grains.

Sugar cane is a kind of grass that is used to make sugar.

Woody grasses like **bamboo** are strong enough to use as building material.

Types of grasslands

Grasslands can be divided into three main types; **steppes** (with short grasses), **prairies** (with tall, thick grasses) and tropical/subtropical **savannas** (with scattered woody vegetation).

Some famous steppes are the Great Plains of North America, western Pampa of Argentina and the Veld of South Africa.

Large prairies can be found in the Midwest of North America, eastern Pampa of Argentina and northeast China.

Venezuela, the Campos of southern Brazil, India and Africa are home to tropical savannas.

Just to name a few

Kinds of grasses: Bamboo, barley, bentgrass, bluegrass, brome, corn, fescue, foxtail barley, kafir, millet, oats, reed, rice, rye, sandbur, sorghum, partina, sudan grass, sugar cane, timothy, wheat.

Grassland regions — North America, South America, Eurasia, Africa, Australia

Most grasses are small plants consisting of a group of **tillers** (shoots) that are tightly rolled leaves called **sheaths**. Joints in the sheath are called **culms**. Joining the sheath at the **ligule** are the leaves (**blades**). Grass flowers (**spikelets**) contain pollen, and are contained in protective base coverings called **glumes**. The **lemma** and **palea** are petal-like and attach to a central spike called the **rachilla**. Hairlike spines called **awns** project from each lemma.

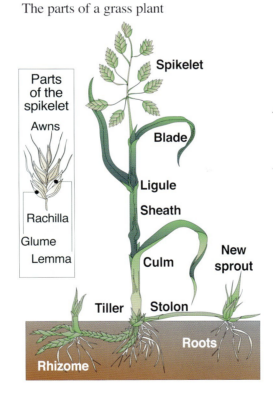

The parts of a grass plant: Spikelet, Blade, Ligule, Sheath, Culm, New sprout, Tiller, Stolon, Roots, Rhizome

Parts of the spikelet: Awns, Rachilla, Glume, Lemma

AVENEAE
Bluejoint grass
(11 to 22 inches tall)
Widespread in North America. An important forage for animals.

FESTUCEAE
Meadow bluegrass
(1.8 to 18 inches tall)
Widespread in temperate and cool regions.

ORYZEAE
Rice
(14.5 to 30 inches tall)
Grows in moist tropical regions. Cultivated for food.

PANICEAE
Elephant grass
(3 to 9 feet tall)
Grows in **Africa** along streams and moist savanna.

Family tree of the Artiodactyls – grass-eating mammals with an even number of toes

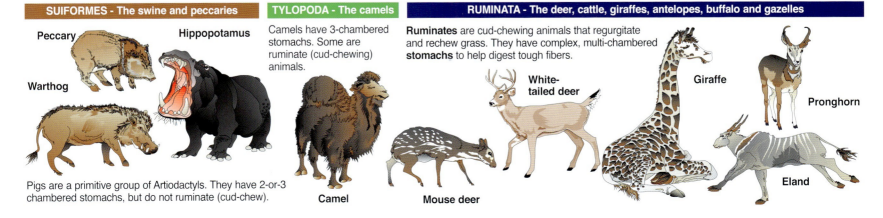

SUIFORMES - The swine and peccaries
Peccary, Hippopotamus, Warthog
Pigs are a primitive group of Artiodactyls. They have 2-or-3 chambered stomachs, but do not ruminate (cud-chew).

TYLOPODA - The camels
Camels have 3-chambered stomachs. Some are ruminate (cud-chewing) animals.
Camel

RUMINATA - The deer, cattle, giraffes, antelopes, buffalo and gazelles
Ruminates are cud-chewing animals that regurgitate and rechew grass. They have complex, multi-chambered **stomachs** to help digest tough fibers.
Mouse deer, White-tailed deer, Giraffe, Pronghorn, Eland

All about Groundhogs and other marmots

How much wood would a woodchuck chuck, if a woodchuck could chuck wood?

Also known as the woodchuck, this member of the marmot family can be found across North America. Here is a look at the facts and myths surrounding this unimposing animal that is famous for one day every year.

Marmotophiles
People who like groundhogs very much are called marmotophiles. Scientists who study groundhogs and marmots are called marmotteers or marmotologists.

All in the family
Groundhogs or woodchucks belong to the marmot family. The scientific or Latin name for a woodchuck is marmota monax.

Marmots are a kind of rodent closely related to the ground squirrel and prairie dog.

Getting around
Groundhogs have been known to climb trees, but they are generally more comfortable on the ground. They are also quite good swimmers.

What big teeth...
Like all rodents, groundhogs have two front gnawing teeth called incisors. Except during hibernation, the incisors grow continuously and require constant grinding and gnawing to keep them from piercing the roof of the groundhog's mouth.

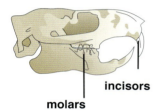

Hibernation
Groundhogs enter their dens for hibernation in early **autumn** (Sept. - Oct.) They curl into a ball and go into a deep sleep. Their breathing slows and their body temperature **drops** to between 43° and 57°F. During hibernation the groundhog cannot hear or feel. It would take several hours in a warm room to wake a groundhog from deep hibernation. In early spring, the groundhog wakes up and begins to look for food and a mate.

Babies
Groundhogs mate in early spring, usually in March. About a month later, the mother gives birth to four or five babies, that she raises alone. Born tiny, naked and **blind**, the babies spend the first month of life entirely dependent on their mother. They open their eyes at about a month old. Soon they are large enough to venture out of the den and begin foraging for plants and grasses. Unlike most marmots, the groundhog is a **solitary** creature and does not live in colonies. In mid to late summer the youngsters leave the family unit and set off to make their own dens a few miles away.

What's for dinner
Woodchucks are **herbivores** (plant eaters). They like to eat young plants and grasses, but they also get into gardens and farmers' fields and eat bulbs and produce. They do not store their food like squirrels, but eat enough in the summer to sustain them through winter hibernation.

Sensible senses
Groundhogs have excellent hearing and very good vision. They make a short, sharp whistling sound when alarmed or frightened, which is why they have the nickname "whistlepig."

North American marmot ranges*
There are 14 known marmot species throughout the world. Six of these live in North America.

* Ranges indicated are approximate

Home sweet home

Groundhogs live 2 to 4 feet underground in **dens** or **burrows** that consist of several tunnels and rooms. They like to build summer dens near sunny open fields and where the food supply is plentiful. Winter dens are often near dry wooded areas.

Sometimes they will dig a burrow under a barn or shed. You can spot a groundhog den by looking for the pile of dirt that often marks the main entrance.

The groundhog's large feet and sharp claws are ideal for **digging** and tunneling. All dens have an entrance and a secret back door, used as an escape route. They build several rooms, one for nesting, one for nursing and another for waste. Abandoned groundhog dens are often taken over by foxes and other animals looking for a safe secondhand home.

Enemies and defense
Groundhogs have a number of enemies. Eagles and hawks are always on the lookout for unsuspecting woodchucks. Red foxes, wolves, and domestic **dogs** are also dangerous to groundhogs.

Humans are the most dangerous enemy of all. Farmers try to protect their crops by trapping, hunting and poisoning. And many people hunt these little rodents just for the fun of it.

The groundhog is generally very timid and will run and hide in its den when threatened. But if cornered, (like all wild animals) the groundhog can be **vicious**. They have been known to badly injure dogs and they will fight until exhausted.

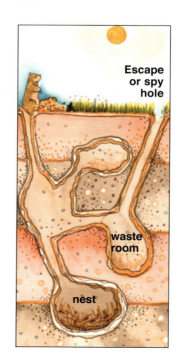

Groundhog day
According to **superstition** and **legend**, if a groundhog sees its shadow on Feb. 2, there will be six more weeks of winter. If it does not see its shadow, there will be an early spring.

Groundhog Day has roots in early Roman history, when the tradition of seeing a hedgehog shadow in mid-winter predicted a severe winter. The Germans continued this tradition when they came to North America, using the groundhog as a weather forecaster on Candlemas Day.

Groundhog Day may also be linked to the early Delaware or Lenni Lenape people, who believed that the woodchuck, Oijik (Wejak) or Wojack was their ancient grandfather.

The most famous of weather predicting groundhogs is Punxsutawney Phil from Pennsylvania. But many towns across North America have their own Groundhog Day celebrations and traditions.

Predicting the weather
Punxsutawney Phil and his ancestors have been predicting the weather since 1887. Unfortunately, his forecasts have been correct only about 39 percent of the time.

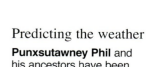

Where in the world

The river hippopotamus needs fairly deep water and grazing land to survive. In the past, hippopotamuses thrived along the many rivers and lakes of **Africa**, but hunting and habitat destruction have taken their toll, and the hippopotamus range is now restricted mostly to wildlife parks and refuges. The river hippo can be found in central and south Africa. The pygmy hippo lives in Liberia, Sierra Leone and Guinea.

What is in a name?

The scientific name for the river hippo is hippopotamus amphibious, which, translated loosely from **Greek,** means "river horse that leads a double life" (because it needs both water and land to survive). The river hippopotamus is also known as the Nile or common hippopotamus. Hippopotamuses and hippopotami are both correct plural forms. A group of hippos is sometimes called a **bloat**. Hippos are **pachyderms**, which means they are thick-skinned, with skin up to 2 inches thick in some places.

Following the herd

The common river hippo usually lives in **herds** of about five to 30, but larger groups have been observed. The herd is led by a dominant male that defends his territorial right to the females in his group. The pygmy hippo is a more solitary creature, preferring to live **alone** or in pairs.

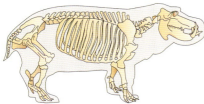
River hippopotamus skeleton

Dinner at 8

Hippos are **herbivores**. The river hippo eats mostly grass, but it also feeds on leaves, vegetables and fruit. This giant creature feeds for about six hours and can eat up to 100 pounds (45 kg) of grass in one night. Some travel long distances in search of food and new waterways.

Enemies

With the exception of man and rival hippos, the river hippopotamus has few enemies. The very young, old or sickly are sometimes the victims of crocodiles, lions and hyenas. When threatened, a hippo will head for the safety of water, but if water is not nearby, the hippopotamus can be very dangerous and aggressive.

HIPPOS

There are two species of hippopotamus — the river hippo (also called the common hippo) and the smaller and extremely rare pygmy hippo. The river hippopotamus is one of the world's largest land animals. Both species are related closely to cetaceans (whales and dolphins).

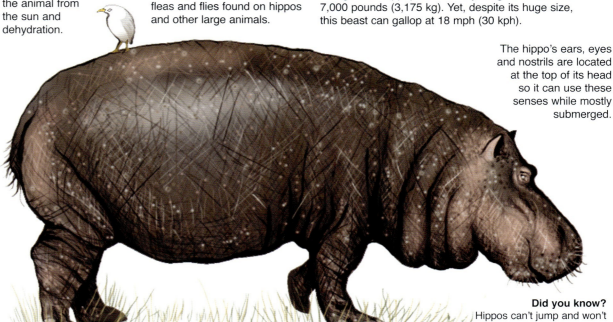

It was once thought that hippos sweat blood, but the fact is that hippos do not sweat at all. They do, however, secrete an oily red-pink substance that early observers mistook for blood. This fluid protects the animal from the sun and dehydration.

The river hippopotamus has a huge head and mouth. When it opens its mouth wide, it is usually posturing in a threatening manner. Males will not hesitate to use their long, tusk-like canines to fight off rival hippos — sometimes fighting to the death.

The **oxpecker bird** eats ticks, fleas and flies found on hippos and other large animals.

A large river hippopotamus may weigh as much as 7,000 pounds (3,175 kg). Yet, despite its huge size, this beast can gallop at 18 mph (30 kph).

The hippo's ears, eyes and nostrils are located at the top of its head so it can use these senses while mostly submerged.

Did you know?
Hippos can't jump and won't even step over objects.

River hippopotamus

The river hippopatomus (hippopotamus amphibious) is well adapted to life on land and in water. This hairless animal ranges in size from 12 to 15 feet (4 to 5 m) long. The life span of hippos is about 30 years in the wild and 50 years in captivity.

Pygmy hippopotamus

The pygmy hippopotamus (hexaprotodon liberiensis) is considerably smaller than its cousin, the river hippo. The pygmy weighs an average of 400 to 600 pounds (180 to 270 kg) and is about the size of a large hog. It lives near water but is less aquatic than the common hippo. This rare animal forages for roots and plants in forests and swamps near lakes, streams and rivers.

Water babies

The river hippo does not have **sweat** glands and depends on water to keep it cool. For this reason, it spends most of the day resting or sleeping while submerged in water. The river hippo has webbed feet that make underwater movement easier. The hippo is too dense and heavy to float, so it can't really swim, but by pushing off the bottom it appears to do a slow and graceful dance. This huge beast also walks and gallops underwater. It is capable of staying underwater for five minutes or more. While submerged, its ears and nostrils close to stop water from getting in.

River hippos mate and usually give birth in the water. A calf weighs about 100 pounds (45 kg) at birth. Once born, the calf will even nurse underwater.

HORSES

This powerful beast is respected for its beauty and its strength. People have relied on the horse as a beast of burden, a weapon of war and as a best friend.

The evolution of the horse

The relationship between horses and men is over 2 million years old. But horses have been on earth for about 54 million years, starting in the **Cenozoic Era.**

Holocene epoch
10,000 years ago to present
Glaciers in Antarctica and Greenland. Giant mammals become extinct. Widespread human development. Man domesticates the horse.

Pleistocene epoch
1,800,000 to 10,000 years ago
The final evolution of the horse, about 2 million years ago, occurred about the time that man had evolved into homo sapiens. The new horse was called Equus.

Pliocene epoch
5,000,000 to 1,800,000 years ago
Pliohippus had a single toe, ending in a hoof. A grazer, it could see well and run quickly on long, strong legs. The Pliohippus was about 50 inches (127 cm) tall.

Pliohippus

Miocene epoch
26,000,000 to 5,000,000 years ago
Beginning in the **Miocene,** these horses lived on open prairie land. Teeth changed to flat, grinding molars. The muzzle and head became longer. **Merychippus,** this form of the horse, was a little over 3 feet (0.9 m) tall. The foot changed to allow the horse to escape predators quickly.

Merychippus
Skull
Front foot

Oliogocene epoch
38,000,000 to 26,000,000 years ago
During the **Oligocene,** about 38 million years ago, gradual changes took place in the Eohippae family. Some strains died out, others evolved into **Mesohippus,** a three toed, 2-foot (0.6 cm) tall animal.

Mesohippus
Skull
Front foot

Eocene epoch
54,000,000 to 38,000,000 years ago
Modern horses are all descendants of the tiny **Eohippus,** or Dawn Horse that lived in swamps and forests. Fossils of this 10-inch (25.4 cm) tall animal have been found in North America. The four-toed Eohippus was a slow-moving pig-shaped animal with sharp teeth. Scientists speculate that it had a dappled brown coat, like a young deer, to camouflage it on the forest floor.

Eohippus
Skull
Front foot

Forelock, Poll, Mane, Muzzle, Cheek, Neck, Withers, Shoulder, Back, Loin, Croup, Tail, Chest, Belly, Buttock, Elbow, Stifle, Point of rump, Gaskin, Forearm, Knee, Cannon, Hoof, Fetlock, Pastern, Hock

Parts of the hoof
Heel, Center cleft, Bar, Frog, Sole, Wall

The Arab
Arabs are the oldest purebred horses in the world. It has been bred all over the world and has improved nearly every other breed of horse.

Colt — A male less than 4 years old.
Dam — The mother of a foal
Filly — A female less than 4 years old
Foal — A newborn
Hand — A height measurement. A hand is four inches. Horses are measured from the ground to the top of the withers in hands.
Mare — A female more than 4 years old
Purebred — Bred from horses of the same type
Stallion — A male more than four years old

Horses have different face markings. Here's how they're named:

Star, Stripe, Blaze, Baldface, Snip

Origins of modern horses

Prehistoric horse herds migrated from North America to Asia in response to a hotter, drier climate. None remained in the Western Hemisphere until they were reintroduced by Spanish conquerors to Mexico in 1519.

The earliest horse migrants travelled to the arid regions of Africa's savannah and the Asian steppes, becoming the **Zebras** and **Asses** of today. These primitive horses have changed very little.

Later migrants, called the Southern Group, had moved south during the ice age, but remained on the grasslands of Eurasia. They became the **Steppe Horses.** Steppe horses were lean, fast and large-headed. Their coats were fine and thin.

The next group of migrants became more adapted to harsh and cold conditions of the North American ice age. They stayed further north as they traveled to Asia and Europe. This group became the shaggy, tough and adaptable **Ponies.**

The slow-moving horses were the last to leave North America, and they became the Tundra Horses. These large animals grew big feet and thick coats to survive in snow and ice. They are ancestors of the **Work and Draft horses** of today.

Zebra, African wild ass, Viatka, Shetland pony, Clydesdale

Horses and man

No one knows when man first captured and domesticated the horse. Primitive man hunted the horse for meat. Discoveries at the ancient city of Susa in Southwest Asia reveal that the horse was ridden about 5,000 years ago. Here are some historic facts about how man has used the horse:

The Ancient Egyptians
Many tomb paintings, scrolls and carvings illustrate horses pulling chariots for Pharaoh.

The Scythians
The Scythians were nomadic Eurasian people who lived in the steppelands. They were fierce warriors who used the horse in warfare.

The Tartars
These Mongolian horse warriors of the steppe were a fierce army that first united under Genghis Khan in the 13th century and were still a force to be reckoned with in the late 1800s when British Imperialism spread to China. They excelled at fast maneuvers on the tough little ponies of the region.

Age of Chivalry
During Medieval times, the Renaissance, and Baroque, elaborate suits of armor were fashioned for kings, noblemen, knights and their steeds. Here is a German suit of horse armor from the 18th century.

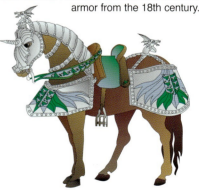

The Pony Express
Fast horses and brave riders carried the mail across the Wild West in America until 1861, when the telegraph linked the East and West coasts.

KOALAS

Wild koalas can only be found in **Australia**. Fossil evidence suggests that koalas evolved more than 25 million years ago. These extinct koala species were much larger than the 20- to 30-pound koalas of the present. The map shows where koalas were found when Europeans arrived (A.D. 1788) and where they can be found today. Two hundred years of hunting and habitat loss has drastically affected populations.

- ■ Present ■ Before 1788

250 million years ago — Pangaea
130 million years ago — Laurasia / Gondwana
Today — North America, South America, Eurasia, Africa, Antarctica, Australia

Habitat loss, dogs and cars are the koalas greatest enemies.

Prized for their soft fur, the koalas were hunted to near extinction. In 1937, they became a protected species. But despite conservation efforts, their numbers have continued to decline. It is estimated that there are 100,000 koalas in the wild today, compared with more than a million 100 years ago.

Koalas live alone or in small groups high in the forest canopy. Koalas don't build nests, but like to wedge themselves between forks in the tree branches. They only leave the trees when they absolutely have to. (For example, to cross a road to get to another tree.)

Land of the marsupials

The plants and animals of Australia have evolved differently from those on other continents. This is because Australia was separated from the rest of the world about 200 million years ago.

Marsupials first appeared about 250 million years ago, when all the planet's land areas were joined as one giant continent called "Pangaea." About 130 million years ago, Australia and Antarctica were one landmass. When they broke apart about 45 million years ago, the marsupials that lived in Antarctica did not survive the cold as the continent drifted farther south, but the marsupials of (warmer) Australia thrived.

There are about 200 kinds of marsupials living in Australia today. South America has about 200 species. North America has only one — the **opossum**.

What's in a name?

The word "koala" is believed to be from an aboriginal word that means "no drink." This is because koalas get almost all of their water from gum leaves. It is very rare to see a koala drinking.

Relatively close

Koalas are closely related to the Australian **wombat** and opossum. Koalas are distantly related to the opossum of North and South America. The kangaroo is an even more distant cousin on the genetic family tree. What all these mammals (milk-drinking animals) have in common is that they are marsupials. **Marsupials** are a group of animals that are not fully formed when born — they are in an almost embryonic stage. They continue their development in their mother's special pouch.

Behavioral traits

Koalas are **nocturnal** and are active at night. (Koalas sleep about 18 to 21 hours a day.) They are also **arboreal**, which means they live in trees. They communicate with each other using smell and a variety of growls, clicks, snorts and bellows.

Skeleton

Esophagus, Stomach, Caecum, Small intestine, Proximal colon, Distal colon, Anus

Koalas are awkward on the ground. Here they are vulnerable to predators and automobiles. They are capable of running and swimming if they need to.

There are more than 600 kinds of eucalyptus trees in Australia. But koalas only eat about 120 kinds. (Some will only eat four to six kinds.)

Footprints

Grooming claw

Front paw **Rear paw**

Koalas have adapted to life in the trees. They have powerful legs and sharp claws that are well suited for climbing. The front paw of the koala has two thumbs, excellent for gripping tree limbs. Two of the toes on the hind paws are joined together for most of their length. These joined toes are used for combing, scratching and grooming thick fur.

Each koala has a home range made up of several trees. These home trees provide both food and a place to live.

Special diet

Koalas only eat the leaves and bark of certain types of eucalyptus (gum) trees. They have sharp teeth for the job. They also have cheek pouches (like hamsters), where they store leaves until ready to eat.

Eucalyptus leaves are thick, fibrous and oily, but not high in nutrition (some are even poisonous). Koalas will carefully choose the young and tender leaves. A koala eats about 2 lbs. of leaves a night and takes three days to digest them. Koalas have a special digestive chamber called a **caecum** (SEE-kum) that helps break down and extract extra nutrients from the gum leaves.

The diet of eucalyptus gives the koala a unique odor, which some people compare to cough drops.

Just call me "joey"

Baby koalas are called joeys. A joey is born about 35 days after its parents mate. Newborn koalas are about the size of a jellybean. A newborn is pink and has no fur. Despite being tiny, blind and deaf, a joey must make its way from the birth canal to the mother's pouch.

When the joey is 5 or 6 months old, it will begin to peek its head out of the pouch. Its mother begins to feed it a runny mix called **pap**. Pap is made with the mother's droppings and is needed to pass on microorganisms required to digest gum leaves. By 7 months the joey will be leaving the pouch more and more often — clinging to its mother. At 1 to 3 years, it will leave to live on its own. Koalas are fully grown by age 3 or 4.

Joey

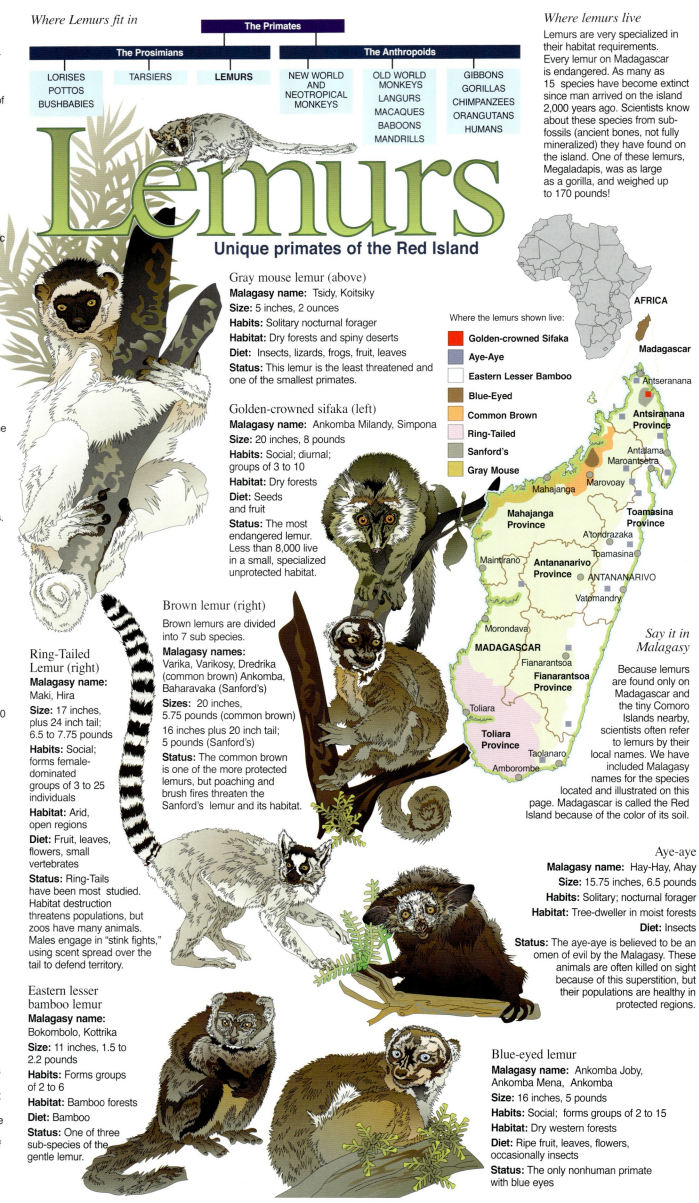

Lemurs
Unique primates of the Red Island

The primate family tree

There are more than 200 species of primates living today. Primates are mammals with flexible hands and feet, each with five digits. There are nails on the hands and feet instead of claws. Special bones in the ear, chest and limbs as well as vertical posture, large brains, and short snouts separate primates from other animals. Humans, great apes, monkeys and lemurs are all primates.

Scientists who study primates are called primatologists. Scientists arrange animals using a system called taxonomic classification. The system arranges animals into groups based on their resemblances to each other.

The primate order is divided into two suborders: prosimians and anthropoids.

The Anthropoids
Humans, great apes (chimpanzees, gorillas and orangutans), gibbons and monkeys have lived on Earth for about 30 million years. Scientists believe they evolved from similar ancestors, called the Early Simians, about 36 million years ago.

The prosimians
Lemurs, tarsiers, galagos and lorises are primates that have been around the longest. They are prosimians, or pre-monkeys. Scientists believe they are related to ancestors called **omomyids** and **adapids**, who first lived on Earth about 60 million years ago. All of the prosimians living today live on the island of Madagascar, sub-Saharan Africa and parts of South and Southeast Asia.

What is a Lemur?

Lemurs are unique prosimians because they have evolved in isolation on the island of Madagascar. Human beings arrived on the island about 2,000 years ago. At that time there were at least 49 species of lemurs. Today, around 15 of those species are extinct.

Lemurs are varied, ranging in weight from 1 ounce for the pygmy mouse lemur to 16 pounds for the indri. They live in the treetops or on land, are social or solitary, and have diets that include all or some of the following foods: fruit, plant parts, tree gum, small animals and insects.

The name lemur derives from the Latin word **lemures**, which means ghosts.

Lemurs don't blink. They have a special eyelid called a **nictitating membrane** which moves over the eyeball to keep it wet.

Lemurs depend on their sense of smell much more than other primates. Many have special scent glands they use to mark territory. Lemurs that live in social groups form strong bonds by grooming each other. To do this, they have special teeth that serve as a **tooth** or **grooming comb**. Another grooming feature of lemurs is the **toilet claw**, a special nail on the second toe of the hind foot that is used to spread scent through the fur.

Where Lemurs fit in

The Primates
- **The Prosimians**: LORISES, POTTOS, BUSHBABIES | TARSIERS | LEMURS
- **The Anthropoids**: NEW WORLD AND NEOTROPICAL MONKEYS | OLD WORLD MONKEYS, LANGURS, MACAQUES, BABOONS, MANDRILLS | GIBBONS, GORILLAS, CHIMPANZEES, ORANGUTANS, HUMANS

Gray mouse lemur (above)
Malagasy name: Tsidy, Koitsiky
Size: 5 inches, 2 ounces
Habits: Solitary nocturnal forager
Habitat: Dry forests and spiny deserts
Diet: Insects, lizards, frogs, fruit, leaves
Status: This lemur is the least threatened and one of the smallest primates.

Golden-crowned sifaka (left)
Malagasy name: Ankomba Milandy, Simpona
Size: 20 inches, 8 pounds
Habits: Social; diurnal; groups of 3 to 10
Habitat: Dry forests
Diet: Seeds and fruit
Status: The most endangered lemur. Less than 8,000 live in a small, specialized unprotected habitat.

Brown lemur (right)
Brown lemurs are divided into 7 sub species.
Malagasy names: Varika, Varikosy, Dredrika (common brown) Ankomba, Baharavaka (Sanford's)
Sizes: 20 inches, 5.75 pounds (common brown)
16 inches plus 20 inch tail; 5 pounds (Sanford's)
Status: The common brown is one of the more protected lemurs, but poaching and brush fires threaten the Sanford's lemur and its habitat.

Ring-Tailed Lemur (right)
Malagasy name: Maki, Hira
Size: 17 inches, plus 24 inch tail; 6.5 to 7.75 pounds
Habits: Social; forms female-dominated groups of 3 to 25 individuals
Habitat: Arid, open regions
Diet: Fruit, leaves, flowers, small vertebrates
Status: Ring-Tails have been most studied. Habitat destruction threatens populations, but zoos have many animals. Males engage in "stink fights," using scent spread over the tail to defend territory.

Eastern lesser bamboo lemur
Malagasy name: Bokombolo, Kottrika
Size: 11 inches, 1.5 to 2.2 pounds
Habits: Forms groups of 2 to 6
Habitat: Bamboo forests
Diet: Bamboo
Status: One of three sub-species of the gentle lemur.

Where lemurs live

Lemurs are very specialized in their habitat requirements. Every lemur on Madagascar is endangered. As many as 15 species have become extinct since man arrived on the island 2,000 years ago. Scientists know about these species from sub-fossils (ancient bones, not fully mineralized) they have found on the island. One of these lemurs, Megaladapis, was as large as a gorilla, and weighed up to 170 pounds!

Where the lemurs shown live:
- Golden-crowned Sifaka
- Aye-Aye
- Eastern Lesser Bamboo
- Blue-Eyed
- Common Brown
- Ring-Tailed
- Sanford's
- Gray Mouse

Say it in Malagasy

Because lemurs are found only on Madagascar and the tiny Comoro Islands nearby, scientists often refer to lemurs by their local names. We have included Malagasy names for the species located and illustrated on this page. Madagascar is called the Red Island because of the color of its soil.

Aye-aye
Malagasy name: Hay-Hay, Ahay
Size: 15.75 inches, 6.5 pounds
Habits: Solitary; nocturnal forager
Habitat: Tree-dweller in moist forests
Diet: Insects
Status: The aye-aye is believed to be an omen of evil by the Malagasy. These animals are often killed on sight because of this superstition, but their populations are healthy in protected regions.

Blue-eyed lemur
Malagasy name: Ankomba Joby, Ankomba Mena, Ankomba
Size: 16 inches, 5 pounds
Habits: Social; forms groups of 2 to 15
Habitat: Dry western forests
Diet: Ripe fruit, leaves, flowers, occasionally insects
Status: The only nonhuman primate with blue eyes

LIONS

Lions are powerful animals, respected for their beauty, power and mighty roar. Sometimes called the king of beasts, the lion is the second largest of the big cats after tigers.

Where in the world

There was a time when wild lions roamed much of Europe, the Middle East, Asia and Africa. But hunting and habitat loss reduced their numbers drastically. Today, lions are found only in the **grasslands** of central and southern Africa. (There are about 300 lions left in northwest India.) Protected national parks called **reserves** have been formed to give lions a place to live without fear of hunters.

Feast or famine

Lions are meat-eating **carnivores** that hunt mostly large, hoofed animals such as zebra or antelope. If food is scarce, they will catch smaller prey or scavenge for carrion. Catching dinner can be a challenge, as most potential meals can run faster than the lion. A week may go by without a successful hunt, but lions usually manage to eat every two or three days. Hunting in small groups and at night may give the potential advantage of surprise. Females do most of the hunting, but the males usually get to eat first. After a successful hunt, the lions gorge themselves. Some can eat 75 pounds (34 kg) of meat in one sitting.

Example of what a pride of six lions ate in one year.

- 5 Elands
- 5 Hartebeeste
- 9 Giraffes
- 9 Impalas
- 12 Buffaloes
- 25 Gazelles
- 33 Zebras
- 107 Wildebeests (antelope)
- 14 Other

Hear me roar

Lions roar for many reasons: to call a pride member, to announce territorial rights or to intimidate rivals. Social bonds are strengthened when the pride roars as a group. Some roars can be heard miles away.

Pride of place

Lions are the only wild cats that live together in a family group, called a **pride**. A pride ranges in size from six to 30 animals. The size of a pride depends on the availability of food. A pride consists of several related females and their cubs, led by one male or a **coalition** of two or three males. Members of a pride hunt, sleep and eat together. Each pride has its own hunting territory, which is guarded jealously by the males in the group.

Lions may spend 20 hours a day just relaxing.

Just the facts

Scientific name: Panthera leo
Scientific classification: Lions are members of the class Mammalia and the order Carnivora. They are part of the cat family Felidae.
Size: The adult male is about 9 feet (2.7 m) from nose to the end of the tail. The adult lioness is smaller at about 8 feet (2.44 m).
Weight: Adult males weigh 330 to 500 pounds (150 to 225 kg). Adult females weigh 260 to 330 pounds (120 to 150 kg).
Sexual maturity: 3 to 4 years
Gestation period: About 3 1/2 months

The jaws of a lion are strong enough to bite through bone. Lions don't chew their food; they swallow large chunks. Lions have 30 teeth. Their four sharp, pointed canines are perfect for holding down prey, and their four **carnassials** (cheek teeth) are sharp enough to cut through skin and tendons.

Perfect paws

Lions have retractable claws that can be pulled back into a protective covering called a **sheath**.

A lion's sharp, curved claws are weapons that help it catch prey.

A lion's paws have thick pads that provide grip and allow for quiet movement.

Front feet

Back feet

Front feet

Back feet

Unsheathed claw

Retracted or sheathed (pulled back) claw

The male lion can be distinguished by its large **mane**. This protects its head and neck and also serves to make the animal look larger to potential enemies.

A lion's color is similar to the grasses of its savanna habitat.

Growing up

Lions spend most of their time sleeping or resting. During the day, they can be found snoozing in the shade of a tree. They hunt only when hungry. A lion in the wild lives up to about 15 years. In captivity, the life span averages 25 years.

A cub's spotted and lightly striped fur will fade to a more uniform coat.

Lions breed at any time of the year. The lioness leaves the pride when it is time to give birth. She can give birth to one to six cubs, but two or three is most common. Cubs are born after 100 days of gestation and weigh about 3 pounds (1.4 kg) at birth. Born blind and helpless, the babies are vulnerable, especially while the mother is away hunting. (It is estimated that 50 percent to 80 percent of cubs die before 2 years of age.)

Cubs are introduced to the pride at about 10 weeks of age. It is not uncommon for nursing lions to share responsibility for each other's cubs. Males are generally tolerant of cubs, but if a new male takes over a pride, it will kill all cubs that are not its own.

Cubs are considered full grown at about 18 months old. At this time, their mother may breed again, and young males may be forced to look for a pride of their own.

What are marsupials?

Marsupials are an ancient, unique group of animals often called pouched mammals. Like all mammals, marsupials are warm-blooded, have hair, and mothers nurse their young. They differ from placental mammals in that they give live birth without long gestation times. Marsupials give birth to a helpless embryo. The embryo climbs from the mother's birth canal to her pouch. There it attaches with its mouth to the mammae (nipple) and continues to nourish and develop for weeks or even months, depending on the species. Placental mammal mothers instead nourish their developing embryo in the uterus with the blood supply, during a longer gestation.

Today, marsupials have fewer species worldwide than placentals, but are very diverse in body structure. They range from tiny four-footed forms to large, two-legged kangaroos.

When they evolved

Cases of convergent evolution exist between marsupials and placentals. This means that two different animal species fill the same ecological niche in different parts of the world, evolving independently. Today, most marsupials are found in Central and South America (around 70 species) and Australia (around 200 species).

North America

The only living marsupial found here is the opossum. During the Mesozoic Era, marsupials were more common than placentals, persisting until the mid- to late Tertiary period.

South America

Marsupials began to go extinct in the late Miocene and Early Pliocene Epochs here. At that time, a land connection with North America allowed many competing placentals to cross into South America.

Australia and Tasmania

Marsupials are the dominant native mammals and include kangaroos, koalas, Tasmanian devils, wombats and others. Thylacinus lived there until 1936, when the last living individual was seen in Tasmania.

The marsupial orders

Traditionally, scientists have classified marsupials (Metatheria) into these orders:

Didelphimorphia American opossums

Paucituberculata "Shrew" opossums

Microbiotheria Monito del monte

Dasyuromorphia Australasian carnivorous marsupials

Peramelemorphia Bandicoots Bilbies

Notoryctemorphia Marsupial "moles"

Diprotodontia Kangaroos wallabies, opossums koalas, gliders, wombats

Kangaroo locomotion

When feeding at ground level, the tail is used as a "fifth limb" while the rear legs are lifted and repositioned.

The tail also acts as a rudder, providing balance during leaps and turns.

At full speed, a kangaroo can leap 30 feet or more.

BROWSING/FEEDING — **SHORT LEAPS** — **ESCAPE/LONG LEAPS**

Marsupials
The "pouched mammals"

Virginia opossum (Didelphis)
North America
Habitat: Variety of environments. Prefers wet areas, especially streams and swamps.
Diet: Insects and carrion. Also plants, including fruits and grains in season.

Coarse-haired wombat (Vombatus)
Australia, Tasmania and Flinders Island
Habitat: Wet, humid climate with suitable burrowing conditions. Mainly solitary, except during breeding season. Individuals live in a series of burrows called warrens.
Diet: Feeds on grass, roots, sedges, matrushes and fungi.

Red kangaroo (Macropus)
Central Australia
Habitat: Scrub and shrub land, grassland and desert, where rainfall is less than 500 millimeters yearly. Of all marsupials, only the kangaroos are bipeds, moving more naturally on two legs than four.
Diet: Plants, preferring green grasses and flowering plants. They can go without water for long periods of time.

Brown antechinus (Antechinus)
Eastern and southeastern Australia
Habitat: Wet forest with dense cover and fallen trees for nest building. Usually ground dwelling; may become arboreal in dry areas
Diet: Insects

Koala (Phascolarctos)
Eastern Australia
Habitat: Arboreal, mostly in eucalyptus trees, where they feed and avoid predators. They are slow-moving and sleep up to 18 hours a day.
Diet: Feeds at night, on eucalyptus trees.

Feathertailed glider (Acrobates)
Mainland Australia
Habitat: Open and closed forests. Forages in trees, bushes and tall grasses.
Diet: Insects, arthropods, occasionally nectar.

Tasmanian devil (Sarcophilus) Tasmania
Habitat: Hollow logs, caves or burrows in forests. The Tasmanian devil resembles a small bear. They are nocturnal and usually solitary. They make nests of bark, grass and leaves, which they inhabit during the day.
Diet: Carrion. An efficient scavenger, the devil eats both bones and fur. Other food includes insects, insect larvae, snakes and some vegetation.

How the marsupials and placental mammals differ

Key anatomical differences distinguish the mammal groups. A third group of mammals, the monotremes, is an ancient and primitive egg-laying group of animals. The only living monotremes are the duck-billed platypus (which lives in Australia) and the echidna (which lives in Australia and New Guinea).

In marsupials, the embryo passes down through the vaginal sinus and into a single body exit called the cloaca. In placentals, there are three separate body exits.

Migration

The word migration is usually used to describe the seasonal or periodic movement of an animal from one habitat to another and then back again. Many species of insects, birds, sea creatures, mammals and reptiles are known to be migratory. People also migrate, but not always for biological reasons; they will sometimes migrate for political and/or social reasons.

About 245 species of birds migrate from the United States to Central or South America. Herons, swallows, flycatchers, hawks, falcons, owls and warblers are just a few of these migrants. In Europe, many birds migrate back and forth to Africa. About half of the 9,500 species of birds found around the world migrate.

In late summer and early fall, **monarch butterflies** gather for the annual southern migration.

Monarchs are the only butterfly to make such an extreme, two-way journey. Their route can be more than 3,000 miles (4,828 km) long. Monarchs begin the return trip in the spring. They breed along the way and then die. The new generation completes the journey.

On the move

Migration occurs in a huge variety of animals. From microorganisms to giant whales, migration is commonly a round-trip response to climate, food availability and/or ideal breeding conditions.

There are many types of migration. Daily and seasonal migrations are the most common kind, but some animals migrate on lunar or cyclical intervals.

One-way, irregular movements are called mass movements or emigrations. When an emigration is the result of a population explosion it is called an irruption. Lemmings and some insect and bird species experience cyclical irruptions.

Daily migrations

Daily migrations are quite common in creatures that live in oceans and lakes. These daily movements are usually triggered by changes in light and/or temperature. Huge numbers of zooplankton (collections of tiny organisms that drift in bodies of water) move toward the surface at night and return to the deep during daylight hours.

Some terrestrial (land) animals make daily migrations. The tree-living daddy longlegs can be observed each evening moving from its tree trunk to the forest floor. As dawn approaches, the spider returns to its tree trunk.

Seasonal migrations

Seasonal migrations generally take place twice a year. They are usually triggered by changes in temperature, light or rainfall.

There are three main types of seasonal migrations: **Latitudinal, altitudinal** and **local**. Most migrating birds, bats, seals and whales move in a north-south or latitudinal direction. Many mountain dwellers, such as the great panda or mountain quail, move up and down their mountain range in an altitudinal migration. Local migrations are usually when animals relocate looking for water.

Some species of **salmon** will travel up to 800 to 900 miles (1,287-1,448 km) from spawning stream to ocean and back again.

Gray whales breed and winter in the warm waters of Mexico. They migrate north to the seas around the Bering Strait.

Baby **loggerhead turtles** embark on an 8,000-mile (12,875 km) migration that takes five to 10 years to complete. When they are born along the eastern Florida coast they are only 2 inches (5 cm) long.

The **green turtle** migrates a distance of more than 2,000 miles (3,219 km) from its feeding grounds off the coast of Brazil to lay eggs on Ascension Island, in the middle of the southern Atlantic Ocean.

Lemmings have a 3- to 5-year cycle of migration, and animals (like the snowy owl) that depend on lemmings as a food source will sometimes migrate with these small rodents.

Cyclical migrations

Cyclical migrations are not linked to climate or seasons, but happen at irregular intervals and often take a **lifetime** to complete. Some species of salmon have cyclical migrations where the young hatch in small rivers and streams and then move into the ocean for two or three years. To breed, the adult salmon make their way back to the river where they were born. There they lay their eggs before dying.

Reasons for travel

Scientists have been studying the migrational habits of animals for many years, but they still cannot explain what triggers many animals to migrate. Daylight plays an important role for many migrations. It is believed that under certain light conditions, hormones are released that tell the animal it is time to move. Experiments reveal that some animals do not need any outside stimulants or cues, but are just born knowing when to migrate.

The **Arctic tern** migrates from the Arctic to Antarctica (11,000 miles, or 17,703 km) and back again, one of the longest migrations of any animal.

The **ruby-throated hummingbird** eats until it has gained nearly 40 percent of its original body weight. This extra fat is needed to fly the 500 miles (805 km), across the Gulf of Mexico.

How do they do that?

Many species have migration routes and navigation skills that are instinctive. Some animals rely on the Earth's magnetic field to navigate. Some use the sun, moon and stars as a compass, while others may use landmarks such as mountains or rivers. Many birds and insects use polarized light to find their way (this lets them find their way even on cloudy days). Salmon use their sense of smell and water currents to find their way back to their spawning stream.

Lunar migrations

Lunar migrations are most common in aquatic animals and are usually associated with reproduction. From March through July, California smelt (or grunion) ride the night tide of the full moon in order to deposit their eggs and sperm in sandy burrows on the beach. Two weeks later, the fish's offspring are washed out to sea by the high tide of the new moon.

During droughts and the dry season in Africa, thousands of **wildebeests and zebras** migrate to areas with more water.

Human migrations

People have been known to migrate as well. For example, the Kung bushmen of the **Kalahari** Desert continue the tradition of following migrating game animals, which they rely on for food. During drought or dry seasons the Kung bushmen will migrate to areas where water is more plentiful.

MUSHROOMS

Mushrooms are not plants, but a kind of fungi. Lacking chlorophyll they rely on the decay of dead plants for their nutritional needs.

Nature's recyclers

There are more than 5,000 kinds of mushrooms. Most species grow in shady forests or in damp, grassy fields. Most mushrooms are saprotrophs (they break down organic debris). These mushrooms play an important role in their ecosystems by enriching the soil. They turn decaying matter into helpful chemicals such as amino acids and sugars which feed the mushroom and the plants around it. Some fungi are parasitic (they feed on living organisms). Symbiotic fungi have a beneficial give and take relationship with an organism (some orchids rely on fungi for healthy growth).

Life cycle

Mushrooms produce and release spores that grow into new fungi. A spore is a nearly microscopic cell that contains the genetic information of the mushroom. When a spore germinates it grows thread like filaments that make up the mycelium. Eventually a button forms on the mycelium and develops a cap and stalk, becoming a mature mushroom that releases spores.

Button, **Mature mushrooms**, **Spores**, **Mycelium**

Tiny basidia on the gills or tubes produce reproductive spores.

Gilled cap of the agraric group

Tubed cap of the boletes group

Cap (pileus), **Ring (annulus)**, **Stem (stock or stipe)**, **Volva**, **Mycelium**

The mycelium has threadlike filaments called hyphae that absorb water and nutrients. Some species have long strands called rhizomorphs that serve the same purpose.

Anatomy 101

A mushroom has two main parts the mycelium and the fruiting body. The mycelium can live for many years. It is usually found in soil or wood and is responsible for absorbing nutrients.

The fruiting body consists of the stalk and umbrella-shaped cap, it grows from the mycelium and generally lives up to several days.

What is in a name?

Mushrooms are part of the scientific group called basidiomycota. This group is divided into classes, orders and families of mushrooms and other fungi. A mycologist is a scientist who studies fungi. Some mushrooms are edible and some are poisonous. Poisonous mushrooms are sometimes called toadstools (a term that dates back to the 14th century). There are two main types of mushrooms, agarics and boletes. Agrarics have gills under their caps, boletes have tubes.

A historic favorite

In ancient Egypt mushrooms were food for the gods and could only be eaten by Pharaohs. The Greek physician Hippocrates (c.460 BC) recorded the use of mushrooms in medicinal potions. The ancient Romans seemed to have agreed with the Egyptians and referred to mushrooms as food of the gods.

Myths and madness

Mushrooms have been associated with frogs, fairies and little people for centuries. When mushrooms grow in a circle they are sometimes called fairy rings and folklore suggests that it is where fairies dance. In South Africa mushrooms are sometimes called duiwelskos (devils food). Many cultures, past and present, have used hallucinogenic mushrooms in mystical and spiritual rituals. When eaten, the toxins contained in these "magic" mushrooms can damage the body's nervous system and may result in serious illness.

Nutritional facts

The common white mushroom or table mushroom, has a mild flavor and is used in many dishes. Wild mushrooms, such as chanterelle, morel, shiitake, portobello and oyster, have a more intense flavor. Generally, mushrooms contain 90 percent water and have few calories. They are rich in protein and contain vitamins such as B, C and D. Cooking depletes some vitamins.

Nonpoisonous

There are more than 2,000 kinds of edible mushrooms. Most people are familiar with the table or button mushroom.

Poisonous

Poisonous mushrooms contain chemical toxins that (if eaten) may cause abdominal pain, vomiting, weakness, hallucinations or even death.

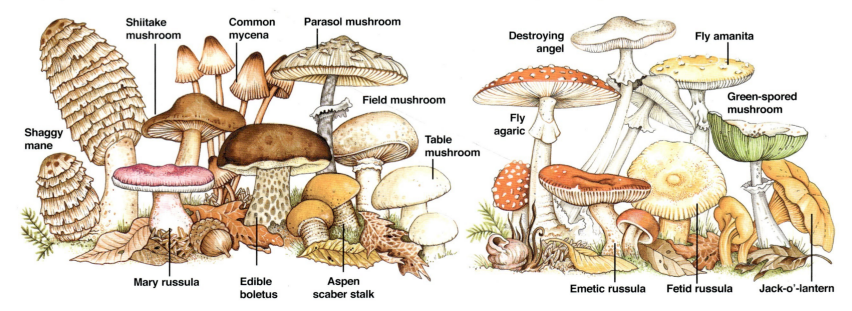

Nonpoisonous: **Shaggy mane**, **Shiitake mushroom**, **Common mycena**, **Parasol mushroom**, **Field mushroom**, **Table mushroom**, **Mary russula**, **Edible boletus**, **Aspen scaber stalk**

Poisonous: **Destroying angel**, **Fly amanita**, **Fly agaric**, **Green-spored mushroom**, **Emetic russula**, **Fetid russula**, **Jack-o'-lantern**

Mythical creatures

Man has used Mythology for centuries as a way to explain the mysteries and troubles of the world. Myths and legends from many lands and cultures have been used to address human concerns such as birth and death, love and hate, fortune or misfortune, creation and afterlife, magic power or forces of nature. These common themes, or **motifs**, are used to classify myths into groups by the mythologists who study them.

A motif common to all cultures is that of fantastic creatures with extraordinary powers. These creatures usually fall into two categories: those to be feared, and those that were accepted as a part of life. Some of the creatures were helpful, some mischievous. They may have existed once as real animals or people, but over time, and through the storyteller's art, enhancements made them fantastic and magical beasts. Often stories about them were used to entertain or even scare children into behaving. Every culture has an interesting collection of fantastic beasts in their mythology and describing them all would take many volumes.

Unicorn

Legends about the unicorn are common in Europe, Asia and parts of North Africa. In medieval Europe, it was believed that only a pure, unmarried **maiden** could tame a unicorn. The maiden would wait alone in a forest grove until the usually swift and wild animal would slowly approach her and lay his head in her lap. From that moment on, the unicorn would follow the maiden wherever she went.

According to legend, the unicorn's horn could cure any poison. If a river or pond were tainted, the unicorn could purify the water by dipping its horn. Sometimes, hunters would kill a tamed unicorn in order to possess the magical horn. Kings made goblets from the horn to guard against being poisoned.

Mermaid

Sailors often returned from seafaring with tales of beautiful women with tails like fish, who sang sweetly on rocks by the shore. Mermaids were considered dangerous, because they held power over the sea, and could bring storms, floods and giant waves that could sink ships.

It was thought that mermaids could entice men to live under the sea by showing them a magic mirror — as long as the man held the mirror and could see his reflection, he had the ability to breathe underwater.

A **sailor** could force a mermaid to live on land by finding and hiding an object belonging to a mermaid. Often, she would remain for many years. But if she ever came across her possession, the mermaid would return to the sea, forgetting the life she once had on land.

Griffon

Legends about the griffin are common to Europe and the Middle East. Griffons had the body and hind legs of a lion and the head, wings and claws of an eagle. Griffons were thought to be very wise with great **treasures** hoarded in their nests, which were built high up on craggy mountaintops. If a brave hero could take even tiny amount of a griffon's treasure, he would be rich for the rest of his life, but the risk of climbing high into the nest, and the attacks of the sharp-beaked beast, resulted in many men being killed.

Dragons

The dragon is common in the mythologies of Europe and Asia. In Europe, dragons were usually evil and ferocious, but in Asia, they were benevolent and wise.

In China, dragons are wingless and snakelike. A dragon dance celebrates the new year. Many dancers dress as one giant, writhing creature, moving in unison as various parts of the dragon. Dragons are believed to protect the new year from being spoiled by evil spirits, and the dancers travel from house to house through the town in order to scare those spirits away.

European dragons were large and fire-breathing. Tales told of treasure hoards in underground lairs attracted dragon-slaying heroes like **St. George**, the patron saint of England or the ancient Greek god **Apollo**, who fought with a dragon called **Python**.

But men didn't always win in fights with dragons. **Beowulf** was killed while fighting a dragon for its treasure. Perhaps the most famous dragon-slayer story is that of the **Siegfried**, who killed **Fafnir**. Fafnir guarded the treasure of the Nibelungenlied. When Fafnir's blood covered Siegfried during the fight, it gave him the power of protection. A famous opera by Richard Wagner, called **The Ring**, tells the story in detail.

Basilisk

Europeans in the Middle Ages feared a certain positioning of the stars and planets, because at that time, a **seven-year-old rooster** could lay an egg. When the rooster crowed at his achievement, a snake and toad would come to coil around the egg or sit upon it to help it hatch. When it did, a fearsome creature known as the basilisk — **part rooster, part snake, and part toad** — came out of the egg.

The basilisk was small, but so deadly that anything it breathed on would die. The only way it could be killed was to see its own reflection in a mirror.

Night creatures

When evening falls, a strange and different world awakens. It is full of night creatures, **nocturnal** animals that have adapted to living and hunting in the dark. You may discover that some of them live right in your own back yard.

Flying squirrel (Glaucomys)
These shy squirrels are mostly active at night. They don't really fly but use special skin flaps under their arms to help them **glide** from branch to branch.

Opossum (Didelphis virginiana)
This solitary, cat-sized **marsupial** lives in trees and carries her babies in a pouch. When cornered and frightened, she "plays possum" (dead) to fool her enemies.

Great horned owl (Bubo virginianus)
Cottontail rabbits are the favorite prey of this sharp-eyed hunter, but it also eats many other small animals. Its horns are really tufts of feathers.

Greater horseshoe bat (Rhinolophus ferrumequinum)
When hibernating and during the day, this parkland creature roosts upside down in shaded areas. At night he awakens to enjoy large insects as a mid-air snack and to devour bigger prey at his nighttime perch.

Cat (Felidae family)
Although not entirely nocturnal, a cat's eyes are well designed for nighttime hunting.

Raccoon (Procyonidae family)
One might think that these rascals spend all night getting into the garbage, but raccoons that live in forests eat fruit, frogs, crayfish and fish.

Mice (Murinae family)
Under the protection of darkness, many species of mice scurry about, collecting food. Some are caught by owls and cats and they become part of a food chain.

Spring peepers (Pseudacris crucifer)
During the night, male peeper frogs use inflatable air sacs beneath their chins to make loud breeding calls. Female peepers do not make sounds.

Night eyes
Animals with good night vision usually have a special layer of cells behind their retina called **tapetum**. These reflector cells mirror even small quantities of light and give eyes the appearance of glowing in the dark. This phenomenon is called **"eyeshine."**

The pupils of a cat's eyes close to tiny slits in bright sunlight and open wide in the dark. Human eyes also work this way, but not as much as cats'.

Bats

These are the only mammals that can truly fly. There are some bats that eat fruit and others that eat fish. And almost all of them like to eat flying insects. Bat eyes are small and not well developed, but they can see a little bit. Some bats use a kind of sonar, emitting high-frequency sounds that humans can't hear. The sounds bounce off objects and help the bats to navigate.

Sonic fishing
Echolocation

A fisher bat dives toward the water, emitting high-pitched sounds.

When a fish breaks the surface, it reflects back the bat sound, creating an **echo**.

Beeping again, the bat uses its curved talons to hook the fish.

While biting into the fish the bat remains silent.

Insects

Although bugs are sometimes thought to be pests, they are really an essential part of nature.

Crickets
Beginning at sunset, male crickets sing all night long as a way of marking out their territories.

Mosquitoes
Only the female of the species drinks blood. Mosquitoes use light, heat and scent to seek out their victims and can locate a lighted building from a great distance.

Moths
Moths use moonlight to navigate. They become confused by bright light and this is why they often circle around street lamps. To assist them in avoiding attack by predators such as bats, moths are equipped with an ultrasonic hearing system.

Cecropia moth (Hyalophora cecropia)

Fireflies
Fireflies are sometimes called lightning bugs, but they are really **beetles** and not bugs or flies at all. Every firefly species has its own unique flashing pattern. This has helped scientists to identify more than 130 different types of fireflies.

Eyes
Feelers

Slugs and snails
Slugs and snails are closely related and there are more than 1,200 kinds in North America. Both have two sets of tentacles. The long tentacles are tipped with eyes, and the short pair are used as feelers.

Color blind
Human eyes contain two kinds of cells – **rod cells** and **cone cells**. Cone cells help us tell one color from another and require lots of light to do this. Rod cells make it possible to see in poor light conditions, but they can't distinguish between colors. Night creatures have mostly rod cells and for this reason most of them are colorblind.

OCEANS

Scientists believe that life began in this wet, salty world. The largest animals on Earth (whales) and the smallest (bacteria and viruses) live in our oceans. Oceans play a vital role in global weather by regulating air temperature and supplying moisture for rainfall. Oceans provide us with food, minerals and energy. We also use oceans as water transportation and for recreation.

The sunlit zone

Most of the animals that live in the sunlit or **epipelagic zone** are strong swimmers. They have to be in order to cope with strong surface currents. This zone extends from the surface to 656 ft. (200m).

Always on the move

The global ocean is in constant motion. Gravity pulls at the water, creating the rise and fall of **tides**. Wind and earthquakes result in **waves** and whitecaps breaking on the surface. And **currents** move like underwater highways.

Making waves

Most waves are the result of wind moving over water. The size of a wave depends on wind speed, and how long and far the wind blows. Some waves are caused by the movement of tectonic plates below the sea floor. Called **tsunamis**, these waves can move across an entire ocean, reaching speeds of up to 600 miles an hour.

Ocean waves move up and down, not forward.

The **trough** of a wave.
The **crest** of a wave.
Breaking crest on the shore.

Tides

Tides are the rise and fall of the **oceans** caused by the **gravitational** pull of the moon and the sun. Because the moon is closer, its pull has more influence on tides than the sun. Generally, there are **two** high and two low tides every day (lasting for about 6 hours each). **Spring tides** happen when the sun, moon and Earth are in a straight line, causing the tides to rise and fall more than usual.

Where in the world

Oceans (also called seas) cover almost three-quarters of the Earth and contain 97 percent of the world's water. **The Pacific Ocean** is the largest and deepest ocean. It covers about 70 million square miles and contains about half of all the world's ocean water. **The Atlantic Ocean** has an area of about 36 million square miles. **The Indian Ocean** covers about 29 million square miles. The world ocean has an average depth of about 12,200 feet, but is much deeper in spots.

- ☐ 0 to 656 ft.
- ☐ 656 to 19,700 ft.
- ☐ Deeper than 19,700 ft.

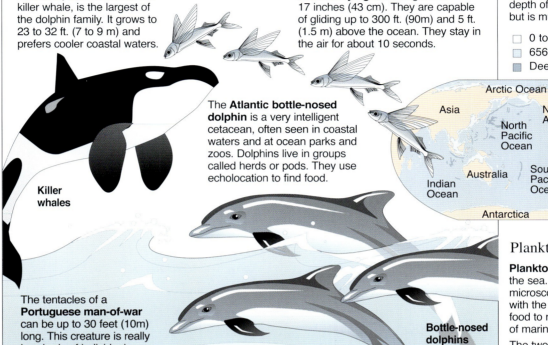

The **orca**, also known as the killer whale, is the largest of the dolphin family. It grows to 23 to 32 ft. (7 to 9 m) and prefers cooler coastal waters.

Atlantic flyingfish can grow to 17 inches (43 cm). They are capable of gliding up to 300 ft. (90m) and 5 ft. (1.5 m) above the ocean. They stay in the air for about 10 seconds.

The **Atlantic bottle-nosed dolphin** is a very intelligent cetacean, often seen in coastal waters and at ocean parks and zoos. Dolphins live in groups called herds or pods. They use echolocation to find food.

The tentacles of a **Portuguese man-of-war** can be up to 30 feet (10m) long. This creature is really hundreds of individual animals living jointly.

Skipjack tuna swim in large schools of up to 50,000 fishes. They are an important commercial fish.

Dolphinfish travel in small schools. A popular game fish, they should not be confused with mammalian dolphins.

The **Garfish** is usually found in surface waters along the coast. It grows to about 37 inches (94 cm).

The **moray eel** is found near rocky shores. Known to be an aggressive predator it will bite if disturbed.

Lionfish (15 inches, 38 cm) are found in the shallow waters of the Indian and Pacific oceans. They are extremely poisonous.

Herrings are a major food source for fish and people. There are more than 290 species belonging to the herring family. They vary in size and eat mostly plankton.

Weedy seadragons are considerably larger than their cousin, the dwarf seahorse, growing up to 18 inches long.

Dwarf seahorses and **weedy seadragons** are spiny creatures that resemble tiny horses or dragons and swim standing up. They live in all the oceans of the world and are related to sea urchins and sand dollars.

Dwarf seahorses are found in shallow waters and grow to about 1½ inches (4 cm).

The **hawksbill** is a small to medium-sized sea turtle, (30 to 36 inches, 76-91 cm). Listed as an endangered species since 1970, this turtle has been hunted for its beautiful carapace (shell).

Plankton

Plankton is the basic food of the sea. These tiny, often microscopic, organisms travel with the currents and provide food to more than 90 percent of marine life.

The two main types of plankton are tiny plants called **phytoplankton** that travel on ocean currents and swimming animals, such as water fleas and jellyfish, called **zooplankton**.

Phytoplankton use the sun's energy to make food out of sunlight and minerals in a process called **photosynthesis.** It is estimated that phytoplankton make more than 60 percent of the Earth's oxygen.

Zooplankton feed on phytoplankton. Then larger zooplankton eat the small zooplankton and these in turn provide food for larger creatures.

Phytoplankton

Zooplankton

You can catch plankton by submerging a bucket in the sea and dragging it. Pull it up and put the contents in a glass. Use a magnifying glass or a microscope to see it even better.

The twilight zone

The **mesopelagic zone** is also called the twilight or midwater zone. It extends from 656 ft. to 3,281 ft. (220m to 1000m). Here the light becomes fainter and the water gets colder.

Water temperature

The temperature of the ocean varies depending on currents and water depth. Warm surface water generally reaches depths of about 500 ft., double that in some tropical waters. As we move into deeper water, the temperature drops quickly. Below the warmer surface waters is a band of colder water called the **thermocline**. Below the thermocline layer the water cools more slowly.

Currents

Currents are the result of two main forces: surface wind and the difference in temperature and salt content of the water.
Wind circulation produces the major ocean currents or great streams that travel in general circular patterns. **Thermohaline circulation** happens when colder, saltier water sinks, resulting in vertical currents that flow from the surface to the bottom and eventually to the surface in a never-ending cycle.

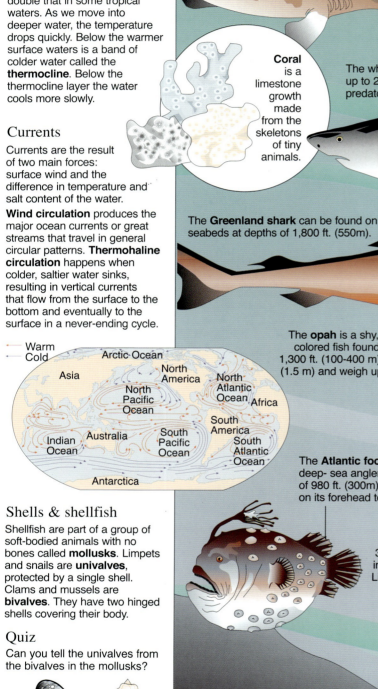

Shells & shellfish

Shellfish are part of a group of soft-bodied animals with no bones called **mollusks**. Limpets and snails are **univalves**, protected by a single shell. Clams and mussels are **bivalves**. They have two hinged shells covering their body.

Quiz

Can you tell the univalves from the bivalves in the mollusks?

Mussel **Moon**
Limpet **Oyster**
Clam **Scallop**
Conch **Top**

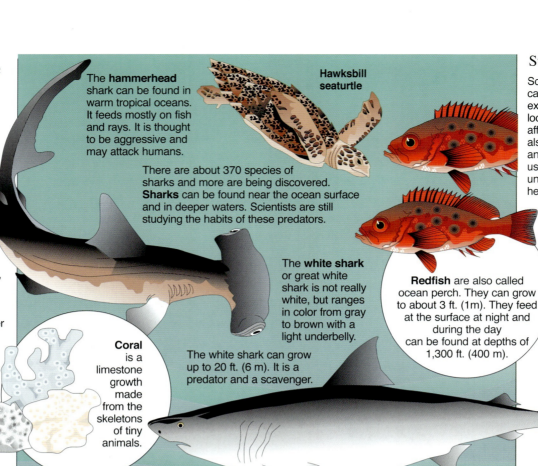

The **hammerhead** shark can be found in warm tropical oceans. It feeds mostly on fish and rays. It is thought to be aggressive and may attack humans.

Hawksbill seaturtle

There are about 370 species of sharks and more are being discovered. **Sharks** can be found near the ocean surface and in deeper waters. Scientists are still studying the habits of these predators.

The **white shark** or great white shark is not really white, but ranges in color from gray to brown with a light underbelly.

Coral is a limestone growth made from the skeletons of tiny animals.

The white shark can grow up to 20 ft. (6 m). It is a predator and a scavenger.

Redfish are also called ocean perch. They can grow to about 3 ft. (1m). They feed at the surface at night and during the day can be found at depths of 1,300 ft. (400 m).

The **Greenland shark** can be found on seabeds at depths of 1,800 ft. (550m).

Sharks are related to chimaeras (ratfish) and rays. These fish have a skeleton of cartilage instead of bone.

The **opah** is a shy, rarely seen brightly colored fish found at depths of 330 to 1,300 ft. (100-400 m). It can grow to 5 ft. (1.5 m) and weigh up to 161 lbs. (73kg).

The **Atlantic football fish** is a deep-sea angler found at depths of 980 ft. (300m). It uses the lure on its forehead to attract prey.

Roughie can be found at depths of 3,300 feet (1,000m) in the North Atlantic. Little is known about their habits. They grow to about 11 inches (30cm).

Sperm whales are the largest of the toothed whales and grow between 36 and 66 ft. (11-20 m). Their bulging skulls protect an organ made up of weblike pipes containing waxy yellow oil called **spermaceti**. Scientists think this organ helps with echolocation and controlling buoyancy.

Sperm whale

Eagle ray

Studying the deep

Scientists who study oceans are called **oceanographers**. They examine the secrets of the seas, looking at how oceans move and affect climate. Oceanographers also examine life in the oceans and study the sea floor. They use computers, satellites and underwater submersibles to help collect information.

People who study fish are called **ichthyologists** (pronounced IHK thee AHL uh jihsts). Ichthyologists divide fish into two main groups; jawed and jawless. Most fish have jaws; only lampreys and hagfish do not.

Marine algae

Large **marine algae** are also called **seaweed** and help purify the air and water through photosynthesis. Here are some algae that can be found on wharves and rocky beaches:

Mermaid's hair   **Codium**

Sea lettuce   **Sargassum**

Agarum   **Alaria**

Press and dry seaweed

You can dry seaweed and kelp by hanging them over railings or on laundry lines. Later you can place the dried seaweed in saltwater and take a closer look at how it is made. Here's what to do:

1. Float specimen in a pan of seawater.

2. Slide heavy paper underneath the seaweed and use the paper to slowly lift the weed.

3. Place cheesecloth over the seaweed to dry it. Once dry, mount the specimen on another piece of paper and label it.

The dark zone

The **bathypelagic** or dark zone extends from 3,281 ft. to 13,124 ft. (1,000m to 4,000m). Despite the lack of light and the immense water pressure, many creatures can be found here. Sperm whales dive to this level in search of food and bioluminous creatures begin to appear.

Bioluminescence

Many ocean creatures use **bioluminescence** (pronounced BY oh LOO muh NEHS uhns) to attract prey and to warn predators away. These fish have a special **enzyme** that changes stored energy into light. This light does not give off any significant amount of heat. Sailors often see bright lights flickering in the waves at night. This is usually caused by algae that light up when movement is sensed.

The **Alvin** was designed for deep-sea research. In 1977, the Alvin team of scientists discovered deep-sea vents and previously unknown species.

Octopuses belong to the **mollusk** family, which includes clams, oysters and snails. There are about 100 species. They have soft, round bodies with eight legs. Some live in shallow water, others live in the deep. As a means of defense, the octopus can discharge an inky fluid; it can also change color to match its surroundings or to scare a predator.

The **skate** is a valuable commercial species, caught for food. They feed on fish, crabs, lobster and octopus. Skates live in depths from 98 to 2,000 ft. (30-600 m) and grow to about 8 ft. (2.4 m) wide.

Most **squid** have light-producing organs called **photopores** and some can eject a glowing cloud of **ink**.

Lanternfish are named for their ability to make light. During the day, they stay in the deep ocean, but at night they swim to the surface to feed on plankton. Lanternfish can be found at depths of 3,000 ft. (914.4 m)

The **Greenland halibut** can grow to up to 4 feet (1.2 m) long. This fish has strong, fanglike teeth. It feeds on fish, crustaceans and squid. Both of its eyes are on the right. Greenland halibuts can be found at depths of 6,600 feet (2,000 m).

Whale diving depths

Diving depths and underwater times for various whales:

Whale	Depth	Minutes
Porpoise	984 ft.	6
Finback	1,148 ft.	20
Bottlenose	3,000 ft.*	120
Sperm	9,000 ft.*	75-90

* possibly deeper

Larger shrimp or **prawns** are an important food for many fish and a valuable commercial catch. Related to crabs and lobsters, these **crustaceans** come in a variety of colors and sizes.

There are 10 species of **swordfish** ranging in size from 6 to 16 ft. (2 to 4.9 m). They are found in deep waters, but also at the surface. Generally solitary predators, they feed on fish and squid.

Roughhead grenadier can be found at depths of 650 to 3,300 ft. (200 to 1000 m). They are members of the cod family and grow up to 3¼ ft. (1 m).

The oarfish is the longest bony fish in the sea. It can grow more than 50 ft. and weigh as much as 100 lbs. Ancient stories about sea serpents were probably based on sightings of these strange animals.

How fish swim

Most fish swim by moving their tail from one side to the other, while their body moves in the opposite direction. Fins are used to make turns and other maneuvers. Fast swimmers often have deeply grooved, crescent shaped tails and large, pointed pectoral fins. Slow swimmers tend to have round or squarish shaped tails and fins.

Dogfish	Tuna	Eel

Ratfish are also known as chimaeras. They live in deep waters, feeding on starfish, mollusks and crustaceans. Ratfish can grow to about 5 ft. (1.5 m).

The **snipe eel** is a deep-sea fish found at depths of 3,300 ft. (1,000 m) or more. They can grow to about 4 ft. (1.2 m) long. Although they are fairly common, little is known about their habits.

The abyss

The **abyssopelagic zone** extends from 13,124 ft to 19,686 ft. (4,000 m to 6,000 m). The word abyss is from the Greek and means "no bottom." Except for bioluminous flickers and super hot spews from deep-sea vents, the deepest parts of the ocean are incredibly dark and cold.

The **Triest I** submersible was conceived and built by Auguste Piccard. It is famous for its 1960 dive to 35,800 feet at the bottom of the Mariana Trench in the Pacific Ocean.

Lanternfish are one of the most populous and widely distributed deep sea fish. Named for their bright bioluminescense these creatures play a vital role in their ecosystems, being dinner for many larger fish.

A deep-sea chimney spouts magma-heated seawater into the cold ocean.

The chemical reaction caused by the temperature difference gives a "black smoker" its color.

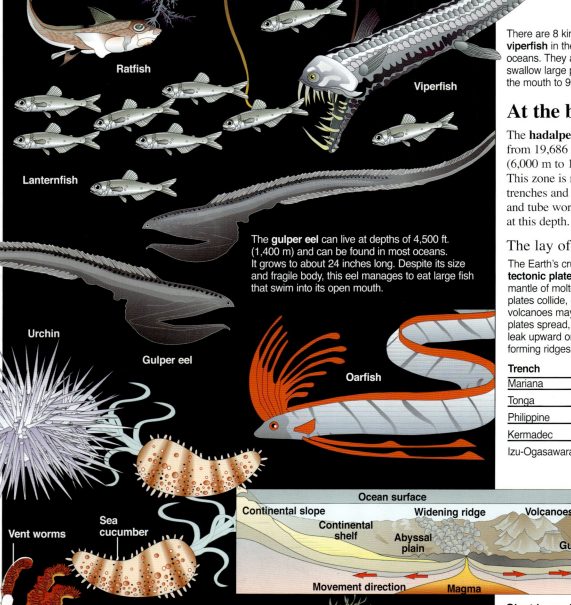

Silver hatchetfish grow up to 4 inches in length and have flattened, scaleless bodies and upward-facing eyes.

Linophryne A tiny deep sea angler

Anglerfish There are many types of deep-sea **anglerfish**. Most are black and have "lures" called illicium growing from their heads. Some are light-producing.

Black swallowers can consume animals twice their size.

The **gulper eel** can live at depths of 4,500 ft. (1,400 m) and can be found in most oceans. It grows to about 24 inches long. Despite its size and fragile body, this eel manages to eat large fish that swim into its open mouth.

Weird and wild

The creatures that live at the bottom of the sea could almost be called monsters, they are so strange and scary looking. Many use bioluminescent light to attract prey or ward off predators. Others have evolved in such a way as to get all of their nutrients from chemicals in the ocean in a process called **chemosynthesis**. Many deep-sea creatures are enormous. This is where the sperm whale comes to feed on squid.

Tripod fish balance on projections from their fins waiting on the bottom for falling food.

There are 8 kinds of **viperfish** in the world's oceans. They are able to swallow large prey by opening the mouth to 90 degrees.

At the bottom

The **hadalpelagic zone** extends from 19,686 ft. to 32,810 ft. (6,000 m to 10,000 m). This zone is mostly found in trenches and canyons. Starfish and tube worms can be found at this depth.

The lay of the land

The Earth's crust is covered with **tectonic plates** that float on a liquid mantle of molten rock. When the plates collide, earthquakes and volcanoes may result. When the plates spread, rifts allow **magma** to leak upward on to the crust, forming ridges.

Trench	Ocean	Depth
Mariana	W. Pacific	36,198
Tonga	S. Pacific	35,433
Philippine	W. Pacific	32,995
Kermadec	S. Pacific	32,963
Izu-Ogasawara	W. Pacific	32,087

Giant isopods are carnivorous crustaceans that feed on anything they can find on the deep ocean floor.

Sea urchins are related to starfish and found in seas around the world. These small creatures have a shell called a test which is covered in spikes.

Night hunters

A closer look at owls

What are owls?

Owls are mysterious, mostly nocturnal birds that have been worshiped by primitive peoples, associated with magic, superstition and sorcery and made companions or advisors to gods and goddesses. The owl has figured prominently in the folklore and legends of people around the world. The owl is often portrayed as wise, or as a sign of things to come.

Because owls are seldom observed by the average person, many of their traits or habits are not so obvious. Owls are extraordinary and unique birds.

Efficient hunters

Owls are **raptors**, like hawks, eagles and falcons. They capture living prey using specialized **talons** on their feet. The beak is razor sharp, but unlike other raptors, the owl swallows its prey whole, or in rough, torn chunks.

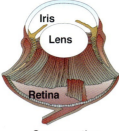

Cross-section of an owl eye

270 degrees

Super vision

The owl has the most versatile eyesight of any bird. It has what scientists call a **tubular eye**. It differs from other animal's eyes in that it allows more light to be gathered and concentrated on the back of the eyeball. This is why an owl can capture small prey like mice or voles in a dense wood in complete darkness. But the trade-off for such a large eye is that the owl cannot swivel its eyes in their sockets like other animals can. Instead, it must turn its neck, but has an amazing range of motion and can rotate its head a full 270 degrees.

Primary wing feather

On the flight deck

The owl's nocturnal lifestyle has led to some effective adaptations in its feathers. The plumage of an owl is fluffy, and the leading edge of the primary wing feather is finely toothed to absorb any sound made by air rushing over the wing.

Eating too much junk food . . .

Owls eat a huge amount of food. They can consume the equivalent of their own body weight each night. But because they don't chew the food they eat, owls end up with lots of fur, feathers, bones, beaks and nails in their **gizzard**. As with other predatory birds, the owl has evolved the ability to regurgitate the animal parts it can't digest as neat little **pellets**, which can be found under nests and around feeding areas.

Owls and humans

Owls have had a long relationship with the folklore and myths of humans. The earliest known drawing of a bird was of snowy owls in the cave of Les Trois Freres in Southern France.

One of the oldest coins made depicts a saw-whet owl, a symbol of Athena, the goddess of wisdom, from ancient Greece. It is dated from about 500 B.C.

The owl was associated with death by the Aztecs. Above is a wooden drum called a teponaztli. It is carved with the image of an owl's face.

The **great horned owl** is the largest eared owl in North America. It can grow to 22 inches in length and has the power to take skunks and Canada geese as prey.

Snowy owls live in far North America. They inhabit the frozen tundra and feed mostly on lemmings and hares. During the Arctic summer, they hunt in the daytime. This large owl grows to about 23 inches long, and the female's plumes are more heavily barred, or speckled, than the male's.

Saw-whet owl

The short-eared owl grows to be about 15 inches long. It lives in all of North America but is becoming endangered due to habitat loss. It lives in open country, tundra, marshes and weedy fields. The bird nests on open ground.

Owl anatomy

The owl has many features common to all birds, as well as some specialized features. Here are a typical owl's parts:

- Greater wing coverts
- Alula
- Median wing coverts
- Lesser wing coverts
- Mantle
- Primary wing feathers (10)
- Secondary wing feathers (11-19)
- Upper tail coverts
- Tail feathers (12)
- Undertail coverts
- Flank
- Vent
- Breast
- Belly
- Tibia
- Tarsus
- Toe
- Talon
- Forehead
- Nape
- Crown
- Cere
- Bill
- Facial disc

Barn owls grow to be about 16 inches long. They like to roost in old buildings, eaves and farm buildings. They have smaller eyes than most owls and a clearly defined heart-shaped facial disc. Females are paler in color than males.

Barn owl egg

Owls' eggs

All owls lay pure white, round eggs. They do not build nests, but often use ready-made sites like abandoned nests of other birds, the holes in trees made by woodpeckers, or the aerie of a raptor. Owlets leave the nest before that can fly. They keep in touch with their parents by directional sounds and begging calls.

The **elf owl** is North America's smallest owl. It lives in the Southwestern desert, where it usually hollows out a nesting cavity in the tall saguaro cactus. It is strictly nocturnal, and only grows to be about 5 inches long.

PANDAS

Despite efforts to protect it, the giant panda is still in danger of extinction. Habitat destruction and hunting have taken a toll on populations. Only about 1,600 of these black-and-white bears remain in the wild.

The giant panda can grow 5 to 6 feet (1.5 to 1.8 m) long. An adult weighs 150 to 275 pounds (68 to 125 kg).

For many years scientists debated whether pandas are bears, **raccoons** or in a special group of their own. DNA tests have indicated that the giant panda is related to bears.

Location, location

Wild pandas can only be found in **China**. They prefer the wet mountains of the southwest and live at altitudes between 3,000 and 10,000 feet.

In addition to poaching and a low birth rate, one of the main threats to the giant panda is habitat destruction and fragmentation. To address habitat loss, the Chinese government has created 12 nature preserves where **bamboo** is plentiful and giant pandas are known to roam. Strips of land, called "bamboo corridors," are being planted to help the pandas migrate when they need to.

Range of the giant panda

What's in a name?

In China, the giant panda is a symbol of **peace** and is called "da xiong mao," which means "giant bear cat."

The scientific or Latin name for the giant panda is Ailuropoda melanoleuca.

Female pandas are called sows, males are called boars, and the young are called cubs.

Close relatives

The red panda (also known as the **lesser** panda) is a close relative of the giant panda. Scientists once thought the red panda was related to the raccoon (which it resembles), but DNA tests have shown that it is genetically similar to the giant panda.

This shy and solitary creature can be found in southern Asia. Red pandas are listed as endangered.

Red Panda
Ailurus fulgens

The red panda is about the size of a cat. It is primarily nocturnal, and feeds on bamboo and fruit.

A taste for bamboo

Pandas are picky eaters and live almost exclusively on bamboo. If the bamboo forests disappear the panda would die of starvation. And this bear eats a lot! At least 12 hours of every day are spent eating. The giant panda consumes up to 40 percent of its weight (up to 85 pounds, or 38.5 kg) every day.

In the forests of China there are many kinds of bamboo, but only a few species grow in the mountains where pandas live. Every 10 or 12 years, bamboo plants flower and die off. This forces the pandas to migrate to a new area. It is becoming more and more difficult for the panda to find suitable bamboo forests.

Because bamboo is not highly nutritious and pandas do not have very efficient digestive systems, they need to eat large amounts in order to stay healthy.

Besides being adorable, the giant panda has many interesting and unique characteristics.

Bamboo is a very sinewy and tough plant, and strong jaws are needed to chew it. The panda has large teeth and well-developed muscles to make eating easier.

Pandas tend to eat in a seated position. Their front paws have adapted to help them hold bamboo. Their paws have five clawed fingers, plus a bone on each palm that looks and acts much like a thumb. Unlike other bears, pandas do not walk on their hind legs.

Panda molars

Human molars

Molars are teeth used for grinding food.

Giant panda

Other bears

The giant panda has excellent eyesight, but it has unusual eyes for a bear. Most bears have round pupils, but the panda has vertical slits, like a cat's pupil.

Shy and solitary

Giant pandas are not social creatures and prefer to live alone. Small groups may share a feeding range, but they only get together to breed.

Because this animal is very shy, scientists know very little about its habits in the wild. Giant pandas do not live in a permanent den, but take shelter wherever it is convenient. In winter, they do not hibernate, but move to lower altitudes where it is warmer and food is more plentiful.

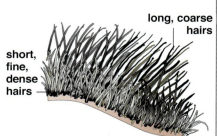

long, coarse hairs

short, fine, dense hairs

Pandas have oily, waterproof fur (similar to seal fur) with a dense undercoat that protects them from the wet and cold.

Having babies

The giant panda breeds from March to May and gives birth in August or September.

The female can give birth to one, two or three cubs, but usually only one cub will survive. At birth, the cubs are white, furless and blind. They are exceptionally tiny, weighing about 3 to 5 ounces (85 to 141 g). Cubs develop their black and white coloring at about 4 weeks old. They open their eyes at 6 to 7 weeks and become mobile at 3 to 4 months. They begin to eat bamboo at around 6 months. Cubs nurse for about nine months and often remain with the mother for one or two years. They are not considered fully grown until they are 4 to 6 years old.

In captivity, giant pandas have been known to live for more than 30 years.

Captive breeding

In 1955, China began attempts to breed the giant panda in captivity. But it was eight years before they succeeded. On Sept. 9, 1963, a giant panda named Li Li gave birth to Ming Ming at the Beijing Zoo.

There are about 110 to 120 giant pandas in captivity. Most of these are in China.

Did you know?

Giant pandas are technically carnivores (meat eaters). Despite the fact that they live almost exclusively on bamboo, they will eat small mammals if they can catch them.

Giant pandas have unusually thick and heavy bones for their size. They are also very flexible.

About birds

Living birds include more than 9,000 recognized species and inhabit every biome of the world. Whether modern birds are most closely related to dinosaurs and other reptilian ancestors is currently under scientific debate. Orders of living birds appear to have evolved closely, but the age of birds is uncertain. Estimates place the earliest birds between 60 to over 90 million years old based on morphology, fossils and molecular data.

Bird characteristics

Birds are warm-blooded, produce external eggs, and engage in complex parental and reproductive behaviors. They have highly developed color vision, use vocalization and social interactions.

Birds have feathers, enabling flight. Feathers insulate, camouflage, and are used by birds to communicate via sound and sight. In waterfowl, feathers aid in swimming, water repellence and support of the body.

Features shared with reptiles

Unlike mammals, birds have nucleated red blood cells, one middle ear bone, and a single occipital condyle (a knob at the back of the brain case, which joins the skull to the spine).

Adaptations for flight

Lightweight bones in birds are fused or reinforced. A keeled sternum supports the flight muscles in the breast. Birds are able to detect and react to magnetism.

Birds have distinctive bills, with many variations in shape, size and color based on diet and habitat, and for sexual display and identification.

Characteristics

All three families of parrots share a distinctive feature: they have crooked bills. It is commonly thought they are all brightly colored, but this is not the case. Many canopy-living species have green plumage in order to camouflage themselves. Some parrots have grey or black feathers.

Parrot classification

Kingdom	Animalia
Phylum	Chordata
Subphylum	Vertebrata
Class	Aves
Subclass	Neornithes
Order	Psittaciformes
Family	Psittacidae
Family	Cacatuidae
Family	Loriidae

Feet
Parrots are zygodactyls — two toes face forward and two back. This is common in arboreal (tree-dwelling) birds.

Beak
Parrots have a hooked beak. The hinged upper jaw is more mobile and developed than the lower.

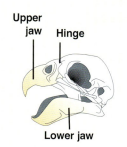

Upper jaw · Hinge · Lower jaw

Habitat
Parrots live in tropical and subtropical regions.

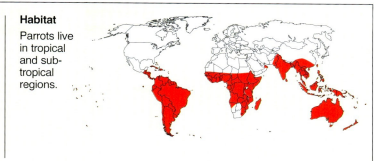

Parrots

Cockatoos — Family cacatuidae

- **Cockatiel** — *Nymphicus hollandicus*
- **Palm cockatoo** — *Probosciger aterrimus*
- **Sulphur-crested cockatoo** — *Cacatua galerita*

Parrots and Macaws — Family psittacidae

- **Rosy-faced lovebird** — *Agapornis roseicollis*
- **Budgerigar** — *Melopsittacus undulatus*
- **Mustached parakeet** — *Psittacula alexandri*
- **Hyacinth macaw** — *Anodorhynchus hyacinthinus*
- **Brown-throated parakeet** — *Aratinga pertinax*
- **African gray parrot** — *Psittacus erithacus*

Lories and Lorikeets — Family loriidae

- **Red Lory** — *Eos bornea*
- **Rainbow lorikeet** — *Trichoglossus haematodus*
- **Purple-crowned lorikeet** — *Glossopsitta porphyrocephala*
- **Scaly-breasted lorikeet** — *Trichoglossus chlorolepidotus*

Penguins

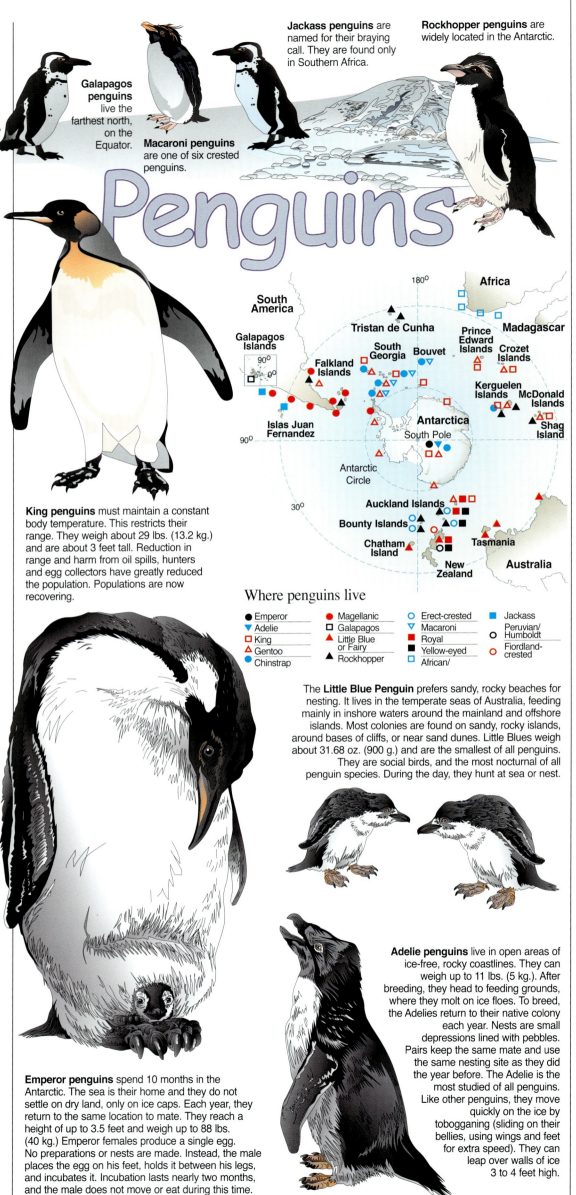

What is a penguin?

Penguins lay eggs, have compact, hard feathers, breathe air, have clawed feet and horny beaks. They are short-legged, flightless birds that live in cold regions in the Southern Hemisphere, such as Antarctica. Penguins have webbed feet and wings that work like flippers.

The first animal called a penguin was a flightless bird of the Arctic Ocean, known as a Great Auk. Despite a similar anatomy to today's penguins, it was from a different order of birds. The Great Auk, hunted to extinction, was last seen in 1844.

When similar animals were found in the southern seas, they were called penguins. The word originally was thought to mean "fat one" in Spanish/Portuguese, but may have originated from the Welsh pen gwyn (white head), or from the Latin pinguis (fat).

Classification

Kingdom
Animalia
They have spinal cords.

Phylum
Chordata
Have strong skeletons.

Subphylum
Vertebrata
Their horny beaks, lack of teeth, large muscular stomachs and feathers make them birds. Another trait of birds is that they lay large-yolked, hard-shelled eggs. Parent birds usually care for the young until grown.

Class
Aves

Order
Sphenisciformes

Variety

Today there are 17 species of penguins. Fossil records show that there were more species in the past. The living penguin species are: Adelie, African (Jackass), Chinstrap, Emperor, Erect-crested, Little Blue, Fiordland, Galapagos, Gentoo, Peruvian (Humboldt), King, Macaroni, Magellanic, Rockhopper, Royal, Snares Island and Yellow-eyed.

Two species, Adelie and Emperor, are often studied because they live on Antarctica year-round. Permanent research stations make it easier for scientists to study and monitor the population. Scientists estimate that 2,300,000 mated pairs of Adelie penguins and 220,000 mated pairs of Emperor penguins live on Antarctica. The exact population is unknown, but it is estimated that 175 million live near Antarctica.

Galapagos penguins live the farthest north, on the Equator.

Macaroni penguins are one of six crested penguins.

Jackass penguins are named for their braying call. They are found only in Southern Africa.

Rockhopper penguins are widely located in the Antarctic.

King penguins must maintain a constant body temperature. This restricts their range. They weigh about 29 lbs. (13.2 kg.) and are about 3 feet tall. Reduction in range and harm from oil spills, hunters and egg collectors have greatly reduced the population. Populations are now recovering.

Where penguins live

- ● Emperor
- ▼ Adelie
- ▢ King
- △ Gentoo
- ● Chinstrap
- ● Magellanic
- ▢ Galapagos
- ▲ Little Blue or Fairy
- ▲ Rockhopper
- ○ Erect-crested
- ▽ Macaroni
- ■ Royal
- ■ Yellow-eyed
- ▢ African/
- ■ Jackass
- ○ Peruvian/ Humboldt
- ○ Fiordland-crested

The **Little Blue Penguin** prefers sandy, rocky beaches for nesting. It lives in the temperate seas of Australia, feeding mainly in inshore waters around the mainland and offshore islands. Most colonies are found on sandy, rocky islands, around bases of cliffs, or near sand dunes. Little Blues weigh about 31.68 oz. (900 g.) and are the smallest of all penguins. They are social birds, and the most nocturnal of all penguin species. During the day, they hunt at sea or nest.

Emperor penguins spend 10 months in the Antarctic. The sea is their home and they do not settle on dry land, only on ice caps. Each year, they return to the same location to mate. They reach a height of up to 3.5 feet and weigh up to 88 lbs. (40 kg.) Emperor females produce a single egg. No preparations or nests are made. Instead, the male places the egg on his feet, holds it between his legs, and incubates it. Incubation lasts nearly two months, and the male does not move or eat during this time. Chicks hatch in early September.

Adelie penguins live in open areas of ice-free, rocky coastlines. They can weigh up to 11 lbs. (5 kg.). After breeding, they head to feeding grounds, where they molt on ice floes. To breed, the Adelies return to their native colony each year. Nests are small depressions lined with pebbles. Pairs keep the same mate and use the same nesting site as they did the year before. The Adelie is the most studied of all penguins. Like other penguins, they move quickly on the ice by tobogganing (sliding on their bellies, using wings and feet for extra speed). They can leap over walls of ice 3 to 4 feet high.

Arctic penguins?

There are no penguins in the Arctic (North Pole). The Great Auk lived there at one time, but it was hunted to extinction in the 1800s. Predators such as bears, wolves, foxes and rats live in the north and may prevent penguins from establishing colonies because nesting chicks are virtually defenseless on land. Antarctica and the other southern islands where Penguins nest are free from predators.

Unique adaptations

Hearing
Penguins do not have external, visible ears, but have a protected ear canal under the feathers. This allows them to hear sound in the air and underwater. They can recognize each other and their young by sound.

Staying warm
Penguins don't get cold because of their fat. Fat has two main purposes in the body; It is a good insulator against cold and is an energy reserve. Usually, the colder the habitat, the larger the penguin. Penguins can overheat on warm summer days. When temperatures are high they erect their feathers to increase airflow near the body. They also separate from each other, or lie on ice, panting to release excess body heat.

Emperor penguins are very social, which helps them survive the hardships of winter. During cold and windy nights, they cluster into groups called turtles. When the birds in the center become warm, they exchange positions with colder outsiders.

Feathers
The structure of penguin feathers gives them increased protection against cold. An outer layer of long, hard and smooth feathers aids fast swimming by streamlining the body and protects them from wind.

A layer of fluffy down feathers underneath provides insulation by trapping warm air close to the body for warmth.

Protective coloration
Penguins have white bellies and dark backs. These colors help the penguins appear less visible in water. When seen from above the black blends into the darkness of the sea; when seen from below the light belly hides blends into the shimmering surface.

Krill

Finding food
Penguins swim fast and can dive 1,640 ft. (500 m.) and stay submerged for five minutes. They feed on krill, small fish, octopus and other sea creatures found in the cold waters of the Antarctic Ocean.

The age of mammals

Dinosaurs and many forms of plant life died out in global mass extinctions 65 million years ago. Their demise left room for new animals to dominate the Earth's ecosystems. Over time, tiny primitive mammals grew larger and larger, and became more specialized, filling **niches** in the food chain by adapting in their quest for food and habitat.

In the Miocene epoch, mammals had reached their largest ever **diversity.** Ancestors of all of today's 26 orders of mammals spread over every continent, and many were huge in size compared with their modern relatives.

How did they evolve?

Four main groups evolved from a common ancestor called a **therapsid** about 190 million years ago. The Therapsids were more advanced reptiles who had special jaw and skull development and unique teeth. These features allowed them a greater diet range, leading to their evolutionary success.

Two of the main mammal groups died out: **eotheria** (dawn mammals) were tiny, shrew-like animals that lived with the dinosaurs, and **allotheria** were primitive rodents who had special cheek teeth for chewing plants. They became extinct 50 million years ago.

The two remaining mammal groups are the **prototheria** (egg-laying, or monotreme, mammals) and **theria,** which includes **marsupials** (pouched mammals) and **placentals** (babies develop in the mother and are nourished by a special organ called a placenta.) All modern mammals are descendants of these groups.

Key mammal features

Specific physical features distinguished mammals from the reptiles they evolved from. Most modern mammals share these **traits:**

- Hinged jaw with one large bone on each side of the lower jaw
- Teeth on the rim of the jaw; teeth in the cheek more complex and with more than one root
- Three bones in the ear
- One bony nasal opening
- An enlarged brain case
- Warm-blooded
- A diaphragm muscle to work the lungs
- Body hair
- A four-chambered heart
- Give birth to undeveloped young (monotremes lay eggs)
- Mothers produce milk to feed young. Marsupials from a vent or in a pouch. Placentals from specialized mammary glands.

The rise of Mammals

Land of Giants: filling every niche with diversity in size, shape and diet

MEGATHERIUM
Pleistocene epoch; 20 feet long
An immense ground-dwelling relative of the sloth. It probably weighed 3 tons and lived in South America. It walked on its knuckles and probably used its front claws to pull down tree branches for food.

MEGALOCEROS
Late Pleistocene epoch; 8 feet long, 12-foot antlers
A giant relative of modern deer, it is often called the Irish elk, because most known fossil remains have been found there.

PLATYBELODON
Late Miocene epoch; 10 feet tall
An elephant called a shovel-tusker. Scientists think it used its wide, flat teeth to root in lakes for plants to eat.

EQUUS
Late Pleistocene epoch; 5 feet long
The modern horse evolved from descendants of this animal.

Rapid evolution: after the KT event a burst of adaptive radiation

The land was nearly empty of life after the extinctions following the KT event. Large reptilian animals were wiped out, along with most of the earliest marsupials. All of the early placental mammal groups survived the KT extinctions and continued on with rapid bursts of adaptation.

HYRACOTHERIUM
Early Eocene epoch; 8 inches to 2 feet long
This tiny animal is the earliest known ancestor of the modern horse. Sometimes called "The Dawn Horse," this animal is known from fossils found in Asia, Europe and North America.

BRONTOTHERIUM
Early Oligocene epoch; 8 feet tall
This giant animal is known from fossils found in North America. It is a relative of the modern rhinoceros. The heavy nose horns are thought to be ornaments or weapons.

EUSMILUS
Oligocene epoch; 8 feet long
One of many examples of predatory saber-toothed cats. They had stabbing teeth and a lower jaw that opened almost 90 degrees.

Pioneers: Mammals and mammal-like reptiles of the Mesozoic

The earliest mammals had to compete with dinosaurs, so they were generally small and secretive. Discoveries of these animals are rare, so the fossil record from this period of mammal evolution is poor.

THRINAXODON
Early Triassic Period; 20 inches long
This Therapsid was the first to show a distinct division between the chest and lower back. Scientists believe it was one of the first animals to develop a diaphragm muscle.

CRUSAFONTIA
Early Cretaceous Period; 4 to 8 inches long
This tiny animal is known from a nearly complete skeleton that was found in Portugal. Scientists believe it was a marsupial and ate insects and fruit.

Time and rock

In the 19th century, scientists began to date fossil rock using a **geologic time scale.** Layers of rock contained specific fossil animal species called **indicators.** Using the indicator fossils, prehistoric time was divided into three great eras. Eras were subdivided into periods, and periods into epochs.

The earliest known mammals appeared in rocks of the Mesozoic, during the Jurassic Period, which started about 206 million years ago. The Mesozoic Era is called the Age of Dinosaurs because they were the most dominant life form of that time. The Age of Mammals began at the **KT boundary,** about 65 million years ago. KT rocks contain a rare mineral substance called **iridium.** Most scientists believe the iridium came from a giant meteorite that crashed into the Earth, causing environmental havoc and the mass extinction of the dinosaurs. Mammals then rose to become the dominant life form on Earth.

The geologic time scale

The earliest forms of life were plants that evolved about a billion years ago. Animals evolved after plants, and the oldest fossil **vertebrates** (animals with backbones) are about 500 million years old. Here we show the uppermost portion of the geologic time scale of mammals and their ancestors:

▼ Going back through time

CENOZOIC ERA	QUATERNARY PERIOD	HOLOCENE EPOCH — 10,000 years ago to today
CENOZOIC ERA	QUATERNARY PERIOD	PLEISTOCENE EPOCH — 2 million to 10,000 years ago
CENOZOIC ERA	TERTIARY PERIOD	PLIOCENE EPOCH — 5 million to 2 million years ago
CENOZOIC ERA	TERTIARY PERIOD	MIOCENE EPOCH — 23 million to 5 million years ago
CENOZOIC ERA	TERTIARY PERIOD	OLIGOCENE EPOCH — 36 million to 23 million years ago
CENOZOIC ERA	TERTIARY PERIOD	EOCENE EPOCH — 53 million to 36 million years ago
CENOZOIC ERA	TERTIARY PERIOD	PALEOCENE EPOCH — 65 million to 53 million years ago
MESOZOIC ERA		CRETACEOUS PERIOD — 144 million to 65 million years ago
MESOZOIC ERA		JURASSIC PERIOD — 208 million to 144 million years ago
MESOZOIC ERA		TRIASSIC PERIOD — 248 million to 208 million years ago

KT Boundary

Prehistoric Oceans

A look at life of the Mesozoic seas

Water world

All life on Earth came from the sea. Scientists believe life was present in oceans more than 3.5 billion years ago – shortly after the oceans formed. At the time, the Earth was water, bare volcanic islands and an atmosphere thick with carbon dioxide. Marine fossils of bacteria filaments date to the early seas of 3.2 billion years ago.

One-celled organisms appeared in the oceans first. Scientists continue to debate how life began and how it evolved.

Stromatolites are structures formed from communities of micro-organisms (mostly those capable of photosynthesis). These odd sedimentary structures are one of the earliest signs of life. Scientists believe they are responsible for large amounts of oxygen being released into the atmosphere, paving the way for modern life.

Triassic world

248 to 212 million years ago

During the Triassic, the supercontinent Pangea expanded to reach its maximum size. A small tongue of ocean reached into Pangea, forming the Tethys seaway. Increased distance from the ocean dried the interior continent, and it became very arid. Merging world land masses and evaporation of the inland seas allowed animals to colonize the entire supercontinent. Mass extinctions, called the end-Permian event, opened evolutionary niches for creatures to evolve into. Because of this, an evolutionary race led to the rise of dinosaurs and many animal groups, including crocodilians, pterosaurs, turtles and mammals. In the sea, relatives of nearly every group of modern fish thrived, along with invertebrates, the great marine reptiles and some amphibians.

Jurassic world

211 to 143 million years ago

In the Jurassic, dinosaurs dominated the land and birds had evolved. Ichthyosaurs and plesiosaurs shared the seas with giant crocodiles, sharks and rays. Cephalopods — early relatives of squids, nautilus and octopi of today — filled the shallow seas. They included ammonites, with coiled, external shells, and belemnites, which had heavy, bullet-shaped, partially internal shells. Plankton diversified and were numerous. Pangea began to break up during Jurassic times, and the North American and Eurasian landmasses formed. The North Atlantic ocean began to open due to rifting.

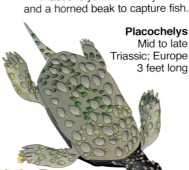

Spathobathis
Late Jurassic; Europe
About 20 inches long

The ancient relatives of the dogfish, chimaeras, sharks, skates, sawfish and rays first evolved about 400 million years ago. Spathobathis is the earliest known ray and is similar to modern guitar or banjo fish of the North Atlantic ocean.

During the Mesozoic, several groups of reptiles returned to aquatic life. Marine turtles like Placochelys had knobby armor and a horned beak to capture fish.

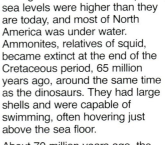

Placochelys
Mid to late Triassic; Europe
3 feet long

Cretaceous world

142 to 65 million years ago

During the late Cretaceous period, sea levels were higher than they are today, and most of North America was under water. Ammonites, relatives of squid, became extinct at the end of the Cretaceous period, 65 million years ago, around the same time as the dinosaurs. They had large shells and were capable of swimming, often hovering just above the sea floor.

About 70 million years ago, the Earth's continents and oceans began to resemble the shapes we are familiar with today. The Atlantic Ocean separated the Americas from Europe, Asia and Africa.

Ammonite species
Late Silurian to Cretaceous; worldwide
9 inches average; some species to more than 6 feet.

Ammonites are index fossils – different species link rock layers to specific geological time periods. Their closest living relatives are octopus, squid and cuttlefish. Their spiral shells resemble rams' horns, and Plinius the Elder named them ammonis cornua (horns of Ammon) after the Egyptian god Ammon, who was depicted wearing horns.

Hybodus
Late Permian to late Cretaceous; worldwide
Average 6 feet

One of the most common fossil sharks, Hybodus, had two types of teeth. Like modern sharks, males had "claspers" on the pelvic fin to assist with mating.

Opthalmosaurus
Late Jurassic; Europe
11 feet long

The Opthalmosaurs evolved from a land-dwelling reptile that returned to the sea. They were streamlined, fast-swimming and abundant. A strong tail and flexible spine allowed them to flourish into the Cretaceous.

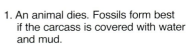

Macropoma is closely related to the "living fossil" fish named coelacanth. Like the modern fish, it had a 3-lobed tail.

How fossils form

1. An animal dies. Fossils form best if the carcass is covered with water and mud.
2. The flesh rots away, and the bones are covered slowly with layered sediment.
3. Permineralization occurs if the bones decay and are replaced by minerals dissolved in the water.
4. Petrification occurs if the bony structures are replaced entirely by minerals.
5. Earth movements cause the fossil to become exposed.

Macropoma
Late Cretaceous; Europe
22 inches long

Pycnodus was a deep-bodied fish with blunt, grinding teeth. This fish probably preyed on mollusks and hard-shelled reef dwellers.

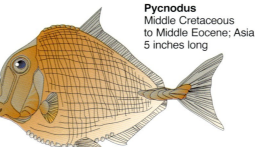

Pycnodus
Middle Cretaceous to Middle Eocene; Asia
5 inches long

PRIMATES

Of all mammals, primates are the ones that most resemble humans in both appearance and genetic makeup. There are more than 350 species of primates (some have only recently been discovered).

Location, location, location

With a few exceptions, such as humans, mountain gorillas and Japanese macaques, most primates live in the tropical or subtropical forests of Africa, Asia and South America. Due to habitat loss and hunting, almost one-third of all primates are at risk of extinction.

Big and small

The smallest primate is the pygmy mouse lemur. This tiny mammal can fit in the palm of your hand at 4 inches long (10 cm) and weighs about 1 ounce (28 grams). The largest primate is the gorilla, which can stand more than 5 feet (1.5 m) tall and weigh more than 400 pounds (181 kg). In between is a great variety of primate shapes and sizes.

The same ...

Primates share many characteristics. The early primates were arboreal (tree dwellers). Life in the trees resulted in the development of forward-facing eyes that resulted in excellent vision and a greater ability to judge distances. Most primates have better vision than a sense of smell or hearing. Long limbs and grasping hands, feet (and some tails) enable them to move through the forest canopy with great agility. Generally, primates have five fingers and nails instead of claws.

Relative to body weight, the brains of primates are larger than other animals. Primates are among the most intelligent and social of all animals. Smaller species are generally solitary foragers, but larger primates often live in large groups and exhibit complex social behavior.

Compared to other mammals, primates have long pregnancies. Infants are usually born in a more mature state than other animals and they rely on their mothers for longer periods.

... but different

Despite their similarities, primates are a diverse group of mammals. The most primitive of primates are called prosimians or lower primates. The word prosimian means "before monkey" because these animals more closely resemble their early primate ancestors. Most prosimians have wet (dog-like) snouts and a long claw on the second toe for grooming. Lemurs, lorises, galagos (bushbabies), pottos and tarsiers belong to this group.

One of the biggest differences between monkeys and apes is that most apes are larger and don't have tails. Apes have broader snouts and are capable of making tools.

The family tree

Fossil evidence suggests that the earliest primates appeared about 65 million years ago. The first known primate-like creature was **Purgatorius**. It lived in what is now North America at the end of the Cretaceous Period and the start of the Paleocene Period. During the middle to late Paleocene Period, **Plesiadapiforms** evolved. These mammals lived in North America and Europe. Modern primates first arose during the Eocene period.

Scientists who study non-human primates are called **primatologists**.

Taxonomy is the scientific method of classifying and grouping animals.

It is estimated that 10 percent of all primate species are acutely endangered and will likely become extinct during the next 20 years.

Many primates look cute and it can be tempting to want one as a pet. But primates are difficult to care for, are extremely active, messy and they can be very aggressive

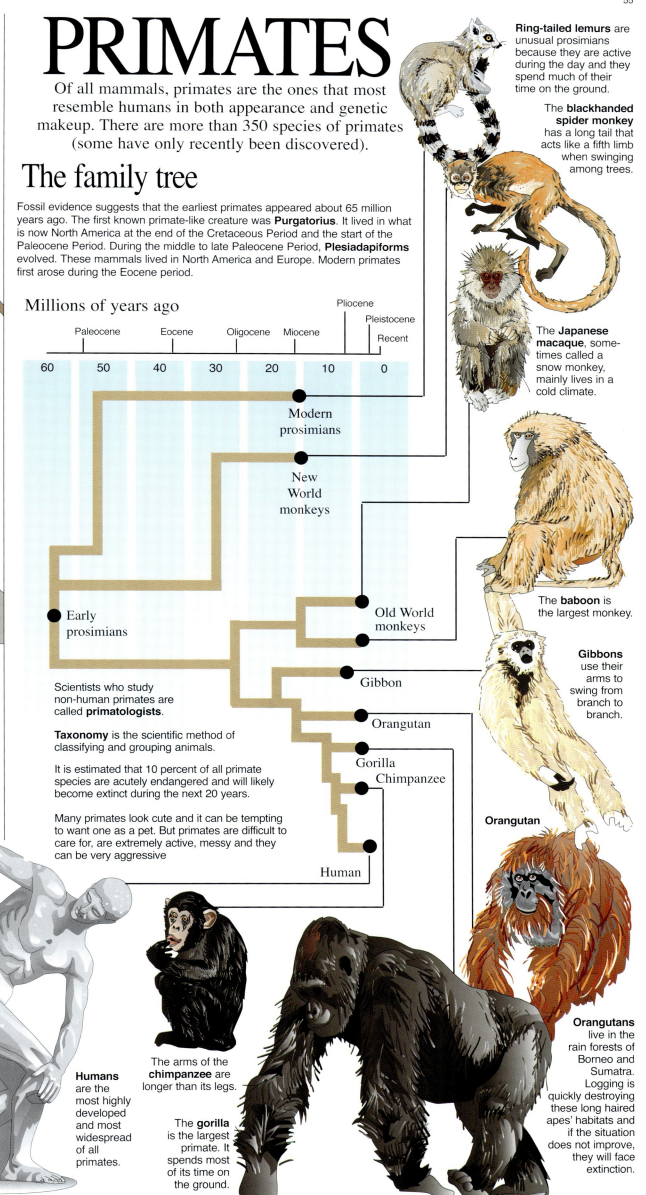

Life in the trees

Almost all prosimians are arboreal and live in the trees. They represent the most primitive or earliest primates on the evolutionary family tree. This group includes the tree shrew, lemur, loris or bush baby, the potto, the rare aye-aye and the tarsier. (Some scientists question whether the tree shrew and the tarsier are true prosimians, but they are included in this article.)

Where in the world?

Most prosimians are native to Madagascar, an island off the southeast coast of Africa. Some species can be found in Asia and on the continent of Africa. Prosimians are not native to the Americas.

Lorises (pottos, angwantibos, galagos)

Lemurs, indris, sifakas, aye-ayes

Tree shrews

Tree shrews have been around for about 70 million years, and they have not changed very much in all that time. Most are 6 to 10 inches long, with a tail that is just as long. They resemble rodents and have long snouts and small ears. Although the tree shrew shares many characteristics of a squirrel, its large brain suggests it may belong to the primate order.

Lemurs

There are 22 species of lemurs, divided into three families: **Lemuridae** (true lemurs and dwarf lemur, **Indriidae** (indris, avahis and sifakas), and **Daubentoniidea** (aye-ayes).

Lemurs vary in size, from as small as a mouse to as large as a cat. They live in the trees and are graceful when jumping from tree to tree. They use their long, bushy tails for balance as they navigate the forest canopy. Lemurs have projecting front teeth that serve as a "tooth comb" for grooming and a special grooming claw on the second toe of each foot. Some lemurs are **diurnal** (active during the day); others are **nocturnal** (active at night).

Lorises and galagos

There are about 11 species in the loris family. They are arboreal, nocturnal and **omnivorous.** (They eat plants and meat.) One way to distinguish between species is to observe how they move. Lorises and their close relatives, the pottos and angwantibos, move slowly, creeping through the treetops, while their close cousins, the African galagos (bush babies) are known for their speed and long jumps.

Tarsiers

Tarsiers are found in Southeast Asia. These small (rat-sized), nocturnal animals have huge eyes (bigger than their brain). They have large hands to aid in hunting and large feet to assist with aerial leaps.

Prosimians
The lower primates

There are six families of prosimians and about 50 species. One of the most interesting things about these mammals is their highly specialized hands and feet.

The **indri** is the largest of prosimians and the most monkey-like.

Today, the **feather-tailed tree shrew** is more often seen in zoos.

The **slender loris** weighs about 2 ounces. It creeps slowly through the trees, eating a variety of insects.

Lesser bush baby

Bush babies are also known as **galagos.** There are several species, each with its unique food preferences. Generally they feed on insects, fruit and tree gum. Some can leap up to 15 feet; others prefer to scramble along the tops of branches.

Diadem sifaka

The **potto** moves very slowly to avoid predators. It can stay still for hours if it has to. This endangered primate lives in Western and Central Africa.

The **aye-aye** is an extremely rare and solitary creature. It lacks the dental comb and grooming claw of other prosimians. This nocturnal omnivore feeds mostly on insects and eggs.

Aye-Aye

Western tarsier

No bigger than your hand, the **tarsier** sleeps in the trees in an upright position. But don't let that cute face fool you. The tarsier is a skilled killer. It is carnivorous and feeds on insects, lizards, snakes, birds and bats. The tarsier can turn its head almost 360 degrees.

Getting a grip on things

The shape of a primate's hand can reveal how it lives. Indris and tarsiers cling and leap through trees, while tree shrews and aye-ayes climb.

The tree shrew has long, clawed fingers.

The loris has a short index finger and a wide hand span.

The Indri's large thumb helps it cling to branches.

The aye-aye digs into a tree limb with its claws.

The tarsier's large pads give it a stronger grip.

Monkey business

More than 90 percent of anthropoids are monkeys. (The rest are apes and humans.) Most anthropoids are larger and smarter than prosimians. There are two main groups or orders of anthropoids: **New World monkeys** (platyrrhini) and **Old World monkeys** (catarrhini).

Two worlds

New World monkeys evolved separately from Old World monkeys 20 million to 30 million years ago. They are found only in the tropical forests of Southern Mexico, Central and South America.

Old World monkeys inhabit a more diverse range and can be found in Africa, South and East Asia and even the southern tip of Spain. They can be found in tropical forests, dry deserts, arid grasslands and in mountains.

What's the difference?

Apart from where they live, many things distinguish a New World monkey from an Old World monkey. New World monkeys tend to be smaller and almost all are arboreal. Some New World species have **prehensile** tails that can grasp branches like a third hand. No Old World monkey has this kind of tail. New World monkeys have flattened noses with nostrils farther apart and facing sideways. Old World monkeys have larger noses with narrow, forward-facing nostrils. In general, New World monkeys have smaller thumbs than their Old World cousins, and some species have no thumbs at all.

Most Old World monkeys have a hairless, callous pad of skin on their rumps. It is not unusual for Old World monkeys to be **semi-terrestrial** (living in the trees and on the ground). When you see a monkey traveling on the ground, you can be sure that it is an Old World monkey.

Old World monkey with narrow face and prominent nose

New World monkey with wide face and flattened nose

Old World monkeys

There are about 78 species of Old World monkeys. They are divided into two families or groups: **cercopithecinae** and **colobinae**.

Cercopithecines are the larger group and include baboons, mangabeys, mandrills, guenons, patas monkeys and macaques. The colobinae family are **herbivores** (plant eaters) and include the colobus, langurs and proboscis monkeys.

New World monkeys

There are at least 53 species of New World monkeys. They are divided into three families: **callithricidae**, **cebidae** and **atelidae**. The callithricidae family consists mostly of smaller monkeys and includes marmosets and tamarins.

The cebidae group includes the squirrel, capuchin and owl monkeys. Atelidae are generally larger and include the spider and howler monkeys

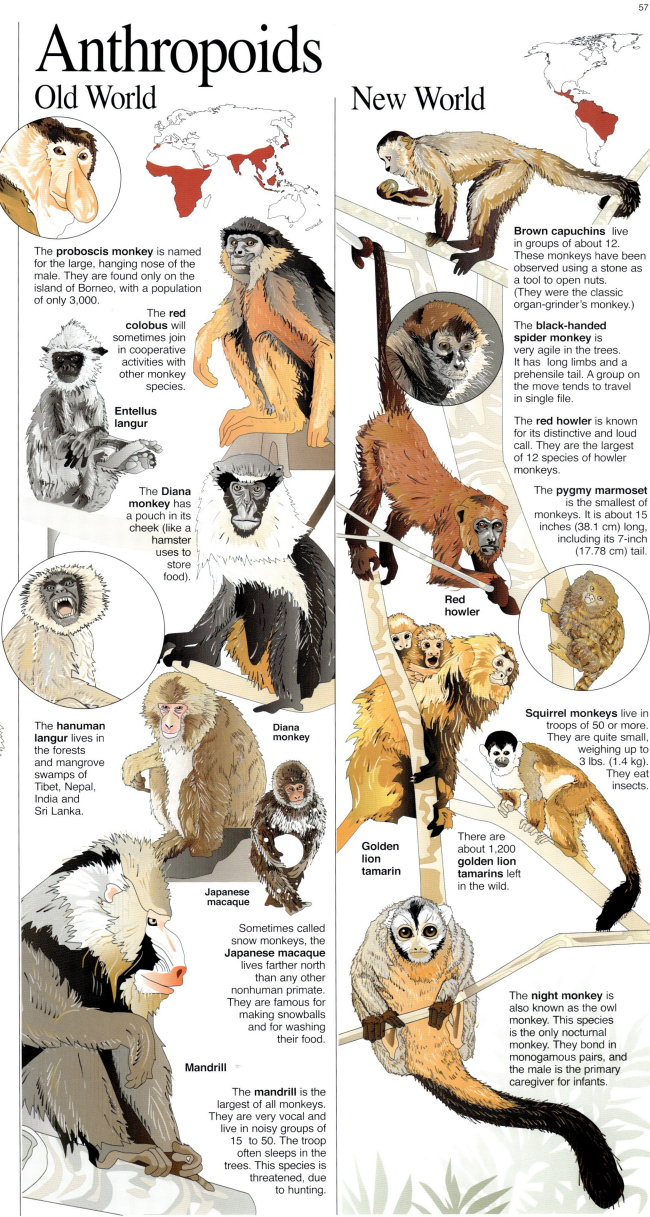

Anthropoids
Old World

The **proboscis monkey** is named for the large, hanging nose of the male. They are found only on the island of Borneo, with a population of only 3,000.

The **red colobus** will sometimes join in cooperative activities with other monkey species.

Entellus langur

The **Diana monkey** has a pouch in its cheek (like a hamster uses to store food).

The **hanuman langur** lives in the forests and mangrove swamps of Tibet, Nepal, India and Sri Lanka.

Diana monkey

Japanese macaque

Sometimes called snow monkeys, the **Japanese macaque** lives farther north than any other nonhuman primate. They are famous for making snowballs and for washing their food.

Mandrill

The **mandrill** is the largest of all monkeys. They are very vocal and live in noisy groups of 15 to 50. The troop often sleeps in the trees. This species is threatened, due to hunting.

New World

Brown capuchins live in groups of about 12. These monkeys have been observed using a stone as a tool to open nuts. (They were the classic organ-grinder's monkey.)

The **black-handed spider monkey** is very agile in the trees. It has long limbs and a prehensile tail. A group on the move tends to travel in single file.

The **red howler** is known for its distinctive and loud call. They are the largest of 12 species of howler monkeys.

The **pygmy marmoset** is the smallest of monkeys. It is about 15 inches (38.1 cm) long, including its 7-inch (17.78 cm) tail.

Red howler

Squirrel monkeys live in troops of 50 or more. They are quite small, weighing up to 3 lbs. (1.4 kg). They eat insects.

Golden lion tamarin

There are about 1,200 **golden lion tamarins** left in the wild.

The **night monkey** is also known as the owl monkey. This species is the only nocturnal monkey. They bond in monogamous pairs, and the male is the primary caregiver for infants.

Where in the world?

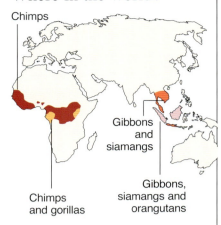

Chimps
Chimps and gorillas
Gibbons and siamangs
Gibbons, siamangs and orangutans

All in the family

Apes and humans belong to the **Hominoid** family of primates. Hominoids do not have tails and their skeleton has evolved to allow for standing upright. They have barrel-shaped chests and flexible shoulders and wrists. Scientists have divided hominoids into three groups: hylobatidae (lesser apes), pongidae (greater apes) and hominidae (humans).

The skeletons below show how different the bodies of apes are when compared to humans. Humans have a curve in their backs, which makes walking on two legs possible and allows for an upright posture.

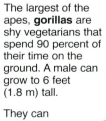

Chimpanzee   Gorilla   Human

Despite their differences, humans and apes share many characteristics: good grasping ability; excellent vision, but a poorer sense of smell; a large brain and increased intelligence; a prolonged period of dependence for young; and complex social behavior. DNA studies have confirmed our place in the order primates.

The largest of the apes, **gorillas** are shy vegetarians that spend 90 percent of their time on the ground. A male can grow to 6 feet (1.8 m) tall.

They can weigh up to 380 lbs. (177 kg)

Hominoids

Lesser apes

The **hylobatidae**, or lesser apes, include gibbons and siamangs of Southeast Asia. They are called lesser apes because they are smaller than other apes. Gibbons and siamangs have extremely long arms that allow them to move through the trees in a special hand-over-hand motion called **brachiation**. Lesser apes are monogamous, which means they choose one mate for life.

Great apes

The **pongidae**, or great apes, include orangutans, gorillas, chimpanzees and bonobos. Great apes are more like humans than lesser apes. They do not have sitting pads on their rumps like lesser apes and some monkeys.

The **orangutan** is the only great ape that lives in Asia. It has strong hands and feet with long digits, but a short thumb and big toe. Orangutans are the largest of all arboreal mammals and are rarely seen on the ground. An adult male can weigh more than 150 lbs (69 kg) and be 4.5 feet (1.4 m) tall. Orangutans are in serious danger of extinction due to hunting and habitat loss.

Gorillas can be found in East-Central and West Africa. There are three kinds of gorillas: the Western-lowland gorilla, the Eastern-lowland gorilla and the mountain gorilla.

2004 gorilla population estimates:
700 mountain gorillas,
5,000 Eastern-lowland gorillas
94,000 Western-lowland gorillas.

Chimpanzees and bonobos share more characteristics with humans than any other animal.

White-handed gibbons live almost entirely in the trees, but they walk erect when on the ground. Gibbons are the smallest of apes and range in height from 15 to 36 inches (38 cm to 91 cm).

The **siamang** inflates a large sac under its chin to make loud calls.

Gibbons, siamangs and some infant apes use **brachiation** (hand-over-hand motion) to swing through the trees. A gibbon can leap 20 feet (6 m) with one swing and travel at speeds of almost 35 miles (56 km) per hour.

Bonobos and chimpanzees are closely related and they can be confused with each other. One way to tell the difference between a **bonobo** and a **chimpanzee** is to look for the pink lips and the large hair part on the forehead of the bonobo. Bonobos are less aggressive and spend more time in trees than their close relative the chimp.

Bonobo

Chimpanzee

Did you know?

- Humans and chimpanzees are 98.5 percent identical when it comes to DNA.
- Gorillas and chimpanzees are so similar to humans that it is possible for them to catch diseases from us (and vice versa).
- Chimpanzees and bonobos have similar blood types to humans.

Rabbits and hares

What's the difference?

Hares and rabbits look a lot alike, but there are differences. Rabbits usually have smaller bodies, legs and ears than hares. Many rabbits dig **burrows**; hares do not. Most rabbits prefer to hide when threatened, while hares are built for running. The surest way to tell a rabbit from a hare is to look at their newborns. Baby rabbits are born **furless** and **blind**. Hares are born with fur and their eyes are open.

Female hares are called **jills** and males are called **jacks**. Baby hares are called **leverets**.

A female rabbit is called a **doe**, the male is a **buck**. Baby rabbits are called **kits, kittens** or **bunnies**.

The March Hare from Alice in Wonderland, the Easter bunny, Bugs Bunny and Peter Rabbit are just a few of the famous long-eared, fuzzy characters so popular in children's stories. Rabbits are cute and can make great pets, but they can also spell trouble for farmers. Rabbits and hares are not rodents. They belong to the order of **lagomorphs**, in the leporidae family. There are about 50 species of **leporids**, and half of these live in North America. Where they were not found naturally, rabbits and hares were introduced by humans — today leporids can be found on every continent except Antarctica.

Anatomy 101

Rabbits and hares have excellent hearing and a keen sense of smell. Their strong back legs allow them to move by hopping. The eyes are located on the side of the head, which allows them a wider view of the world.

Rabbits and hares need to chew constantly to wear down their incisors, which never stop growing.

There is a deep slit on the upper lip. This **harelip** allows the upper front teeth to show, even when the mouth is closed.

Rabbits and hares chew with a sideways motion, not up and down.

Rabbits develop quickly and are fully grown at 2 months of age.

One day old | 11 days old | 20 days old | 28 days old | 7 weeks old

Antelope jackrabbits have long ears that act like a kind of air conditioning for their blood in the hot desert climate.

The term "**mad as a march hare**" originated with the spring mating rituals of jacks fighting.

Home sweet home

Cottontails | Snowshoes
Jackrabbits | Arctic hares

Most hares and cottontail rabbits sleep in shallow depressions called **forms**. The European rabbit often lives in large groups, sharing an underground burrow called a **warren**.

Baby rabbits are born without fur

Baby cottontail rabbits in nest

What's for dinner?

Rabbits and hares are herbivores (plant eaters).* In the spring and summer they like to graze on grasses, clover, sometimes garden flowers and farmers' crops. Rabbits and hares do not hibernate or store food in the winter. During the coldest months they survive on buds, twigs and bark. Leporids eat their meals twice. They have two kinds of waste pellets (droppings). Moist pellets are soft and eaten and digested a second time. (This helps the animal get all the nutrients it needs.) Hard pellets are true waste and not re-eaten.

* Arctic hares reportedly will eat meat.

Wild species

Rabbits and hares seem to live just about everywhere. They can be found high in the mountains, on arctic plains, in deserts, meadows, swamps, forests and even some city parks. In North America all truly wild rabbits are cottontails, but there are many kinds of hares. There are several species of **cottontails** found in North and South America. Named for their fluffy white tail, they make grassy nests above ground.

Cottontail rabbit

The pika

Pikas don't look much like rabbits or hares — they look more like hamsters. But they share many of their cousins' habits. Pikas can be found in the mountains of the northwest United States and Canada, also in the northern regions of Russia, Asia and Europe. Pikas are vegetarians and spend the summer collecting and storing food for the winter. They are shy, vocal animals with a high-pitched squeak.

European hare

Rabbits and people

Since ancient times, people all over the world have raised domestic rabbits for meat and fur. They are also bred for scientific research. Many breeds of domestic rabbit have been bred for show and for pets. The lop-eared rabbit is a popular pet breed. Rabbits make great pets. They are quiet and friendly. Wild rabbits rarely live long in captivity and it is best to leave seemingly orphaned wild bunnies alone. More than likely, their mother is hiding nearby.

Jackrabbits are common in the western United States. They have very long ears and legs and can move at speeds up to 45 mph.

Golden eagle

Enemies everywhere

Rabbits and hares play a vital role in **natural ecosystems**. Because they breed so profusely and have few defenses, they are a plentiful food source for many animals. **Coyotes, foxes, bobcats, minks, weasels, snakes, hawks** and **owls** all depend on rabbits and hares as food for survival. The average life span of a wild rabbit is less than a year. **Humans** are probably the leporids' greatest enemy — rabbits and hares are often hunted as agricultural **pests**, for **sport**, **food** or for their soft **fur**. Domestic cats and dogs are also a danger. Rabbits are usually very quiet animals, but they do scream when in danger or pain. Some rabbits warn of danger by thumping their back legs on the ground.

Black-tailed jackrabbit

Arctic hare

The **arctic hare** is found in the far north. They often live in herds or colonies of 100 or more.

The **snowshoe or varying hare** is found in the forests of central and southern Canada and the northern United States. Like the arctic hare, they change color from brown to white. Unlike the arctic hare, they prefer to live alone, not in groups. They run fast (up to 30 mph) but not far.

Arctic hares change color depending on the season, brown in summer, white in winter.

Snowshoe hare

Snowshoe hare tracks. An unusual feature of rabbit and hare footprints is that the hind leg precedes the front.

European rabbit in a warren tunnel

Domestic dutch rabbit

French lop-eared rabbit

Tropical rainforests

Tropical rainforests are one of the oldest and most valuable ecosystems in the world. Nearly half of the world's plants and animals live there. These forests are being destroyed at a staggering rate, and in 50 years there may be nothing left.

What and where

Equatorial evergreen forests are located near the equator, where temperatures rarely fall below 80° F and the annual rainfall is over 160 inches. Because of this hot, wet weather, these forests stay green and lush. **Tropical moist forests** differ in that they have wet and dry seasons. **Cloud forests** grow in the mountains of the tropics where it is cooler. Because their moisture comes from clouds, they are not dependent on rain.

The emergent layer

The emergent layer consists of the tallest trees in the rainforest. Because of the sun and strong winds, this is where the rainforest is hottest and driest. Among the animals that live here are eagles, monkeys, butterflies and bats. Many of them never leave this layer.

Life at the top

Because of the abundance of sunlight and moisture, rainforest trees grow quickly and to great heights. Some reach 250 feet and have trunks measuring up to 16 feet around. Most are broad-leaved hardwood evergreens. A single region in a rainforest may contain as many as 2,500 species.

Sun conure
Aratinga solstitialis (South America)
Conures are a type of parrot originally from Brazil and the northern Amazon. They travel in playful, noisy flocks, feeding on buds, fruits, seeds and insects.

Tawny rajah
Charaxes bernardus (India, China, Malaysia)
The **tawny rajah** spends its entire life high in the treetops of the emergent layer.

Two-toed sloth
Choloepus didactylus (South America)
Two-toed sloths are slow-moving, nocturnal plant eaters that sleep up to 15 hours a day. Their algae-covered fur is green-tinged and excellent camouflage. Often they are infested with moths found only on sloths.

Aye-aye
Daubentonia madagacarien (Madagascar)
This rare, nocturnal, cat-sized lemur has sensitive ears that help it locate grubs.

Layers of a rainforest
- Emergents 250 ft.
- Canopy 150 ft.
- Middle layer 50 ft.
- Shrub layer 15ft
- Herb layer 2 ft.

Scarlet macaw
Ara macao (South America)
Macaws are the largest bird in the parrot family.

Blue morpho
Morpho peleides

Slow loris
Nycticebus coucang (Asia)

Potto
Perodicticus potto (Africa)

Hummingbirds
usually prefer red flowers.

Other forests

Mangrove forests grow along the sea and are sometimes called **flooded forests**. The long roots of mango trees help to anchor them so they don't fall over. In cooler areas of the world where the seasons are more pronounced, the forests are called **temperate forests**.

Queen Alexandria's birdwing
Ornithoptera alexandrae (Papua, New Guinea)
The world's largest butterfly with a wingspan up to 10 inches. It is endangered due to over-collecting and habitat destruction.

Guereza monkey
Colobus abyssinicus (Africa)

Tropical rainforest area

Tropic of Cancer
Equator
Tropic of Capricorn

Diversity

A four-square-mile area of rainforest may be home to 1,500 species of flowering plants, 750 species of trees, 125 mammal species, 400 species of birds, 100 species of reptiles, 60 species of amphibians and 150 species of butterflies. One study found that a square meter of leaf litter contained 50 kinds of ants.

Toco toucan
Rhamphastos toco (Brazil)
The **toco** is the largest of the toucans. Its bill can be up to 7.5 inches long. Tocos are plentiful in the Amazon forests, living in noisy flocks and eating fruit and sometimes insects and reptiles.

Vampire bat
Desmodus rotundus (Central and South America)
More myth than fact, vampire bats do feed on blood, but they won't attack a human and suck blood.

Transpiration

Rainforests create their own rain, using **transpiration**. In this process, plants and trees absorb rainwater into their leaves. The sun heats this water and turns it into vapor, which then evaporates into the air. Rainforest transpiration has a major effect on the world's climate. While about half of the water vapor falls in the rainforest, the rest is carried by warm air currents to provide rain in cooler, drier parts of the Earth. Rainforests return large amounts of oxygen and carbon dioxide to the air — elements that are essential for a healthy atmosphere.

The canopy

Starting at about eight feet from the ground and rising to over 150 feet is the canopy, a permanently green umbrella that protects the ground and absorbs both rain and sunlight. Thousands of animals live in the canopy, including monkeys, bats, sloths, tree frogs, ants, beetles, parrots, hummingbirds and snakes. Many spend their lives here and never leave the canopy.

Movers and shakers

Fruit and flowers grow in abundance in the canopy, even on tree trunks, and **photosynthesis** is a continuous process. The colors and smells attract birds and insects.

Air plants

Plants that grow on other plants are called **epiphytes**, or **air plants**. They cling to stems, trunks, leaves. **Orchids** are epiphytes and there are over 30,000 different kinds in the world. A single tree may be home to 300 orchids.

Staghorn fern
Platycerium bifurcatum (Australia) This large epiphytic fern uses its fronds to make a hollow to collect debris and water.

Insects lured by the **pitcher plant's** color and scent become trapped in the plant's tube-shaped leaves and are eaten for dinner.

Climbing plants

Lianas or **bush ropes** climb up branches and trunks to the top of the canopy, seeking sunlight. Their thick cable-like vines dangle down in the understory, sending out shoots that root in the forest floor and branch out to support other lianas.

Strangler fig
Ficus walkinsiana (Most rainforests) These plants grow thick and twisted, forming a woody trunk around a host tree and cutting off nutrients until it dies and decays, leaving a hollow place inside the strangler fig.

Monkey ladder vine (Costa Rica) Lianas that look like steps are sometimes called monkey ladders.

Blue-and-yellow macaw
Ara ararauna (South America)

Orangutan
Pongo gypmaeus (Borneo and Sumatra) The **orangutan** is an endangered species whose name means "person of the forest." These shy apes build nests for sleeping high in the treetops and rarely come to the ground.

Photosynthesis
Energy from the sun
Carbon dioxide
Glucose (sugar) is made in the leaves to feed the tree
Oxygen

African moon moth
Argema mimosae (Africa)

Gibbons swing hand over hand.

Primates

There are two kinds of primates: **anthropoids** (humans, apes and monkeys), and **prosimians**, such as lemurs and tarsiers. Most have excellent eyesight and climbing skills.

Gibbon
Hylobates (Southeast Asia) Smallest of the apes, **gibbons** have no tails and use their arms to swing through the branches. They live in families, and hoot and call to warn others away.

Golden lion tamarin
Leontopithecus rosalia (Southeastern Brazil) Endangered because urban growth has destroyed their habitat, these beautiful little monkeys are being reintroduced through captive breeding. Today, there are about 400 in the wild, 500 in zoos.

Lizards and snakes

Green iguana
Iguana iguana (Central and South America) Active during the day, these large (4 to 6 ft.) lizards eat mostly plants. They live in trees and like to bask in the sun. Wild iguanas are endangered by habitat destruction, the pet industry and native people who eat them.

Chameleon
Chameileonidae (Africa and Madagascar) These slow moving, color-changing lizards live mostly in trees and catch insects with long, sticky tongues. They have grasping feet instead of claws.

Clouded leopard
Panthera nebulosa (Asia) Called **mint leopards** in China, these cats hunt day or night. Good climbers, they drop from trees onto small mammals and birds, but often hunt larger prey on the ground.

White-lipped tree frog
Litoria infrafrenata (Australasia) The largest frog in the world, these sticky-toed hoppers can reach up to 14 centimeters.

The understory

The lower canopy gets less than 5 percent of the sunlight received by the upper canopy. The plants here have developed unique ways to survive. Often they have large, dark green leaves that function as solar collectors. Many insects, snakes and frogs make their home in this middle layer, as do parakeets, leopards and jaguars.

Franquet's epauleted bat
Epomops franqueti (Ghana, Africa) These bats have big heads and roost in small groups. At night, they gather in large numbers to feed on fruit trees.

The people

For thousands of years, tribes of **indigenous** or **native people** have made their homes in rainforests around the world. Some still live in traditional ways, finding all they need for survival within the forest. Sadly, since colonists began arriving more than 500 years ago, their numbers have steadily declined.

Not discovered until the 20th century, the **Waorani Indians** are a fierce nomadic tribe in eastern Ecuador who can build a shelter in a few hours and a house in 3 days.

The **Kayapo Indians** of east central Brazil are hunter/gatherers who practice the initiation ritual of lip-stretching. Some lip plugs measure 4 inches wide. Although they use modern devices such as canned foods and the radio, the Kayapo adhere closely to a traditional lifestyle and resent interference from outsiders.

Tribal life & tradition

Rainforest children do not go to regular schools. Instead, they learn forest survival in a family setting, mastering skills such as hunting, fishing, and the selection of plants for food and medicine. Often they know more of the rainforests' secrets than the botanists and biologists who study them. Some of these indigenous people have started making efforts to protect their land and culture. However, although a tribe may have lived in their rainforest for hundreds of years, not all governments recognize this as proof of ownership.

Spider monkey *Ateles Geoffroyi* (Central and South America) These tree-dwellers are active in the daytime and have special prehensile tails.

Ring-tailed lemur *Lemur catta* (Madagascar)

Tarsier *Tarsius tarsius* (Southeast Asia) Tarsiers have huge eyes that help them see in the dark. They can eat up to 40 grasshoppers in one meal.

The **Mbuti** are a **Pygmy** tribe in Zaire, Africa. They refer to their rainforest as ëfatherí or ëmotherí because it is the source of all their food, clothing and building materials.

Indian hornbill *Buceros bicornis* (India)

Leaping lizards
Some creatures have adapted to rainforest life by developing their ability to glide from one branch to another. Lizards and geckos have special membranes that they can open and use like parachutes. The webbed feet on flying frogs serve a similar function.

Green cat-eye snake *Boiga cyanea* (Asia) This nocturnal snake is poisonous and usually lives in trees, close to water.

Ginger *Zingiber officinalis* (China, India, Malaysia)

Small primates

Monkeys belong to the same order of mammals as humans and apes. Most have tails to help them balance themselves. New World monkeys are always **arboreal** (tree-dwelling) and some have **prehensile** tails with bare skin at the end that allow them to grip objects. **Lemurs** usually live in trees and travel in family groups or troops. They eat fruit, leaves, birds, eggs, insects and small animals.

Bush babies
Galagonidae (Africa)
Galagos or bush babies sound like crying human babies and use their hind legs like frogs to jump distances up to 12 feet.

Marmosets
Callithrix jacchus (Central and South America) The common marmoset is a small squirrel-like monkey that feeds mainly on insects, fruit and tree sap. Used for pets and medical research, they are endangered.

Food and furniture

Many products that we use every day come from tropical rainforests. Some are grown on plantations, while others are found in the wild. They include avocados, sugar cane, bananas, coconuts, pineapples, and citrus fruit, as well as papaya, coffee and many kinds of nuts. The chicle in chewing gum comes from a rainforest tree, as does the cacao seed used to produce chocolate. Wood from rainforest trees such as teak, mahogany, rosewood and sandalwood is used for furniture and boats, as well as for many other types of construction work.

Periwinkle
Catharanthus roseus (Madagascar)
The rosy periwinkle from Madagascar is one of many medicinal herbs that grow in the rainforest.

Medicine

The rainforest is the source of approximately 25 percent of today's medicines. **Quinine** from the chichona plant is a treatment for malaria and a tropical vine (strychnos toxifera) provides us with **curare**. Once used by natives to tip poison arrows, it is now an ingredient in anesthetics and muscle relaxants. The **rosy periwinkle** has been found to be extremely useful in combating leukemia. Today, more than 1000 tropical plants are being considered for potential cancer treatment.

The floor

On the floor, except around rivers, and in areas where light breaks through the canopy, very few plants grow. Less than 2 percent of the sunlight shining on the canopy reaches the ground, and the humidity reaches 100 percent. Insects, fungi, bacteria and worms burrow and feast on debris. Large animals such as tigers, anteaters and tapirs roam in the darkness.

On the ground

Because of the heat and moisture, leaves disintegrate in less than six weeks. It is the few inches of this rotted vegetation, rather than the soil, which provides nutrients to most of the rainforests' plants and trees.

Roots

Many of the largest trees have thick above-ground supports called **buttress roots**. These triangle-shaped wedges **prevent erosion** by holding the thin soil around the tree in place. Although shallow, the root systems are wide reaching, they **absorb rainfall** and help **replenish ground water** supplies. By storing and slowly releasing the water over time, they also assist in regulating the water levels in the rivers.

In the water

Riverbanks get lots of light and are rich with silt nutrients left by receding floodwaters. The edges are lush with foliage. The streams are full of living creatures and many animals come out from the forest to feed and drink.

The Amazon

More than 4,000 miles long and in some places 6 miles wide, the Amazon is South America's chief river. It is the second longest river in the world — only the Nile in Africa is longer. The Amazon carries more water than any other river and holds two-thirds of the world's fresh water. Its basin contains the world's largest tropical rainforest and spreads over 2.7 million square miles. The river itself supports a huge diversity of life and contains more than 5,000 known species of fish.

Piranha
Serrasalmus niger (South America) Although they usually feed on fish, piranhas sometimes attack in schools and can remove the flesh from a 100-pound animal in minutes.

Flying frog Rhacophorus reinwardii (Asia)

Malachite butterfly Siproeta stelenes biplagiata (Amazon Basin) One of more than 2,000 butterfly species found in the Amazon, this one likes to feed on overripe and rotting fruit.

Red-kneed tarantula Brachypelma smithi (Mexico)

Frog beetle Sagra buqueti (Malaysia)

Leaf-cutter ants Atta cephalotes (Central and South America) Also called parasol ants, they carry loads up to 12 times their weight.

Malayan Tapir Tapirus indicus (Southeast Asia) These large animals have poor eyesight but are good swimmers.

Some rainforest mushrooms glow in the dark.

Arrow-poison frog Dendrobates auratus (Central and South America) Natives use its skin for poison arrows or darts

The **Amazon water lily** (Victoria Amazonica) can grow to 5 feet across and is valued for its seeds.

Jaguar Panthera onca (Central and South America) Jaguars hunt mainly at night, often leaping from trees to surprise their prey. They are also good swimmers and will eat frogs, fish, and turtles, as well as small alligators.

Amazon dolphin Inia geoffrensis (Amazon River) Endangered by pollution, this pink freshwater dolphin travels more than 1,000 miles upriver. It has poor eyesight and uses echolocation for navigating and to locate food.

Scarlet ibis Eudocimus ruber (South America) This stork is a ground nester and roosts in large colonies. It feeds in the shallow coastal waters of lakes, swamps and lagoons.

Caiman Caiman crocodilus (Central and South America) Caimans are smaller relatives of crocodiles and alligators. They are sometimes hunted for their skins and their babies are captured for pets. Habitat destruction and pollution are a major threat.

Under threat

Over the last 100 years, more than 50 percent of the world's rainforests have been destroyed and every minute, about 100 acres and 2,000 trees disappear forever.

It is estimated that more than 50,000 rainforest plants and animals become extinct each year. Many species will disappear without ever having been recorded or studied.

Slash and burn is an ancient form of agriculture that results in vast areas of rainforest being destroyed. A farmer cuts down a few acres of forest, burns the trees and plants a crop. The soil is made fertile by the ash from the fire and initially crops grow well. But within 2 or 3 years, the soil is worn out and in order to get a better crop the farmer repeats the process, destroying yet another area of the rainforest.

In the Amazon basin in particular, the introduction of **cattle ranching** has caused major damage. Vast acres are burned and turned to pasture for grazing beef. **Logging and mining** also contribute to the destruction of rainforests.

Rafflesia Rafflesia arnoldi (Sumatra, Malaysia and Borneo) This stemless, leafless flower can grow to 3 feet wide and is the largest in the world. They feed on the stems and roots of woody vines and are sometimes called carrion flowers or corpse lilies because they smell like rotten meat. Their scent attracts flies and aids in pollination.

Making a difference

Many individuals and organizations are trying to prevent further destruction of the rainforest. Logging companies and governments are setting aside special **reserves** where only trees of a certain type and size can be cut down, leaving the remainder to replenish the forest. **Extractive reserves** allow a percentage of fruits and plants to be harvested. In addition, many education programs are being introduced around the world to keep people informed of the importance of conservation.

What can you do?

Make rainforest-friendly food decisions. Drink U.S.-grown citrus fruit juice. Consider beef alternatives. Each fast-food hamburger using Amazonian beef equates to destroying a kitchen-sized patch of rainforest. Recycle paper and try to use less. Use less gasoline and plastic. Much of the oil in these products is extracted from rainforest resources. Ride your bike or take the bus instead of the car. Use glass bottles and containers instead of plastic and recycle whenever possible. Contact an organization involved with rainforest conservation and find out how you can help.

RATS & RODENTS

What is a rodent?
Rodents are gnawing animals with front teeth that are well-suited to chewing hard objects. Rats, mice, hamsters, gerbils, guinea pigs, squirrels, beavers, marmots (groundhogs), gophers, porcupines, chipmunks, lemmings, muskrats, prairie dogs and voles are all rodents.

Rodents have two top and two bottom front teeth called **incisors**. The incisors grow throughout a rodent's life time.

Rodents are found all over the world and there are a lot of them. Most rodents are **herbivorous** (plant eaters), but rats will eat just about anything.

These animals are both helpful and harmful to people. Many eat harmful insects and weeds. Others are prized for their fur. Scientist use rats and mice in research. But some rodents damage property and crops or carry diseases like the **plague** and **typhus**.

There are many kinds of rodents, from the often disliked street rat to the cuddly pet hamster. These furry mammals come in lots of shapes and sizes. This page looks at just a few.

Naked mole rat
Brown rat
Capybara
Black rat
Chinchilla
Desert kangaroo rat
Lemmings
Paca
Deer mouse

Squirrel skeleton — Molars, Incisors

Rats
There are about 120 kinds of rats. We are most familiar with the black rat and the brown rat because they often live near people. **Black rats** are sometimes called roof or ship rats. They tend to be found in coastal areas. **Brown rats**, also known as sewer rats, are common in North America and can pose health risks to people.

Rats are larger than mice and have a long scaly tail and sharp claws. They live in large groups or colonies. Rats generally feed at night and will eat just about anything. Rats can mate year-round and may have several litters.

Mice
The word mouse has its origins in an old (Asian) Sanskrit word that means **thief**.

The female **house mouse** can give birth every 20 to 30 days, with an average litter of four to seven babies. Born furless and blind, these rodents are fully grown in three weeks and will begin to mate when they are about 45 days old. House mice, like their cousin the rat, will eat just about anything and prefer to make their homes near people, in houses, sheds and barns. The average life span of a house mouse is two or three months; in captivity they have been known to live six years.

The **American harvest mouse** has large ears, a hairy tail, and is smaller than a house mouse. They build ball-shaped nests 6 to 12 inches off the ground, on bushes or on stems of grass.

Grasshopper mice are found in dry regions, like the deserts of the Western United States and northern Mexico. Most active at night, these animals like to eat grasshoppers and scorpions. They hunt in a similar manner to cats and are the only mice known to howl at night.

Kangaroo rats
Named for the way it jumps like a kangaroo, the kangaroo rat has long, powerful legs, short front legs and a very long tail that ends in a tuft. Found in the deserts of the Southwestern United States and Mexico, these rodents have a kidney that is four times more efficient than humans' and they never drink water. Their large eyes help them find food at night. And like its cousin the hamster, the kangaroo rat has pouches in its cheeks to carry food. This rodent nests in burrows (tunnels) and eats plants.

Agouti

Brazilian agouti
Grasshopper mouse
House mouse

The agouti lives in thick forests from southern Mexico to northern Argentina and in the West Indies. They grow to be about 2 feet long and have small, round ears, long legs and a stubby tail (some have no tail at all). These animals move with little **jumps** (sort of like a deer) and feed on fruit, leaves and roots. Unlike mice and rats, they are born with fur and their eyes open. In the tropics they are hunted for their meat. In North America they have been known to make affectionate pets.

Porcupines
Porcupines have long, soft hairs and strong, stiff **quills** on their backs. The sharp quills are used as defense; the porcupine strikes attackers with its quilled tail and the quills stick into the skin of the attacker. Porcupines grow new quills to replace lost ones. Despite the myth, porcupines cannot shoot quills at enemies. Some porcupine quills have sharp hooks at the end called **barbs** that make removing them painful and difficult. The **North American porcupine** lives mostly in coniferous forests. They have brownish black fur and grow to about 3 feet (91 C) long and weigh about 20 pounds (9 k).

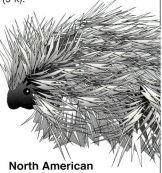

North American porcupine

Tree squirrels
Tree squirrels are found in forests all over the world. The Eastern and Western gray and fox squirrel are common to North America. Many tree squirrels build nests called **dreys** made up of leaves, twigs and vines woven into a ball shape.

Flying squirrels live in trees and are nocturnal, searching for food at night. They have a special fold of skin between their front and back legs that allows them to glide from tree to tree. Most species are from Asia, but two small flying squirrels live in North America.

Eastern gray squirrel

Pacas
Pacas are large rodents that grow to about 24 to 32 inches (62 to 82 c) and can weigh between 14 and 22 pounds (6.3 to 10 k). Pacas live from central Mexico south to Paraguay and in the Andes Mountains of Venezuela, Colombia and Ecuador. They are excellent swimmers and usually live in forests near water. Pacas tend to live alone. They feed at night and eat plants, roots, seeds and fruit. These rodents nest in burrows, caves, woodpiles and rock crevices.

Hamsters
There are about 15 kinds of hamsters. The best known are the golden hamster and common hamster. Originally from Asia and Europe, these furry creatures are popular pets. Most hamsters have special cheek pouches that they use to carry food in.

The golden hamster is also known as the Syrian hamster. It has reddish-brown fur on its back with white fur on its belly. The common hamster is also called the black-bellied hamster (for obvious reasons). These hamsters are most active at night and prefer to live alone. They dig burrows with separate rooms for sleeping, food storage and body waste. Hamsters eat seeds, fruit and vegetables. The average life span of a pet hamster is two to three years.

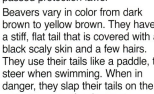

Golden Hamster

Capybaras
The capybara is the **largest** of all rodents, growing up to 4 feet (1.2 m) long and weighing more than 100 pounds (45 k). It is found in eastern Panama and in South America east of the Andes. Capybaras resemble small pigs or giant guinea pigs. They have a coat of coarse hair that ranges in color from reddish-brown to gray with a yellow-brown underbelly. This rodent has **webbed** toes and is an excellent swimmer. For this reason it is sometimes called the **water pig** or water hog. People, alligators and jaguars often eat this animal. In prehistoric times capybaras lived in southeastern North America.

Beavers
Beavers have soft, shiny fur, which made them one of the most hunted animals in North America from the 1500s through the 1800s. In the late 1600s, one beaver pelt would buy four pounds of shot or a kettle. By the late 1800s North American beavers were in danger of extinction and the U.S. and Canada passed protection laws.

Beavers vary in color from dark brown to yellow brown. They have a stiff, flat tail that is covered with a black scaly skin and a few hairs. They use their tails like a paddle, to steer when swimming. When in danger, they slap their tails on the water to warn other beavers.

Beavers are well-known for their ability to cut down trees with their sharp teeth and for building dams and lodges in waterways.

Beaver
Guinea pig (Cavy)

Coral Reefs

What are they?

Coral reefs are rich communities with a diversity of sea creatures. Most coral reef systems form in shallow, tropical ocean waters. In most reefs, the predominant organisms are **stony corals,** which produce rigid formations by secreting exoskeletons of calcium carbonate (limestone).

Although corals are found both in temperate and tropical waters, reefs are formed roughly in the equatorial zone, from about 30°N to 30°S. Reef-forming corals do not grow at depths of over 100 feet (30 meters), or where water temperatures fall below 72°F (22°C).

Corals are not the only, or the major, reef-forming organisms. Other sea creatures, like **coralline algae,** protozoan **foraminiferans,** some **mollusks, echinoderms,** and tube-building **annelid worms** deposit calcium carbonate. But, any reef formed by a biological community is traditionally called a coral reef.

■ Coral reefs

The **regal angelfish** is a beautiful reef dweller. Angelfish have a distinct spine at the base of the gill covering.

The **zebra firefish** is a member of the lionfish family. Many lionfish have toxins in their spiny fins.

The largest coral reef

The **Great Barrier Reef** off Northeast Australia is the largest known complex of coral reefs. It is 10 to 90 miles (16–145 km) wide and about 1250 miles (2010 km) long. A lagoon 10 to 150 miles (16–240 km) wide separates it from the shore. Here's a look at some of its inhabitants:

Brain corals can grow to be very large. Only the outermost layer of stony corals is living. The polyps deposit layer after layer of limestone as they grow, resembling the layers of an onion.

Lettuce corals form shelf-like projections from the reef. Fish and eels often hide in the overhang.

Sea feathers are soft coral. They can grow as tall as a man.

Sponges are hollow filter-feeders. They grow in many shapes and sizes.

Sea anemones are cousins of coral. Their polyps do not deposit limestone. Most have stinging tentacles to capture prey.

Crown-of-thorns

Danger to reefs

In ideal conditions, coral reefs can grow up to a little over 3 feet (100 cm) per year. But, reefs are sensitive to environmental change. Heavy rainfall and runoff from the mainland can kill a reef because of increased sediment and decreased salinity in the seawater. Another danger is the absence of waves, because silt will accumulate and suffocate the coral. Water pollution, dredging and careless boating, or collecting by divers or aquarists, all threaten valuable reef systems.

During the 1990s, many previously unknown diseases began attacking coral reefs worldwide, causing widespread death of coral polyps.

The Great Barrier Reef is threatened by a population explosion of the crown-of-thorns starfish, which eats coral polyps, leaving limestone skeletons behind.

Coral anatomy

Coral reefs consist of many diverse species of corals. Coral is made up tiny organisms called **polyps.** Polyps and structure of the **coral skeleton** combine in one of two ways, forming **perforate** or **imperforate corals.** The perforate corals have porous skeletons with connections between the polyps through the skeleton. Imperforate corals have solid skeletons.

POLYP STRUCTURE
Each polyp has a circle of **tentacles** around the **mouth,** a tube-shaped **gut,** the wedge-shaped **mesentery,** and thin, skeletal walls called **septa.**

THE CORAL SKELETON
Corallite is the part of the coral skeleton deposited by a polyp. A skeletal wall of a polyp is called the **theca.** Skeletal material around individual corallites is called the **coenosteum.**

Polyp cross-section — Tentacles, Mouth, Mesentery, Coenosarc, Gut, Mesenterial filament, Septum, Basal disc

Types of Reefs

Different types of reefs form depending on the conditions. Here's how reefs differ:

➤ **Fringing reefs** form along a coastline, growing on the continental shelf in shallow water. They form on the hard surfaces of rocky shores and are exposed at low tide.

➤ **Bank or barrier reefs** grow parallel to shorelines, farther out. They are usually separated from land by a deep lagoon, and get their name because they form a barrier between the lagoon and the open ocean.

➤ **Coral atolls** are rings of coral growing on top of sunken volcanoes in the ocean. They begin as fringe reefs surrounding a volcanic island. As the inactive volcano sinks, the reef continues to grow. Eventually only the circular reef and calm central lagoon remains.

Fringing reef | Barrier reef | Coral Atoll

Coral growth forms

Corals are **anthozoans,** one of three classes in the phylum **cnidaria.** The anthozoans are roughly divided into two subclasses: **alcyonaria,** the soft corals, or **zoantharia,** the anemones, black and stony corals. Together with the **hydrozoans** (one of the other classes of cnidaria), they are critical to the formation of coral reef communities. The reef-building corals grow in many shapes and sizes.

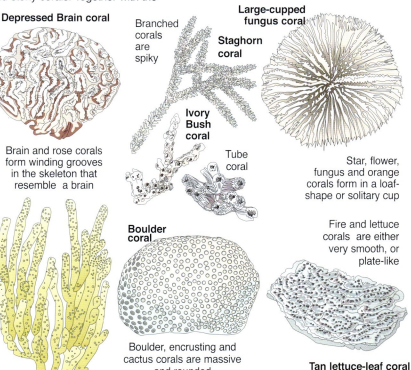

Depressed Brain coral

Brain and rose corals form winding grooves in the skeleton that resemble a brain

Branched corals are spiky

Staghorn coral

Ivory Bush coral

Tube coral

Boulder coral

Boulder, encrusting and cactus corals are massive and rounded

Spiny candelabrum — Soft corals are not rigid

Large-cupped fungus coral

Star, flower, fungus and orange corals form in a loaf-shape or solitary cup

Fire and lettuce corals are either very smooth, or plate-like

Tan lettuce-leaf coral

Reef environment

Ideal reef conditions are somewhat rare. The best places are in **tropical waters** along western coasts of ocean basins, and around oceanic islands. Reefs are usually only found within 30 degrees north or south of the equator.

Reef formation conditions

➤ Growing at or slightly below sea level
➤ In shallow water with strong wave action
➤ In a salinity level of 30-40 parts per thousand
➤ In temperatures of 73-80 degrees fahrenheit

Reindeer

What's the difference?
Reindeer and caribou belong to a species called Rangifer tarandus of the deer family cervidae. Scientists have divided the species into 7 subspecies. Caribou (KAR uh boo) is a French-Canadian name for a large deer. The wild caribou of North America are generally larger than the domesticated reindeer of Europe.

Born to run
Reindeer and caribou are one of the most migratory of all animals. The herd needs to keep moving in order to find enough food and to protect itself against predators. During **migration**, several thousand reindeer may gather into one giant herd. Different migration routes are used to prevent overgrazing. Caribou and reindeer can run at speeds up to 50 mph. (80.5 km) and cover more than 3,000 miles (4,828 km) in a year.

Favorite foods
In summer, caribou eat the leaves of willow and birch trees, various shrubs, sedges (grasslike plants), tundra plants and mushrooms. In winter they eat mostly **lichens** (reindeer moss), small shrubs, twigs and dried sedges.

Did you know?
Male reindeer and caribou are called **bulls** and females are called **cows**. A baby is called a **calf**. Adult caribou stand 4 to 5 feet (1.2 m 70 1.5m) high and can weigh up to 700 lbs. (320kg). Adult reindeer stand about 3 to 4 feet (90 to 120 cm) high and weigh up to 400 lbs. (180kg).

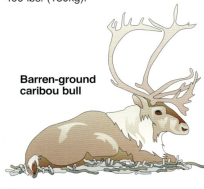
Barren-ground caribou bull

Antlers
Female caribou and reindeer are unique because they are the only deer in the world that have antlers. Males have larger antlers than females, but they drop their antlers in November and December. Females keep their antlers until they give birth in the spring. This means that Santa's reindeer are probably all females or immature males! (Or maybe, the magic dust used to make Santa's reindeer fly also keeps them young forever.)

New antlers grow from knobs on the top of the head. Each year a new branch grows, so the more branches, the older the deer.

Antlers are made of a hard, bone-like substance. As antlers grow they are covered with a smooth hair called velvet. In the fall rutting (breeding) season begins. During this time bulls fight with each other in order to mate. Sometimes the fights get very violent and a rival is injured or killed.

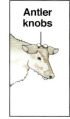
Antler knobs

Velvet

Velvet shedding

Reindeer and caribou are the same species. In Europe they are called reindeer and in North America they are called caribou. They are large members of the deer family and belong to the group of mammals called "ungulates," which means hoofed animals.

Made for snow
Caribou and reindeer live in the far north, in the arctic tundra and boreal forests of Europe, Asia, North America and Greenland. Caribou have large, wide, flexible hoofs. In winter the hoofs are hard and sharp, ideal for traveling over snow and ice. The hoofs make good shovels for digging in snow to reach mosses. In summer the hoofs soften and become more broad to make traveling on the spongy tundra easier. The hoofs also serve as paddles for **swimming** — caribou are strong swimmers. Caribou and reindeer have a special winter hair that is **hollow** and traps air to provide insulation against the cold. These hairs also help them stay afloat in water. In deep winter, when food is scarce, caribou reduce their food intake.

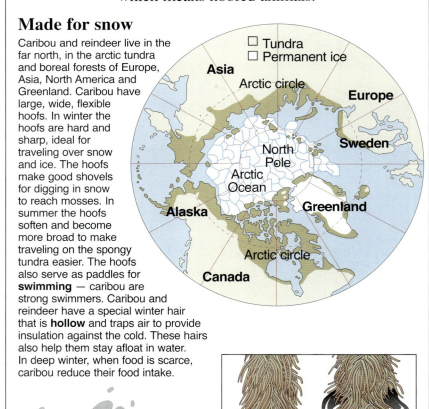

Reindeer tracks

Top of hoof **Bottom of hoof**

Domesticated reindeer
Nomadic people of the north have been herding and taming wild caribou for at least 2000 years (possibly 5,000 years). Today reindeer continue to be herded by many Arctic people, especially those in Europe and Asia. The native people of Alaska and Canada hunt caribou.

The Sami (or Lapps) of northern **Scandinavia** are famous for their way of life, which has centered around migrating herds of reindeer for centuries. The Lapps train reindeer to carry heavy packs and to pull sleds. They depend on reindeer for food, shelter and clothing. They use reindeer skin for their boots, **coats** and tents. Reindeer bones and antlers are used to make needles and knives. They eat reindeer meat and drink reindeer milk and some even keep reindeer as pets.

Some people use snowmobiles, trucks, helicopters and radios to herd the deer. But others maintain tradition and travel with the herds, carrying their goods on **sleighs** pulled by reindeer.

Do reindeer really know how to fly?
If you have ever seen a deer leap across a road, you know how much they look like they are flying. But unless you have some magic dust, reindeer don't really fly.

Santa's reindeer are very rarely seen, which makes it difficult for scientists to study them. Several theories have been presented to explain how Santa's reindeer fly. Perhaps they are a unique and endangered species. Maybe air moving through their antlers helps to create enough lift when leaping to make them airborne, while their large hoofs allow them to row through the air (much like regular reindeer swim through water). Others suggest that Santa's reindeer have a special digestive track that creates lighter-than-air methane gas which is stored in a balloon-like bladder. When released, the gas acts like rocket propulsion and allows the reindeer to reach supersonic speeds. All of these hypothesis have merit, but the fact is, we really don't know how Santa's reindeer manage to fly.

Rudolph (Santa's ninth reindeer) hit the mainstream in 1949 when Johnny Marks wrote the song "Rudolph the Red Nosed Reindeer." Sung by a cowboy named Gene Autry, the song became an instant success and Rudolph became famous.

SALAMANDERS

What are salamanders?
Salamanders are slim-bodied, short legged **amphibians** with long tails. Salamanders resemble lizards (reptiles) in their body shape but are identified by their lack of scales. Amazingly, they have the ability to regenerate lost limbs.

Notable traits
Adults who retain external gills are called **perennibranchiates**. Some salamanders retain their juvenile gilled form but become sexually mature – a process called **neoteny**. Scientists think this happens as a form of protection, keeping them in the relative safety of the water.

Salamanders alternate between swimming and walking, so **herpetologists** (scientists who study reptiles and amphibians) use them to examine the evolution of vertebrate locomotion. Two types of **gaits** (walking styles) have been identified in salamanders.

Salamanders are typically small, but some reach up to 5 feet (1.5 m) long. The hellbender and mudpuppy can grow to a foot long or more. In Japan and China, the giant salamander reaches 5 feet (1.5 m) in length and weighs up to 67 pounds (30.4 km).

Reproduction
Female salamandroidea have glands in their cloacal chamber called **spermathecae**, used to store sperm.

Cryptobranchoidea and sirenoidea have **external fertilization.**

As with all amphibians, salamanders undergo **metamorphosis**, beginning life as an egg, growing as a larvae and finally maturing into an adult.

Habitat
Salamanders are found in moist or aquatic habitats, such as brooks and ponds. Most live in the northern hemisphere; a few live in the northernmost part of South America. They are common on the European mainland.

Habitat destruction threatens many amphibian species worldwide.

Dorsal view — Parotoid gland, Nasolabial fold, Coastal groove, Coastal fold

Ventral view — Belly, Vent, Tubercles, Gular fold, Mental gland

Salamanders have moist skin and live either near water or under protective moist cover, usually in a forest. They are generally nocturnal creatures. Some species are permanently aquatic, some occasionally take to water, and others are exclusively terrestrial (living on land) as adults.

Metamorphosis means "change of body form and appearance." Amphibians are the only quadruped land vertebrates to undergo metamorphosis. In salamanders, juveniles are similar in appearance to adults.

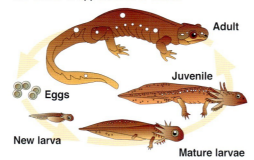

Eggs, New larva, Mature larvae, Juvenile, Adult

Classification and families
Not all scientists agree on the classifications of animals. Here is one method of classifying salamanders.

Kingdom	Animalia
Phylum	Chordata
Class	Amphibia
Subclass	Lissamphibia
Order	Caudata
Suborders	Cryptobranchoidea, Salamandroidea, Sirenoidea

Cryptobranchidae — Giant salamanders
Sirenidae — Sirens
Salamandridae — True salamanders
Ambystomatidae — Marbled salamanders
Amphiumidae — Congo eels
Hynobiidae — Asiatic salamanders
Dicamptodontidae — Pacific giant salamanders
Plethodontidae — Lungless salamanders
Proteidae — Mudpuppies or waterdogs
Rhyacotritonidae — Torrent salamanders

GIANT SALAMANDERS • *Cryptobranchidae*

Hellbender
12 to 29.25 inches long (30 to 74.3 cm)
Long-term survival of this rare animal is threatened by both dam building and pollution. They live in fast-moving streams and never leave the water.

SIREN FAMILY • *Sirenoidea*

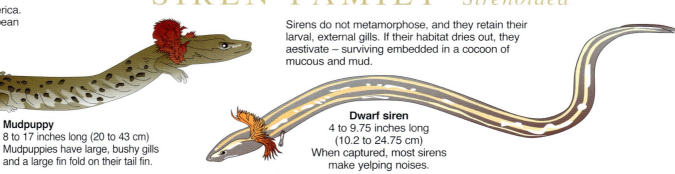

Sirens do not metamorphose, and they retain their larval, external gills. If their habitat dries out, they aestivate – surviving embedded in a cocoon of mucous and mud.

Mudpuppy
8 to 17 inches long (20 to 43 cm)
Mudpuppies have large, bushy gills and a large fin fold on their tail fin.

Dwarf siren
4 to 9.75 inches long (10.2 to 24.75 cm)
When captured, most sirens make yelping noises.

NEWT & SALAMANDER FAMILY • *Salamandroidea*

California newt
5 to 7.75 inches long (12.7 to 19.6 cm)
This species has a warning posture – revealing its belly when threatened.

Red salamander
3.75 to 7.25 inches long (9.5 to 16.4 cm)
Most often found in leaf litter of spring-fed brooks

Newts are members of the 10 genera in the Salamandidrae family that are entirely aquatic or party aquatic as adults.

Salamanders are more often than not terrestrial.

Tiger salamander
6 to 13.5 inches long (15.25 to 34.3 cm)
World's largest land-dwelling salamander

Eastern newt
2.75 to 5.5 inches long (7 to 14 cm)
Adults are aquatic; land-dwelling newts can be found foraging on the forest floor.

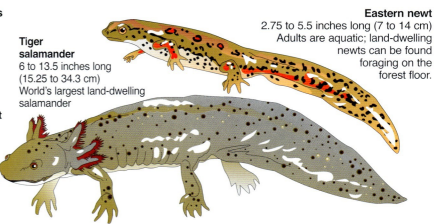

Sargasso Sea

Juvenile eel

Sargassum triggerfish
A vegetarian, unlike other triggerfish that eat coral, sea urchins and other animals. A ball-and-socket joint in the dorsal fin locks it erect, giving triggerfish its name.

Where is it?
The **Sargasso Sea** lies roughly between the West Indies and the Azores and is encircled by two major ocean currents. These currents, the **Gulf Stream** and the **North Equatorial Current,** cause the Sargasso to move in a slow, clockwise drift. Waters of the Sargasso are clear, calm, and filled with seaweed. The currents keep the water quite warm. It rarely rains and the weather is calm, humid, and very hot. The Sargasso has been called "the floating desert." The Sargasso ranges in depth from 5,000–23,000 feet (1,500–7,000 m).

Discovery
When early **navigators** found their ships becalmed in the sea's still waters, they mistakenly believed the ships were tangled in the **Sargassum weed.** Early Greecian, Arabian, Phoenician and Portuguese mariners sailed the edges of the Sargasso. In the 15th century, mariners named the sea "sargaco," the Portuguese word for grape, after the seaweed's bulbous floats. The Sargasso congregates in clusters, and migrates to the middle of the sea, where it is the thickest. Modern motorized ships can sail through it easily.

Serrated frond

Bladder

Freshwater eel
Born in the Sargasso Sea, tightly curled larval eels, called leptocephalli, drift for up to 3 years across the Atlantic. When they reach shore, they undergo metamorphosis, becoming elvers. These transparent juveniles swim into fresh water where they live for 6 to 20 years. Adults grow to 52 inches and are known as yellow or brown eels. As they grow, the undersides turn silver or bronze. At this stage, they are known as silver eels. When sexually mature, they journey back to Sargasso breeding grounds. Spawning takes place in late winter and spring.

Sargassum fish
This 2-to-5-inch long fish has armlike front fins and soft, flabby skin and a flattened body. It sometimes drifts north with the Gulf Stream. Swellings of flesh called illicium function as lures for prey.

Sargassum nudibranch
Nudibranchs resemble slugs. The Sargassum nudibranch has two pairs of flattened lobes which bear small, branched gills. The irregular body shape is good camouflage amongst floating Sargassum, where the nudibranch feeds on tiny animals called hydroids.

Why it is important?
About one-third of the Atlantic's **plankton** — a nutrient-rich mixture of tiny and one-celled plants and animals — is produced in the Sargasso Sea. Many marine animals rely on the weed for food and as a habitat. The Sargasso Sea is an international meeting place for eels. Unknown forces draw the snakelike fish from waters around the world to the Sargasso. Here they mate, spawn and die and their larvae make the journey back to ancestral waters.

Caravels were ships used by the Portuguese

Major currents of the Atlantic Ocean

Greenland
Canada
North Atlantic
Gulf Stream
U.S.A.
EUROPE
Sargasso Sea
AFRICA
Canary
Brazil
North Equatorial

Pelagic sargassum
Sargassum is a type of brown algae. Its golden-green fronds are serrated and feel like plastic. Most seaweeds are anchored to the ocean floor, but the seaweed of the Sargasso is free-floating, or **pelagic**. It stays afloat by growing gas-filled bladders. Accumulated mats of Sargassum support barnacles, sea anemones, worms, crabs, shrimp and fish. The plant produces **asexually** (without seeds) and multiplies when broken by waves. Broken seaweed is sometimes carried by currents to the Gulf of Mexico. Warm waters there accelerate growth, and the Gulf has the second largest quantity of sargassum in the world. Many sargassum leaves are covered with organisms called **bryozoans,** a community of animals attached to the seaweed. As they multiply, they weigh the weed down, pulling it toward the bottom, where it dies, decomposes, and becomes food.

Sargassum also is important to coastal habitats. Fish and turtles feed on shrimp and crabs near the seaweed. When stranded on the beach, the weed holds sand so that land plants may take root, slowing beach erosion.

More than 50 fish species and about 145 invertebrates are linked to sargassum. Four kinds of sea turtles and several marine birds depend on the seaweed for food or shelter.

Sargassum pipefish
Pipefish are relatives of the seahorse. This brownish-green fish has flaps of skin that resemble the blade-shaped leaves, or **fronds**, of sargassum.

Pelagic sargassum

Freaky stuff
Because a portion of the Sargasso lies within the Bermuda Triangle, stories of ghost ships mired in seaweed are often told alongside mysterious tales from the triangle.

Another strange thing about the Sargasso is that it acts as a "catch basin" for the Atlantic Ocean. Objects enter the sea circle and are drawn to its center, where they sink or float forever. This phenomenon has become apparent due to pollution. Currents carry congealed balls of oil from spills (tar balls) into the Atlantic and they become trapped in the Sargasso. Unlike biodegradable waste, they do not sink. The impact this has on the sea life of the Sargasso is being closely watched.

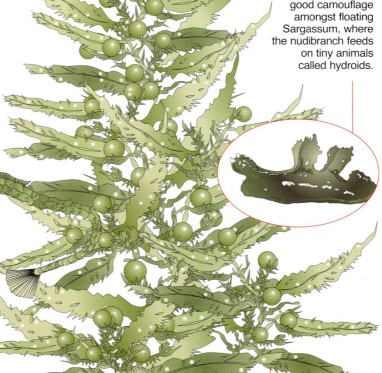

What is a scorpion?

A scorpion is an arthropod, a member of the class of animals called arachnids, and a relative of spiders, mites, ticks and harvestmen. All arachnids have four pairs of legs. There are approximately 1,300 species of scorpions. All have elongated bodies and a segmented abdomen that is tipped with a venomous stinger. As you read the following anatomy section, refer to the diagram to the right.

Scorpion anatomy

Arthropods have an exoskeleton (an outer supportive covering), segmented body and jointed legs. Most arachnids have two body segments. The first segment, or prosoma, has special mouthparts called chelicerae.

The mesosoma:
This section has one pair of pedipalps (pincerlike limbs) and four pairs of legs. The legs, pedipalps and body are covered with thick hairs called setae that are sensitive to the touch. The body regions are protected by a carapace, or head shield.

The metasoma:
The scorpion's body has 12 segments. The last five, called the metasoma, form the curled "tail." At the end is the telson, a bulb-shaped structure containing venom glands and the sharp, curved aculeus to deliver venom.

A scorpion's pedipalps are used for defense and to capture prey. The tips of the legs each have a small organ to detect vibrations in the ground.

On the underside, a scorpion has a pair of sensory organs called pectines. In males, these are usually larger. The pectines sense the texture of surfaces, and are thought to help detect the scent of a mate.

Range and habitat

Although scorpions are thought of as desert animals, they exist in other habitats as well. Grasslands and savannahs, deciduous forests, some pine forests, rain forests and caves are homes to many species of scorpions.

Scorpions have been found under snow-covered rocks at elevations more than 12,000 feet in the Andes Mountains of South America and the Himalayan Mountains of Asia.

About 90 species exist in the United States, and all but four of these are naturally found west of the Mississippi River.

ANCIENT NOCTURNAL PREDATORS
Scorpions

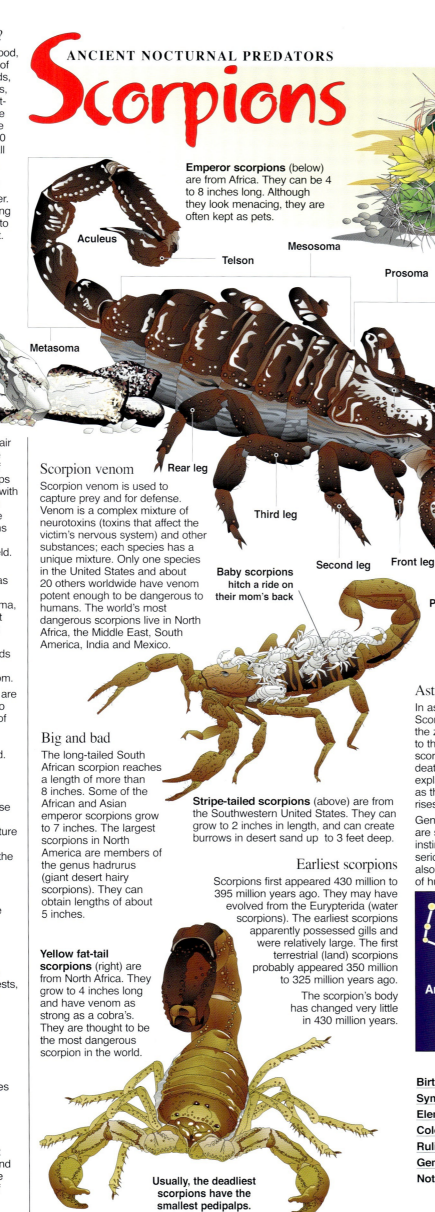

Emperor scorpions (below) are from Africa. They can be 4 to 8 inches long. Although they look menacing, they are often kept as pets.

Scorpion venom

Scorpion venom is used to capture prey and for defense. Venom is a complex mixture of neurotoxins (toxins that affect the victim's nervous system) and other substances; each species has a unique mixture. Only one species in the United States and about 20 others worldwide have venom potent enough to be dangerous to humans. The world's most dangerous scorpions live in North Africa, the Middle East, South America, India and Mexico.

Baby scorpions hitch a ride on their mom's back

Big and bad

The long-tailed South African scorpion reaches a length of more than 8 inches. Some of the African and Asian emperor scorpions grow to 7 inches. The largest scorpions in North America are members of the genus hadrurus (giant desert hairy scorpions). They can obtain lengths of about 5 inches.

Yellow fat-tail scorpions (right) are from North Africa. They grow to 4 inches long and have venom as strong as a cobra's. They are thought to be the most dangerous scorpion in the world.

Stripe-tailed scorpions (above) are from the Southwestern United States. They can grow to 2 inches in length, and can create burrows in desert sand up to 3 feet deep.

Earliest scorpions

Scorpions first appeared 430 million to 395 million years ago. They may have evolved from the Eurypterida (water scorpions). The earliest scorpions apparently possessed gills and were relatively large. The first terrestrial (land) scorpions probably appeared 350 million to 325 million years ago.

The scorpion's body has changed very little in 430 million years.

Usually, the deadliest scorpions have the smallest pedipalps.

Astrological symbol

In astrology, Scorpius (or Scorpio) is the eighth sign of the zodiac. The sign is related to the Greek legend of the scorpion that stung Orion to death. The story was used to explain why the star Orion sets as the Scorpius constellation rises in the sky.

Generally speaking, Scorpios are said to carry with them an instinctive understanding of the seriousness of life, but they also have an excellent sense of humor.

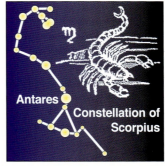

The sign of Scorpio

Birthdates	Oct. 23 – Nov. 21
Symbol	The Scorpion
Element	Water
Colors	Red & black
Ruling planets	Pluto/Mars
Gemstones	Ruby & opal
Notables	Pablo Picasso, Hillary Rodham Clinton, Theodore Roosevelt

Life cycle

In order to survive scorpions' mating behaviors have evolved so that reproduction is ensured.

The breeding season occurs in late spring through early fall. Males may travel long distances to find mates. The male and female scorpion enter into a complicated and characteristic courtship. During the courtship, the male leads the female in a sideways and backward dancelike motion. After this instinctive ritual, the pair mate.

Both males and females may mate repeatedly. Some females will mate while carrying newborn scorpions.

Female scorpions are good mothers. Unlike almost all other animals, female scorpions retain the fertilized eggs in their body for an extended period of time (from several months to a year before the young are born alive), during which time the embryos are nourished.

Birthing lasts several hours to several days. On the average, a female gives birth to about 25 young. They are born live and instinctively climb up on their mother's back as soon as they are born. They will remain there for a period ranging from one to 50 days, until they molt (shed outgrown skin) for the first time. Then they climb down to live an independent existence.

Scorpions periodically molt to reach adulthood. Typically, five or six molts over two to six years are required for them to reach maturity.

Scorpions can live from three to five years, although some may live for 10 to 15 years.

Eat or be eaten

Scorpions are nocturnal (active at night), predatory animals that feed on insects, spiders, centipedes and other scorpions. Larger scorpions may feed on vertebrates, such as small lizards and snakes, or mice.

Although they are equipped with venom to defend themselves, scorpions fall prey to many creatures, such as tarantulas, lizards, birds (usually owls) and mammals (including shrews, mice and bats). Like scorpions, their predators are usually nocturnal.

Seals & sea lions

Seals, sea lions and walruses are ideally suited for life in the frigid waters of the North and South poles. A thick layer of blubber helps keep them warm, and their streamlined body shape allows for speed and grace in the water.

Harp seal (Phoca groenlandica)

The harp seal, named for the harp-shaped mark on its back, is the third most abundant seal in the world, with a population of about 4 million. Baby harp seal pups are famous for their beautiful white fur (which they have for only a couple of weeks).

Harp seals migrate year round, but generally inhabit the North Atlantic and Arctic oceans. During the summer, they migrate to Greenland and the eastern arctic islands. In the fall they move to more southern regions.

These seals can live 35 years or more. They feed mainly on herring, cod and crustaceans.

Threats and dangers

Seals have few defenses against natural predators. In the water, **sharks** and killer whales prey on seals. On land, polar bears hunt them.

Commercial hunting of seals in the 18th, 19th and early 20th centuries severely damaged pinniped populations. Harp seals, especially the white pups, were hunted for their fur. In the late 1980s, public outcry stopped the clubbing of harp seal pups.

Habitat destruction is an ongoing threat to seal populations today. Coastal development and commercial fishermen contribute to population declines. Seals often get caught in fishing nets or tangled up in plastic. Plastic is not biodegradable, so it does not go away, and over time more and more of it ends up in our oceans.

Where pinnipeds live

Most pinnipeds are found in coastal waters, and the majority of them prefer colder climates. The Northern Hemisphere is home to many species. Seals and sea lions come ashore to rest, breed and give birth.

Endangered species

Species	Status
Caribbean Monk Seal	Endangered*
Guadalupe Fur Seal	Threatened
Hawaiian Monk Seal	Endangered
North Pacific Fur Seal	Depleted
Steller Sea Lion	Threatened

* This species is probably extinct; the last known sighting was in 1952.

Earless seals

There are 18 species of phocidae (earless seals). Earless seals are sometimes called **true** seals. These seals do not have ear flaps, but they do have ears. Unlike other pinnipeds, the hind flippers of the seal are angled toward the rear and cannot be rotated forward. This means that they cannot use their rear flippers to walk on land. Instead, they use their front flippers and strong stomach muscles to pull themselves along.

The hooded, or bladdernose, seal is the largest of Arctic true seals. They lead solitary lives on drift ice and eat mostly fish and squid. Males inflate their black hood or blow up the lining of their nasal cavity to attract mates, or when threatened.

Hooded seal (Cystophora cristata)

Ribbon seal (Phoca fasciata)

Banded, or ribbon, seals are found only in the North Pacific. These rare animals are thought to give birth on ice floes, far from the coast.

Bearded seals are named for their abundant whiskers. Their main food sources are crustaceans and mollusks.

Bearded seal (Erignathus barbatus)

Ringed seal (Phoca hispida)

Ringed seals inhabit the far north and are the smallest of seals. They feed on small fish and crustaceans.

Harp seal (Phoca groenlandica)

Harp seals gather in huge groups to breed. Adults can be more than 6 feet long and weigh up to 400 pounds.

Fin-footed friends

Seals, sea lions and walruses belong to a scientific order of mammals called **pinnipeds**, which means "fin-footed" in Latin. There are 34 species of pinnipeds. All are warm-blooded mammals with torpedo-shaped bodies. Pinnipeds can be divided into three families: Earless seals (Phocidae) like the hooded seal; Eared seals (Otariidae) like the **harbor** seal; and Walruses (Odobenidae).

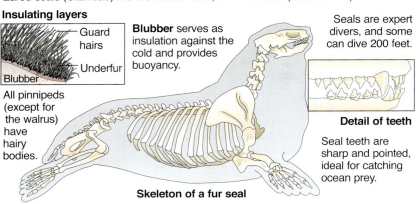

Insulating layers — Guard hairs, Underfur, Blubber

Blubber serves as insulation against the cold and provides buoyancy.

All pinnipeds (except for the walrus) have hairy bodies.

Skeleton of a fur seal

Detail of teeth — Seal teeth are sharp and pointed, ideal for catching ocean prey.

Seals are expert divers, and some can dive 200 feet.

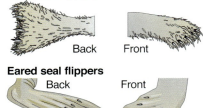

True seal flippers — Back, Front

Eared seal flippers — Back, Front

When swimming, seals use their front flippers to steer. The rear flippers are used in a side-to-side motion (like most fish) to propel them through the water. In the waters, seals can reach speeds of up to 15 mph.

Seals need to breathe air, but when swimming under the ice there is not always a convenient spot to take a breath. So seals chew tunnels up through the ice to create breathing holes. Seals generally need to surface every 7 to 9 minutes, but can stay under water for 15 to 20 minutes.

Eared seals

There are 14 species of fur seals and sea lions. Eared seals have small ear flaps that cover their ears and rear flippers that rotate forward and downward.

Fur seals have fur to protect them from the cold, while sea lions have extra layers of blubber. Sea lions are larger than fur seals and have wider noses. Sea lions are very vocal and are sometimes called "sea dogs" because of their unique **bark**.

These are the seals you see most often at zoos and marine parks. Captive sea lions often bond with their trainers and seem to enjoy performing.

In the wild, eared seals live in the northern Pacific Ocean and along coastal regions in the Southern Hemisphere.

Californian sea lion (Zalophus californianus)

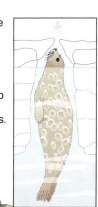

A walrus uses its whiskers to help locate clams and mussels. They live in the Arctic, North Atlantic and North Pacific oceans.

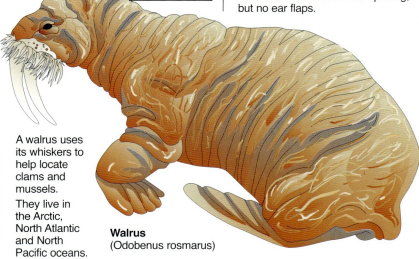

Walrus (Odobenus rosmarus)

Walruses

The walrus is the only pinniped that has **tusks**. Both sexes have ivory tusks, which they use for digging, defense and raking ocean floors for shellfish. Their scientific name, Odobenus, means "tooth walker," reflecting how they pull themselves onto the ice with their tusks. Walruses eat mostly mollusks and fish, but have been known to eat small seals. A large walrus can eat up to 4,000 clams in one day.

A male walrus can can weigh up to 2,700 pounds and grow to 12 feet long. Females are about half that size.

Walruses use their hind flippers for swimming and to walk on land, but like the eared seal they can bend their hind flippers forward. Like the earless seal, the walrus has a small ear opening, but no ear flaps.

Seashells

Parts of a gastropod

Spire — apex, spiral ribs, spines, axial ribs, tubercles, columnella, teeth

Body whorl — columnella folds, lirae, base, anterior canal

What is a seashell?

Seashells are natural objects. They are the exoskeletons of a group of animals called mollusks. The exoskeleton is important to mollusks because it provides shape, rigidity and protection from predators.

What is a mollusk?

The phylum Mollusca includes clams, snails, slugs, octopuses, squid and chitons.

The Latin word mollis means soft. The term malacology (study of mollusks) comes from "malakos," the Greek word for "soft."

Sometimes the term conchology is used for the study of shells alone. Several features are common to all mollusks:

1. A mantle that secretes calcium carbonate in the form of spicules or a shell.
2. A mantle cavity where respiration occurs through gills (aquatic) or through the mantle wall (terrestrial).
3. A body divided into three regions: the head, foot and visceral mass.
4. Three body cavities for kidney, heart and gonad.
5. A ribbon of teeth (radula) used in feeding.

How are they classified?

According to the characteristics of their shells, mollusks are organized into major groupings. Most seashells fall within these groups:

Gastropods (snails) have a single shell, which spirals outward and to one side.

Bivalves (oysters, clams, scallops and mussels) have two-part shells that enclose the body.

Scaphopods (tusk shells) have a single shell that does not coil, but grows in a narrow, slightly curved cone.

Polyplacophores (chitons) have a row of eight overlapping plates.

Cephalopods (octopus and squid) have no shell, although the chambered nautilus does have a shell which coils flatly, in a single plane.

Neopilina are deep-sea creatures that have a single shell which fits over the body like a cup.

Aplacophora are also deep-sea mollusks with no shell. Small spines cover their bodies.

CHITONS

Eight articulating plates make up the shell of the chiton. About 500 species live worldwide in rocky tidal areas. A muscular band surrounds the plates and firmly attaches the chiton to algae-covered rocks.

TUSK SHELLS

The scaphopods, or tusk shells, lie buried in the sandy seabed. A cone-shaped muscular foot protrudes from the hollow base. Tentacle-like filaments help the mollusk capture small prey and feed. Native Americans used shells to decorate their clothing.

Parts of a bivalve

Hinge — lunule, escutcheon

Inside — ligament, lateral tooth, pallial sinus, pallial line, adductor muscle impression

Outside — auricle, spines, scales, radial ornament, concentric ornament, ventral margin

CHAMBERED NAUTILUS

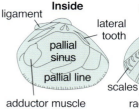

The only cephalopods to produce true external shells are the Nautiloids. The shells are large and lightweight. Inside, closed chambers are filled with gas, allowing the shell to float. All of the Nautiloids live in the Indo-Pacific region.

BIVALVES

Pecten albican — All scallops "swim" by rapidly ejecting water from their shells.

Thorny Oyster — The thorny oyster is actually a scallop. They attach themselves to rocks or coral and grow to 6 inches long.

True Heart Cockle — When the shells are viewed from the side, they resemble a heart.

Black Hammer Shell — This family of mollusks creates a shell with projections along the hinge.

Pen Shells — These shells are thin and brittle.

GASTROPODS

Volute imperialis — Volutes are among the most popular, beautiful and expensive of shells collected.

Black Murex — Most murex shells are heavy-walled and spiny.

Green Turbo — Turbo shells are common worldwide.

Perry's Triton — All Triton shells are thick and have tooth-like grooves on the outer lip.

Hebrew Cone — Markings on the shell resemble the Hebrew language.

Humpback Cowrie — All cowries are highly polished and shiny.

Lettered Cone — Some Pacific cones have venom so poisonous that it can kill humans.

Sundial — These are small to large shells from warm, tropical seas.

Spider Conch — Distinctive finger-like spires project from the shell of these conches.

Tiger Cowrie — Only five species of cowrie are found in North America.

Pacific Triton — Triton shells are large and were used as horns by ancient peoples.

Marlin's Spike Auger — Auger shells are very pointed. The mollusks inside eat marine worms.

Venus' Comb Murex — A very rare and delicate shell from Japan.

Blackened Frog — Members of this family live on or near coral reefs.

Life at the seashore

The best way to find out about seaside plants and animals is to visit the shore and observe them yourself. Go up and down the beach, lift up rocks, look inside the piles of seaweed and dig beneath the sand and mud. Look carefully and you may find creatures such as these.

Great blue heron

Upper beach

Male fiddler crab

Fiddler and sand crabs are burrowers. They like dry, sandy beaches near salt marshes and move with an unusual sidewise gait.

Sandbug

Sand bugs or mole crabs always move backward. They live in the sand and follow the tide as it rises and retreats.

Sand hoppers or beach fleas are tiny crustaceans. Some make their homes in sand and rotting seaweed.

Horseshoe crab

Hermit crab

A **horseshoe crab** has the shape of a horse's hoof. This harmless creature is not really a crab and its closest relatives are scorpions and spiders.

Eastern sand hopper

Herons seek their prey along fresh and saltwater beaches around the world.

Hermit crabs live in tide pools and shallow water all over the world. They make their home inside empty shells and exchange these for larger ones when they have grown too big.

Mermaid's purse Skate egg case

Barnacles are crustaceans that attach themselves to hard surfaces and never leave. Their hard shells protect their soft bodies.

Sand dollar (alive)

Sand dollar (dead)

Gooseneck barnacles

Rock barnacles

Middle beach

Sea urchins have moveable spines. Some live on rocks in shallow water, others live near coral reefs.

Sand dollars or sea biscuits live under the sand in shallow water. They look like large white coins and are often found washed up on the beach.

Sandworms make their home inside a thin tube buried in sand or mud. They can reach 12 to 18 inches in length. Male worms are bright greenish blue and females are reddish orange.

Sea urchin (dead)

Purple sea urchin (living)

Clam worm or Sandworm

Sea anemones are small, slow-moving sea creatures that look like flowers. They attach themselves to rocks and other hard surfaces, and move their tentacles in order to attract shrimp and tiny fish.

Moon jellyfish

Green anemone

Jellyfish or medusa live in the sea, but are often found washed up on beaches and in tide pools. Their jelly-like, umbrella shaped bodies are transparent and their tentacles contain a stinging poison, so be careful not to touch them!

Agarum a large kelp

Blue mussels

Lower beach

Dasya

Sea horses are spiny, fishlike creatures that resemble tiny horses and swim standing up. They live in all the oceans of the world and are related to sea urchins and sand dollars. Found on the Atlantic Coast and the Gulf Coast of Florida in summer, they disappear in winter and we don't know where they go.

Sea horse

Crab larva developing into young crab

Rock crab

Rock crabs like sandy bottoms and rocky beaches. They feed on small plankton-eating sea creatures. Young crabs like tide pools, mature crabs prefer deeper water.

Sea cucumbers have a long fleshy body and are related to sea urchins and starfish. Those that live in the cooler regions of the Atlantic and Pacific are much smaller than tropical sea cucumbers.

Eastern Star

Most starfish have five arms lined with rows of tube feet suckers. They have no brains and a new arm grows when an old one breaks off.

Sea cucumber

Coral is a limestone growth made from the skeletons of tiny animals.

Plankton is the basic food of the sea. These tiny, often microscopic, organisms travel with the currents and tides. They provide more than 90 percent of the food eaten by fish and other marine life.

The two main types of plankton are tiny plants called phytoplankton and fragile swimming animals such as water fleas, called zooplankton.

Phytoplankton use the sun's energy to make food out of sunlight and minerals in a process called photosynthesis. Scientists estimate that phytoplankton make more than 60 percent of the Earth's oxygen.

Small animal plankton (zooplankton) feed on plant plankton (phytoplankton). Then larger zooplankton eat the small zooplankton and these in turn provide food for fish. Some zooplankton stay as plankton all their lives; others turn into larger adult sea creatures.

Catching plankton

You can catch plankton by submerging a bucket in the sea and dragging it. Pull it up and put the contents in a glass. Take a look at it through a magnifying glass or use a microscope to see it even better.

Marine algae

Large marine algae are referred to as seaweed and help purify the air and water through photosynthesis. Here are some algae that can be found on wharves and beaches:

Mermaid's hair

Codium

Sea lettuce

Sargassum

SHARKS

Sharks are one of the oldest vertebrates living on Earth. Sharks were living in the oceans 400 million years ago, 100 million years before dinosaurs evolved. Sharks are found in waters all over the world.

What is a shark?

A shark is a fish, but a fish unlike any other. There are about 360 species of sharks. Sharks are closely related to skates and **rays**, and are cartilaginous. Cartilaginous fish have a skeleton made of **cartilage** instead of bone. Cartilage is a strong, flexible material — human noses and earlobes are made of this.

All in the family

Kingdom	Animalia
Phylum	Chordata
Subphylum	Vertebrata
Class	Chondrichthyes
Subclass	Elasmobranchii
Order	Selachii

Did you know?

- Most sharks can detect blood and animal odors from many miles away.
- Sharks don't blink.
- Small, tooth-like scales cover a shark's body, making the skin of a shark very rough. Dried sharkskin was once used as sandpaper.
- Most fish have a "swim bladder," an organ that helps them maintain certain depths in water. Sharks don't. They have a large liver filled with oil that is lighter than water. This helps sharks float a little, but most still need to swim constantly or they will sink.
- Many sharks have long life spans and can live for 12 or 13 years. Some can even live for 100 years or more.
- Most sharks are cold-blooded. Their inner body temperature matches that of the water surrounding them.

Tiger shark
Galeocerdo cuvier

Interview with a tiger shark

Q. You are a pretty big shark, aren't you?
A. I'm 18 ft. (5.5 m) long, about average for my species.

Q. Where do you live?
A. In oceans all over the world, but I like tropical, warm waters best.

Q. You are considered to be a dangerous shark. Why?
A. Well, it's my nature to scavenge and I will eat just about anything. Can I help it if people fall off boats? Seriously though, I'm not that fond of human meals; I would be just as happy with a seal or a nice turtle, and I love spicy jellyfish.

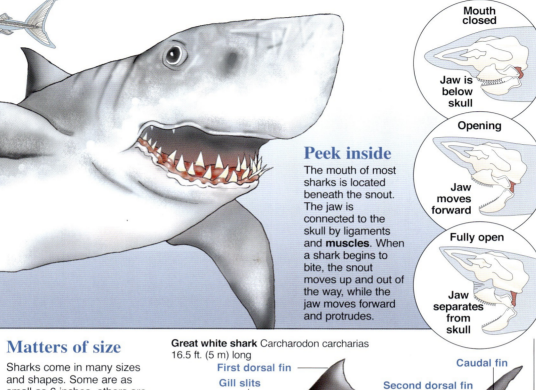

Peek inside

The mouth of most sharks is located beneath the snout. The jaw is connected to the skull by ligaments and **muscles**. When a shark begins to bite, the snout moves up and out of the way, while the jaw moves forward and protrudes.

- Mouth closed — Jaw is below skull
- Opening — Jaw moves forward
- Fully open — Jaw separates from skull

Matters of size

Sharks come in many sizes and shapes. Some are as small as 6 inches, others are as big as a bus and weigh more than two elephants.

NOTE: Great white shark not drawn to scale.

Great white shark Carcharodon carcharias
16.5 ft. (5 m) long

Labels: First dorsal fin, Gill slits, Snout, Caudal fin, Second dorsal fin, Anal fin, Pectoral fin, Pelvic fin

Whale shark
Rhincodon typus
40 ft. (12 m) long

Thresher shark
Alopias vulpinus
20 ft. (6.1 m) long

Smooth hammerhead shark
Sphyrna zygaena
13 ft. (4 m) long

Sand tiger shark
Odontaspis taurus
10.5 ft. (3.2 m) long

Basking shark
Cetorhinus maximus
33 ft. (10 m) long

Sandy dogfish shark
Scyliorhinus canicula
3 ft. (1 m) long

Human
Homo sapiens
6 ft. (1.8 m) long

Feeding frenzy

Sharks are **carnivores** (meat eaters). Most sharks eat fish (often other sharks), squid and octopus. Larger sharks like the great white shark eat just about anything: seals, turtles, small whales, garbage and, very rarely, people. The **whale shark**, the largest of sharks and largest fish in the world, survives primarily on plankton (tiny ocean animals). Shark feeding behavior is stimulated when three or more sharks appear in the presence of food. They can become very excited and vicious, attacking not only the food but each other. This is called a feeding **frenzy**.

Reproduction

One of the ways that sharks differ from most fish is that the majority of sharks fertilize their eggs inside the mother and give birth to already-hatched live young (instead of laying eggs). About 40 shark species lay eggs outside the body. Baby sharks are called **pups**. Some sharks will give birth to more than 100 pups, but that is an exception. Most sharks give birth to much smaller litters — some as small as one or two. Pups begin to swim and hunt almost immediately after birth. Sharks do not look after their young. Some will even eat their pups.

Who is the threat?

Sharks are born **predators**, but that doesn't mean they are man-eaters. There are more than 6 billion people on Earth and about 100 shark attacks each year. About a fourth of those attacks turn out to be fatal. Humans are much more dangerous to sharks: 30 to 100 million sharks are killed by people each year. And 80 shark species face exctinction. Large sharks are suffering the most from over-hunting. But there is hope. Some countries, including the United States, have begun to make laws that protect sharks, instituting sport and commercial fishing limits.

Shark sense

Sharks have highly developed senses. In addition to taste, sight, touch, smell and hearing, sharks also have an "electrical sense" that can detect small **electric** signals of prey. Sharks can also detect vibrations made by animals moving through the water, using a sense called "distant touch."

 Great white shark — Shortfin mako

 Blue shark — Horn-shark

 Goblin shark — Mega-mouth shark

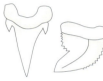 Salmon shark — Tiger shark

Teeth

Sharks have several rows of teeth; many have five to 15 rows. Some sharks have as many as 3,000 teeth at one time. New teeth move forward to replace old or lost ones (a missing tooth can be replaced in about 24 hours). Most sharks do not chew their food very much — instead they swallow large chunks whole.

Gills

Water enters the shark's mouth and passes over the gills, where respiration takes place (oxygen in the water is exchanged for carbon dioxide in the blood), and then passes out of the gill slits. Most fish can pump water over their gills, but the majority of sharks have to swim in order to force water through their mouth and over their gills.

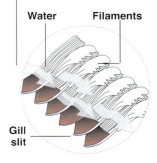

Water — Filaments — Gill slit

SHOREBIRDS

What is a shorebird?
Shorebirds are a diverse group of birds that include avocets, oystercatchers, plovers, phalaropes, sandpipers, stilts, snipes, and turnstones. About 49 species of shorebirds are common visitors to North American wetlands and beaches.

Piping Plover
7-inches
Uncommon and endangered, the delicate Plover nests on sandy beaches, dunes and lakeshores.

Lesser Yellowlegs
10.5-inches
Larger birds with yellow legs and straight bills. They nest on tundra or in woodlands. Most winter in South America.

Red Knot
10.5-inches
Seasonal plumage is pale gray and white in winter, chestnut brown and black in summer. Feeds on sandy beaches and mudflats. Rare in interior wetlands.

American Oystercatcher
18.5-inches
Distinctive orange bill. Feeds in small flocks on coastal beach areas and mudflats.

American Avocet
18-inches
Feeds by sweeping the bill from side to side through the water. Habitat is Lakeshores, marshes and shallow ponds.

Sanderling 8-inches
Plumage is extremely pale in winter. Feeds on sandy beaches, running back and forth with the surf to capture small crustaceans exposed by the waves.

Spotted Sandpiper
7.5-inches
Breeding plumage is beautifully barred. In winter, spotted underparts are pure white. Found in sheltered waterways, marshes, ponds and lakes.

Common characteristics
Shorebirds typically have small bodies, thin legs and webless feet. They range in size from a few ounces to a pound or more and have plumage in many colors.

Shorebird species are residents of wetlands but do not swim. Intertidal mudflats, salt marshes, and estuaries are their habitats. Many species are found on ocean beaches, but many use fresh water wetlands in the interior of North America along their migration paths and for breeding habitat.

They exhibit a wide variety of bill shapes and sizes. These differences allow many species to forage on dry land or in shallow water.

All shorebirds migrate over vast distances. Migratory paths called flyways are used. The birds, geography and the wind determine the direction taken.

Ornithologists (scientists who study birds) believe that an internal compass orients migrating shorebirds. The birds' ability to navigate may depend on the sun, moon and stars. Or light, the Earth's magnetic field, wind, day length, and smell may influence how a bird finds its way.

Help conserve shorebirds
➤ **Support the Federal Duck Stamp Program** Revenues from the sale of Duck stamps provide funds to buy wetlands.

➤ **The Shorebird Sister Schools Program** is designed to educate students about shorebird migration from wintering grounds to nesting sites in the arctic.

➤ **Be a wetlands advocate.** Do what you can to help conserve and protect all wetlands for birds and other wetlands inhabitants.

➤ **Get informed about shorebird issues.** Visit your nearest refuge to view shorebirds and learn about them.

About flyways

The Atlantic Flyway runs from offshore waters of the Atlantic Coast to the Appalachian Mountains. Birds using this flyway usually begin migration from the southern tip of South America or the coast of Chile. Typically, they travel through the interior of South America and cross the Caribbean, reaching the U.S. in the mid-Atlantic states. From there, they move to James or Hudson Bay. This flyway is divided into two regions: Northern Atlantic and the South East Coastal Plain/Caribbean.

The American Central Flyway covers the region extending from the eastern Rocky Mountains to the western edge of the Appalachian Mountains. It includes the Midwest, Mississippi River, and Gulf of Mexico. It is divided into four geographic regions: Northern Plains and Prairie Potholes, Central Plains and Playa Lakes, Upper Mississippi Valley and Great Lakes, and Lower Mississippi and Western Gulf Coast.

The American Pacific Flyway follows the eastern Pacific coastline. It extends from the western Arctic and includes Alaska and the Aleutian Islands. From there, it travels down the Rocky Mountain and Pacific coastal regions of Canada, the United States and Mexico. It blends into other flyways in Central and South America. This flyway is divided into four geographic areas: Alaskan, Northern Pacific, Intermountain West, and Southern Pacific Regions.

FAST FACT:
Though some of these numbers may seem high, studies indicate that the populations of many species of shorebirds are in serious decline.

Shorebird populations
Because they travel so much, it is hard to measure shorebird populations. Estimates put the members of some species in the millions, others at only a few thousand.

Efforts to census shorebirds are taken at specific staging areas during migration. Censuses in recent years report the following numbers in North America:

Delaware Bay: 600,000 shorebirds consisting mostly of Red Knots, Ruddy Turnstones, and Semipalmated Sandpipers

San Francisco Bay, California: 930,000 shorebirds, many species

Bay of Fundy, Canada: 1,000,000 shorebirds, the majority being Semipalmated Sandpipers

South American bird counts show the following populations:

Mar Chiquita Cordoba, Argentina: 500,000 Wilson's Phalaropes and 20,000 Golden Plovers

Bigi Pan, Suriname: 1,000,000 Semipalmated Sandpipers

Wia Wia, Suriname: 2,000,000 Semipalmated Sandpipers and 50,000 Short-billed Dowitchers

Snakes

Many people are afraid of snakes. This may be an ancient and instinctual reaction, because some snakes are deadly. But most of these scaled reptiles are harmless and they play an important role in nature. Snakes are invaluable to people as rodent and pest control aids. There are approximately 2,700 species of snakes around the world, and about 250 of these live in North America.

All in the family

Reptiles are animals with a backbone and scales. Reptiles breathe air and usually lay eggs. Snakes are reptiles, distantly related to the **dinosaurs** of old. Today, the snake's closest relative is the **lizard**. Crocodiles, alligators, turtles and a rare creature from New Zealand called a tuatara are all reptiles.

What's for dinner?

Most snakes will eat any animal they can swallow, so what they eat depends largely on how big they are. Snakes are **carnivorous** (meat-eaters), feeding on a variety of live animals: insects, worms, bird and reptile eggs, frogs, rodents, lizards and even other snakes. Water snakes will eat fish and other marine animals. The largest python is capable of eating a small goat. Some snakes catch their food by striking and grabbing, others by **constriction** (suffocation by squeezing) and some use poisonous venom. Snake jaws are elastic and double-jointed, which allows them to eat their meals whole.

Snake eating a bird

Snake constricting around a rodent

Enemies and defense

Snakes have many enemies, including humans. Hawks, eagles, owls, raccoons, skunks, bears, weasels, hedgehogs, rats, crocodiles and other snakes are just a few of their natural enemies.

Hiding is one of the snake's best defenses, and many snakes use **camouflage** to avoid predators. Many are similar in color to their habitats. Some species use bright colors to warn that they are poisonous, and others use color to pretend to be poisonous. Many snakes will hiss or play dead. Some, like the cobra, try to look bigger by puffing out a special hood near the head. And rattlesnakes use their famous rattles to scare away trouble. **Garter** snakes let off a nasty smell that discourages most enemies.

Snake senses

Sound: Snakes have no ears and use **vibration** instead of hearing to locate prey and avoid danger. They make no vocal sound, but they do hiss and some rattle.

Hissing is the result of air being rapidly forced out of the lungs. Hissing and rattling warn that the snake is frightened or annoyed and may strike.

Sight: Snakes have no eyelids, so their eyes are always open. Most see well enough at close distances and some have excellent night vision.

Taste: The long, forked tongue of the snake is harmless and serves as a feeler and also aids with smell.

Smell: The tongue carries particles to special smelling organs in the mouth.

Anatomy 101

Snakes have long internal organs to match their long and slender bodies. They have more than 300 small, riblike bones attached to a backbone.

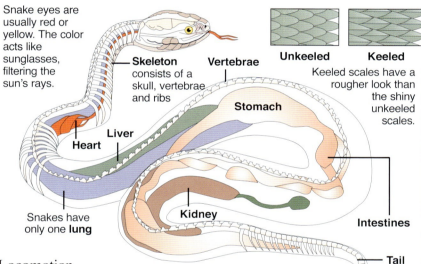

Snake eyes are usually red or yellow. The color acts like sunglasses, filtering the sun's rays.

Skeleton consists of a skull, vertebrae and ribs

Snakes have only one **lung**

Unkeeled **Keeled**

Keeled scales have a rougher look than the shiny unkeeled scales.

There are about 30 species of rattlesnakes living in North America.

Locomotion

Different snakes move in different ways and experts can often identify a snake by its track.

Concertina or climbing motion is similar to the way an inch-worm moves. The snake pulls its body along with its head and upper muscles.

Sidewinding is used mostly by desert snakes like the viper. The snake touches the ground at only two points, leaving parallel tracks on the ground.

Caterpillar crawl or rectilinear motion 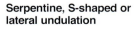 is preferred by large, heavy snakes. Scales act like treads, pulling the body along.

Serpentine, S-shaped or lateral undulation
The snake pulls and pushes against rocks and pebbles. Medium sized snakes use this movement.

Mating and babies

Snakes find their mates by smell and each species has its own mating ritual. Some male snakes will fight each other for the right to mate. Scientists do not know very much about snake courtships.

Most snakes lay eggs, but some (garter snakes for example) give birth to live snakes. Some species lay as many as 100 eggs, while others lay only a few. They nest in warm, damp and shady places, under leaves or rocks, or in hollow logs. The parents do not linger at the nest, leaving the eggs and babies to fend for themselves. Snake eggs are small and not hard like bird eggs, but **soft** and **leathery**.

Baby snakes stay in their eggs for two or three months. They use a special egg tooth to break out of the egg. When they are born they look just like adults, only smaller. Throughout their lives, as snakes grow they shed their old skin. This is called **shedding**, **sloughing** or **molting**.

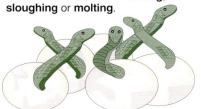

Snake lore — did you know?

During the American Revolution, before the official Stars and Stripes flag, the colonies used a flag with a rattlesnake on it. It had 13 rattles representing the 13 colonies and the words "Don't tread on me."

Some ancient people thought that earthquakes were caused by giant snakes moving underground. Others believed that the earth was born from the egg of a huge snake.

The ancient Greeks believed snakes had powerful healing powers. The early Greek and Roman gods of medicine often held a rod with a snake coiled around it. Today, the caduceus (a winged staff with two snakes) is still used as a medical symbol.

Mambas from Africa are very poisonous and very fast.

Home sweet home

Snakes live just about everywhere in the world, except for New Zealand, Ireland, polar regions and some isolated islands. Most prefer the warm temperatures of the tropics, but many have adapted to the cooler climate of the Northern Hemisphere. Depending on the species, they live on and in the ground, in trees, in water and in sand. All snakes can swim, but only a few (like the giant anaconda) live mostly in the water. Snakes like to bask in the sun to warm up and if they live in colder regions they **hibernate** in the winter.

Poisonous snakes

Snakes almost never attack people unless threatened or surprised.

There are about 600 species of venomous snakes. They use a poison called **venom** to kill their prey. The venom is injected through sharp, hollow teeth called **fangs**.

Poisonous snakes can be divided into three groups: **rear-fanged**, **elapids** and **vipers**.

Rattlesnakes belong to the viper family. They are famous for their rattling tails. **Vipers** strike very quickly. Their long fangs move forward for the bite then retreat.

The largest venomous snake is the **king cobra** from India.

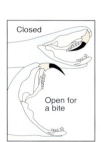

Vipers have long, poisonous fangs that retract when the mouth is closed and jut out when attacking.

As the name suggests, the fangs of **rear-fanged** snakes are at the back.

Elapids have poisonous teeth at the front of their upper jaw.

Spiders

Many people do not like spiders, but they are actually very helpful creatures because they eat insects that might otherwise become pests. Spiders are not insects, but eight-legged animals belonging to the **arachnid** family. There are more than 30,000 kinds of spiders. All spiders have the ability to make silk, but not all spiders spin webs. They are carnivorous (meat-eaters) and most are venomous, using their fangs and poison to catch food. Only a very few spiders are actually dangerous to people.

The life cycle

Spiders are generally solitary creatures who come together only to mate. Males are smaller than females and need to be careful not to be eaten when they come courting.

How long a spider can live depends on the species. Some live a year, others have been known to live 20 years.

Molting

Spiders do not have bones. Their bodies are contained in an outer skeleton covered in hairs and spines called an **exoskeleton**. As they grow they shed their outer skin in a process called **molting**. You may have noticed these empty skins hanging around.

Anatomy 101

Some spiders see better than others. Hunter spiders depend on keen eyesight, while many web-building spiders use a highly developed sense of **vibration** to detect their prey. Most spiders have eight eyes, but some have six, four or only two, and some cave species have no eyes at all. Spiders do not chew; they suck. Their mouths have special appendages that act like straws.

Body of a garden spider

Spiders have two main body parts: the cephalothorax and the abdomen, connected by a thin waist called the pedicel.

Abdomen · **Stomach** · **Pedipalp** are claws used to catch and crush prey
Spinnerets Silk is spun with these organs · **Heart** · **Eyes**
Chelicerae are pointed clawlike limbs with fangs, used to capture and paralyze prey
Leg · **Ovaries**
Silk glands produce the web threads
Detail of foot
Poison gland is connected to the chelicerae and fang

A variety of spider faces

Wolf spider Lycosa carolinensis

Tarantula Lasiodora

Jumping spider Phidippus variegatus

Ogre-faced stick spider Deinopis spinosus

Orb web

Garden spider

Beginning The spider spins and strings a Y-shape.

Extra support More thread is added to the web.

The orb The web gets stronger as it takes shape.

Dinner time The spider waits for its dinner to fly into the web.

Making silk

Spiders use their silk in many ways. Some spin webs or drop lines to catch prey in. Silk is also used for nests. Spiders leave a trail of silk, called a **dragline** behind them. This is used as a lifeline. **Gossamer** is another word for a spider's silk thread.

Spiders make silk using their **silk glands**. Most spiders have five silk glands, but some have as many as seven or as few as three. Each gland produces a different kind of silk. Spider silk does not dissolve in water and is considered to be the strongest natural fiber. Some ancient people used spider silk to wrap wounds and help healing.

Types of webs

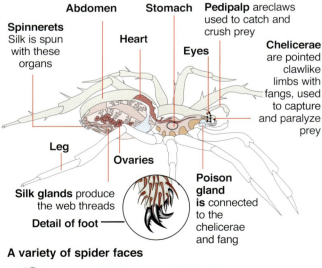

Tangled · **Triangle** · **Bowl and doily** · **Dome**

A few good spiders

Spiders come in many shapes, colors and sizes. They also have many different ways of life. Scientists classify spiders into groups that make studying them easier.

Hunting spiders tend to lie in wait and jump out on their prey from a good hiding place. They generally have large eyes and powerful **chelicerae** to help them find and over-power their prey.

The Lynx spider is a type of hunting spider. It will lie in wait or chase its prey, which often consists of other spiders.

Jumping spider · **Lynx spider**

Jumping spiders are aptly named because they like to pounce on their victims. There are more than 4,000 kinds of jumping spiders.

Trapdoor spiders There are about 20 species of trapdoor spiders. They live in burrows with trapdoor entrances.

Trapdoor spider

Water spiders make silk nests underwater that they fill with air bubbles. They leave the nest only to catch food or get more air bubbles. They are found only in Europe and Asia.

Water spider

Female fisher spider

Fisher spiders live near marshes, ponds and slow moving waterways. They eat insects, but also will catch small fish and tadpoles. Their light bodies make it possible for them to walk on water.

Wolf spiders have hairy bodies and often look and act like other kinds of spiders. They are very quick when chasing down prey.

Wolf spider

Male ladybug spider

Ladybug spiders are one of 20 spider species threatened with extinction.

Bigger is better

Tarantulas are the largest spiders and despite a nasty reputation, are quite harmless to people. Many dig burrows and live in the ground, but some live in trees.

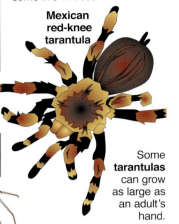
Mexican red-knee tarantula

Some **tarantulas** can grow as large as an adult's hand.

Spiderlings

Most females lay about 100 eggs, but large tarantulas will lay up to 2,000 eggs.

Baby spiders are called **spiderlings**. They hatch inside a special silk sac that their mother spins before laying her eggs. Spiderlings stay in the sac until warm weather arrives. During this time they grow larger and **molt**. When the time is right, they tear a hole in the sac and greet the world. Most spiderlings travel by **ballooning**; soon after leaving the sac they spin silk **draglines** that are caught by the wind. The young spiders are carried by the wind to new areas. Some species of spiderlings will stay with their mother, sharing her web and food for a period of time before moving on.

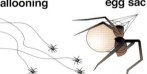
Spiderlings ballooning · **Female with egg sac**

Avoid these spiders

There are only six spiders in North America that are dangerous to people: the brown recluse, the lynx, the black widow, the brown widow, the red widow and the varied widow.

Female black spider

Brown recluse spider

Black widows like warmer climates, but can be found all over North America, except in the extreme north.

Squirrels

These cute and lively rascals can be found just about everywhere except Australia and Antarctica. Some people think of them as pests because they sometimes nest in places they are not welcome (houses, sheds) and they have a knack for getting into bird feeders and taking more than their share. A few species have been known to damage farmers' fields. Most people like squirrels enough to share the back yard and parks with them, but worldwide, the biggest threat to these little animals is the destruction of their forest and grassland homes.

All in the family

Squirrels are a kind of **rodent** (gnawing animals), closely related to mice, rats and **beavers**. There are about 270 species in the Sciuridae (squirrel) family. Squirrels can be divided into three main groups: tree squirrels, flying squirrels and ground squirrels.

Tree squirrels have bushy tails and live mostly in trees. They can be found in forests all over the world. These animals spend most of the day searching for food. The common Eastern and Western gray and fox squirrel are found in North America.

The **Western gray squirrel** is also known as the California squirrel.

Flying squirrels live in trees and are **nocturnal**, searching for food at night. They have a special fold of skin between their front and back legs that allows them to **glide** from tree to tree. Most species are from Asia, but **two** small flying squirrels inhabit North America.

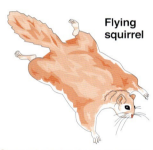

Flying squirrel

Ground squirrels have short tails and tend to be more compact than their cousins. They burrow in open fields. **Chipmunks** are a kind of ground squirrel. So are **marmots** (groundhogs) and **prairie dogs**.

Marmot   Prairie dog

Chipmunk

Squirrels **molt** (shed their fur) twice a year, usually in the spring and fall. Squirrel fur is multi-layered; the inner layer is short and thick to trap air and keep the animal warm. The outer layer is longer and makes up the visible coat. Tree squirrels in North America have many color patterns and variations are often regional.

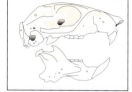

Squirrels have very strong upper and lower **incisor teeth** that grow continually throughout their lives. The incisors are well-suited for cracking nuts, while the back molars grind food into smaller bits.

The tail helps with balance.

The **Eastern gray squirrel** is not always gray. It can be tan, brown or black.

The front feet have four digits and the back have five. Sharp claws and hairless foot pads (some squirrels grow fur on their pads in winter) help the squirrel climb vertical surfaces and give the animal superior gripping control.

Having babies

Squirrels that inhabit the far north tend to mate once a year and have litters of four to eight offspring. Those that live farther south may have a second litter, but the number of offspring is much smaller. The female is pregnant for 36 to 43 days. The newborns are blind and have no hair. The mother raises the young alone. Most tree squirrels become independent in about 8 weeks. Flying squirrels can take 10 or more weeks; this may be because they have to learn how to glide before leaving the nest.

By 5 weeks old, baby squirrels have fur and begin to explore.

Comparing squirrel sizes

Fox squirrel	Abert's squirrel	Gray squirrel	Red squirrel	Northern flying squirrel	Southern flying squirrel
17 to 37 oz. (504-1,062gm)	18 to 33 oz. (681-908 gm)	12 to 34 oz. (338-964 gm)	5 to 11 oz. (338-750 gm)	1.5 to 5 oz. (45-140 gm)	1.4 to 3.5 oz. (40-98 gm)

Dinner time

Squirrels spend a great deal of time eating and collecting food.

They like to eat nuts, seeds, pine cones, bark, sap, insects, eggs, fruit, plant shoots, buds and fungi. What they eat depends on the season and what is available.

If they live in a place with cold winters, squirrels store caches of food in the ground and/or under leaves near their nests. Squirrels usually remember where they have hidden food, but if they forget, they have a keen sense of smell to help them locate a lost meal.

Many squirrels share much of their habitat with humans. They have adapted by nesting close to bird feeders and they can be quite bold if they are used to people feeding them in the park. Some have even developed a taste for human garbage.

Squirrels are helpful to forests when they bury nuts and when they nibble on a certain underground fungus. Unclaimed buried nuts often grow into young trees, helping forest growth. When squirrels eat a **fungus** called **mycorrhizae** they help distribute the fungus spores through the forest. This fungus is beneficial because it aids in the exchange of water, minerals and energy from the sun between soil and plants.

Home, sweet home

Squirrels generally build more than one nest, so that they can move easily if a nest is damaged or threatened. The nest provides essential shelter from the elements and enemies. It is also a safe place to raise young and to store food. Nests are padded with leaves, grasses, chewed bark and other materials. The summer nest is a ball of twigs, leaves and vines woven into the fork of a tree branch. In milder climates some squirrels use a leaf nest year-round. These leaf nests are called **dreys**.

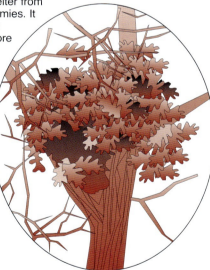

Territories

Most squirrels establish a home **territory** and some will fight to defend it. Territory size depends on food resources and the number of potential mates. Most tree and flying squirrels live alone, but some live with a mate or in a small family group. In winter, some squirrel species will gather in temporary groups called **aggregations**. Aggregations help the animals survive the cold by combining body heat.

Old age

How long a squirrel lives depends a great deal on how large it is. Larger squirrels tend to live longer because they are less likely to be eaten by a predator. Smaller squirrels have shorter life spans, but they compensate by having larger litters more often. Squirrels may live up to 10 or 12 years in the wild, but most die much younger. Hawks, cats, foxes, weasels and snakes are some of the squirrel's natural enemies. Squirrels are also the victims of automobiles and habitat destruction.

Swamp Marsh & Bog

What are wetlands?

According to the U.S. Fish and Wildlife Service, wetlands are defined as areas where "saturation with water is the dominant factor determining the nature of soil development and the types of plant and animal communities living in the soil and on its surface."

In general, wetlands are most often areas between bodies of water and land. Some wetlands are isolated, and most are low-lying. They are areas of great biodiversity, providing habitat for plants and animals. Most North American wetlands are endangered. There were an estimated 220 million acres of wetlands in the continental U.S. in the 1660s. More than half of U.S. wetlands have been lost to development or agriculture in the past 100 years. Many of the remaining ones have been used as dumping grounds and are poisoned by toxic metals, chemicals and pollutants. Continued disregard for these vital areas will negatively affect water supply, flood control, tourism, commerce, and species diversity.

Taking a closer look at the main categories of wetlands and some of the plants and animals that live in them...

Swamps

Like marshes, swamps are populated by grasses, but they also include hardwood and conifer trees and shrubs. The baldcypress grows in the south. Its trunk is wide at the base, forming buttresses that stabilize the tree in wet soil. Knobby projections called knees help the tree to get air.

Bogs

Bogs are acidic wetlands populated by sphagnum mosses, sedge grasses and heath shrubs growing on nutrient-poor soils with rain or snow as their only water source. Thick accumulations of decaying plant materials called peat give bogs their characteristic spongy texture.

Fens

Alkaline wetlands that are nutrient-rich. Dominant plants are sedges, shrubs, and herbs that thrive on calcium. Peat also accumulates in fens, and their bottoms are usually made of limestone. There are two types: Rich fens, fed by flowing surface and ground waters, and poor fens that are sealed off from flowing water, becoming acidic, and transitioning into bogs.

Marshes

Mineral-rich wetlands dominated by grasses, rushes and cattails. Freshwater marshes often transition to swamps. Saltwater marshes form a vital, protective barrier between the ocean and the land. Marshes are shallow wetlands, with water depth of 3 feet or less. They usually form adjacent to rivers, lakes and ponds. Marshes exhibit a high species diversity and are some of the most productive habitat on earth. The rate of photosynthesis is very high, and plant grow this rapid. Here, a water-meadow of wild rice, bulrushes and pondweeds transitions into a pond.

Shrub-carr

Wetland thickets populated by shrubs like red-osier dogwood, willow, alder and chokeberry. Shrub-carr forms between wetlands and uplands and can invade marsh, fen or bog. Here, alder trees and red cedar have established in a grassy marsh. Small rivulets are all that remain of the once open water in this transitional marsh, soon to become a damp meadow with small trees and woody shrubs.

Turtles can be seen basking on roots and logs in swamps. The slider turtle below has a wide red stripe behind its eye, identifying it as the red-eared subspecies.

Carnivorous plants are common to bogs and supplement a nutrient-poor soil with insect food.

Pitcher plant

Amphibians were once common to wetlands, but now are critically endangered worldwide. Below is a tiger salamander, the world's largest land-dwelling salamander, reaching lengths of 13 inches long.

Waterfowl depend on wetland habitats, thousands of birds have adapted to the plants and shelter found there. An American bittern pair (right) hides in the tall marsh grass.

Rodents are common in wetlands. This rodent is a muskrat. Their homes have one or more underwater entrances.

Food chains, webs and ecological pyramids

Wetlands are usually dominant in producer organisms, like plants, bacteria and microscopic protists. Producers are the basis for all food chains, and have the ability to convert raw material (soil nutrients) and energy (solar power) into food, which is in turn, eaten by consumer organisms.

Food chains are a method of showing who eats whom in a habitat. They can be incredibly complex and interwoven because many creatures eat many things.

Usually, producers greatly outnumber consumers, but disruption on any trophic level can negatively impact the balance of an entire food web.

Each layer in this food chain is called a trophic level. If you were able to measure the amount of stored energy or mass of the creatures at each level, you would notice that it reduces with each upward step, forming a wide-based pyramid. Each consumer feeds from one or more of the layers beneath it.

Fourth-order consumer
Raccoon
↑
Third-order consumer
Crayfish
↑
Second-order consumer
Aquatic insects
↑
First-order consumer
Zooplankton
↑
Producers
Phytoplankton and plants

The Leopard frog was once a biology class dissection animal. This frog, like many other amphibians, is in serious decline across North America. They were abundant in most wetlands as few as 20 years ago.

Swans

Swans are water birds closely related to geese and ducks. There are seven species of swan. Four of these are found in the Northern Hemisphere and three live in the Southern Hemisphere. Male swans are called **cobs**. The females are called **pens**, and baby and young swans are called **cygnets**.

Swans are flightless during their annual molt and while their young are still incapable of flight.

Swans cannot take off in sudden flight. Because of their large bodies, swans must run until they get up enough speed to take off.

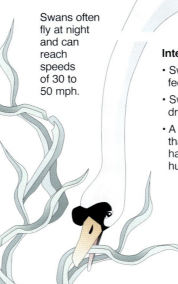

On average, swans in the wild live about 20 years, but they can live 50 years in captivity.

Swans often fly at night and can reach speeds of 30 to 50 mph.

Northern Hemisphere

Mute swan
Cygnus olor

The mute swan is also known as the European swan. Native to Europe and Asia, it can now be found in many parts of the world. The mute swan is named for its **silence**; it is a quiet bird compared with its swan cousins. This bird rarely migrates and tends to live on the same lake or pond year after year. Efforts to reduce populations have been introduced in places where the bird has become competition for native species.

Whooper swan
Cygnus cygnus

The whooper swan is about the same size as the mute swan, but has a straighter neck. The noisiest of swans, the whooper is named for its loud, bugle-like call. Hunting this bird is against the law in Great Britain.

Tundra swan
Cygnus columbianus

The tundra swan is named for where it likes to live — the Arctic tundra. It is the most common swan found in North America. It breeds in the Arctic tundra and winters on the Atlantic and Pacific coasts.

Trumpeter swan
Cygnus buccinator

The trumpeter swan is one of North America's largest birds and the **largest of all the swans**. It has a loud, deep, trumpet-like call. This bird was on the verge of extinction in the early 1900s, but conservation efforts have helped population numbers improve. There are about 6,000 trumpeter swans today. Reintroduction into former ranges is continuing.

Southern Hemisphere

Black swan
Cygnus atratus

The black swan is originally from Australia, where it gathers in huge flocks of up to 50,000 birds.

Black-necked swan
Cygnus melanocoryphus

The black-necked swan is from southern South America. When it honks it sounds a bit like a small trumpet. This swan has been hunted almost to extinction.

Coscoroba swan
Coscoroba coscoroba

Like the black-necked swan, the coscoroba is also from South America. It is small and white with a shorter neck than other swans. It is also the smallest of the swans. This swan sounds a lot like a goose when it calls.

Interesting facts:
- Swans are messy eaters and will often leave a feeding area littered with torn-up vegetation.
- Swans have special glands that allow them to drink saltwater.
- A swan's neck has 24 to 25 vertebrae — more than any other warm-blooded animal. Geese have 18 or 19, and mammals, including humans and giraffes, only have seven.

Dinnertime
Swans feed primarily on underwater vegetation, but they also eat land grasses. They do not generally use their whole bodies to plunge below water for their food. They instead use their long necks to reach lake and pond bottoms. They can keep their heads under water an average of 10 to 20 seconds.

Family units
Swans are very loyal and most stay with the same mate for **life**. They build huge nests of grass and other plant material. An average swan clutch (a nest or brood of offspring) consists of 4 to 6 whitish eggs. The eggs hatch in 30 to 35 days. The young emerge with a thick gray **down** (small, soft feathers). Cygnets often ride on their parents' backs. They can fly at 7 to 14 weeks of age. Young birds often stay with their parents until they have reached full maturity (2 to 3 years).

Myths and legends
- The Greek god Zeus sometimes assumed the form of a swan.
- The ancient **Celts** associated swans with healing waters and the sun. Many myths tell of swans changing into human form, and vice versa.
- It was once believed that the swan only sang right before its death — hence the origin of the expression "swan song."
- Swans were often used as figureheads on ships. As swans don't plunge below the waves, sailors believed the swan brought good luck.

TIGERS

The miacis lived in European forests during the Eocene period. It was about 8 inches long.

What are tigers?
Like many carnivores, tigers descended from a small prehistoric animal called a miacisd. The miacisd lived millions of years ago and evolved into bears, dogs and cats.

Approximately 2 to 3 million years ago, in Central and East Asia, an early group of cats began to develop characteristics that exist in today's tigers. These traits include tawny fur and black stripes. From this region, the striped cats moved north into Russia and south and east into the Indonesian islands. Eventually, they reached as far south as Bali, southwest throughout India, and west as far as the Caspian Sea.

Tiger classification
Scientists use a system called taxonomic classification to arrange animals into progressively smaller groups based on their similarities. Each group contains the groups beneath it in the hierarchy. Here's how tigers are classified:

Kingdom animalia
Cats are animals, not plants, protists or bacteria. Kingdoms are the largest groups.

Phylum chordata
Animals with backbones.

Class mammalia
Mammals give birth to live young, have fur, are warm-blooded, and nurse their young with milk.

Order carnivora
Carnivores eat meat.

Family felidae
Felidae are felines. Three sub-families are included.

Subfamily Acinonychinae
The Cheetah is the only member of this subfamily.

Subfamily Felinae
The "little cats." Although some can grow quite large, they are called little cats. They cannot roar, and most of these cats have pupils that form slits when they are closed.

Subfamily Pantherinae
The "big cats." In bright light, their pupils sappear round, rather than slit.

Tiger habitats

Critical situation
Today, tiger territory is severely limited in the forests and grasslands of Asia. They can range from tropical areas of the Far East to the Arctic Ocean, roaming the snowbound forests in Siberia.

There were once eight subspecies of tigers. Only five live today. Balinese, Javan and Caspian tigers are all extinct. The five remaining subspecies are critically endangered and efforts are being made to preserve what few thousand cats remain. Despite efforts to preserve them, poaching, habitat loss and loss of genetic diversity threaten tigers worldwide. Scientists predict the tiger will survive only with human intervention and complete protection.

Indochinese
Centered in Thailand, this subspecies can also be found in Myanmar, Cambodia, Vietnam, Laos, Malaysia, and southern China. Population estimates are based almost exclusively on secondary evidence. It is believed that 1,000 to 1,700 survive in the wild. Sixty live in zoos throughout Asia and the United States.

South China
This tiger is on the very brink of extinction. Only a few sightings have been reported over the last 10 years. Optimistic estimates place them at two or three dozen. Even if protected completely, such a small wild population is unlikely to survive.

Tiger skull

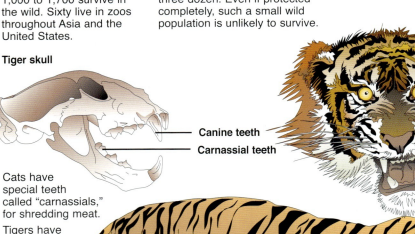

Cats have special teeth called "carnassials," for shredding meat.

Tigers have four sharp canine teeth.

Sumatran
The smallest in size of the five living tiger subspecies. For over a million years, they have lived in the once extensive tropical jungles of Sumatra, Indonesia. Wild populations are now heavily fragmented and estimated to be around 600.

The largest of all the tigers, **Siberians** are the biggest cats on Earth and can exceed 9.8 feet in length. Members of this subspecies are found along a strip of land in far eastern Russia, along the coast of the Sea of Japan. As many as 400 Siberians live there, with some still inhabiting the northern portions of Korea and China.

Bengal
The most commonly known tiger subspecies. Estimates range between 3,000 and 4,500 across India, Bangladesh, Nepal, Myanmar and Bhutan. Several hundred are in captivity, primarily in Indian zoos.

TREES

Trees are the largest plants on Earth and the oldest living things. They can be taller than skyscrapers and some live thousands of years. Trees make up our forests and they shade our houses and gardens. They help clean the air we breathe and keep soil from washing away. We use their wood for shelter, furniture and paper, and they are also a source of food and medicine. Five thousand years ago, trees covered more than three-quarters of the world's land; now as much as 90 percent are gone and more trees disappear every minute.

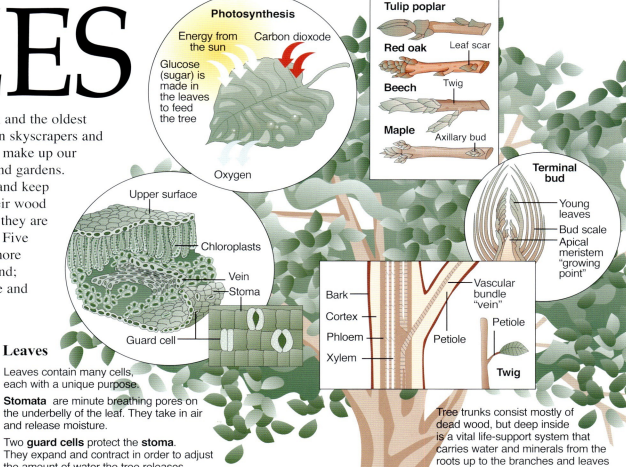

Looking at a tree

There are five basic tree groups. Needle leaf trees (**conifers**) such as pines and firs, and **broadleaf** trees, such as oaks, maples, eucalyptuses and palm trees, are the most common. Unusual tropical and sub-tropical species include the **tree fern**, the **ginkgo** and the **cycad**. Tree ferns can reach over 70 feet and look like slender palms topped with fronds. The ginkgo or maidenhead tree has a silhouette similar to an elm or willow and is often found in parks and botanical gardens. Cycads are cousins to the conifer and resemble squat palm trees with large red or yellow cones.

Broadleaf trees are **deciduous**, they lose their leaves every autumn.

Coniferous trees generally have leaves known as scales or needles.

Tropical trees like the palm are broad-leaved trees.

Redwoods, eucalyptus and sequoias can grow to giant size. The General Sherman Tree, a sequoia in California's Sequoia National Park, is over 275 feet and one California redwood has reached 368 feet. The tallest tree on record was a eucalyptus. Over 430 feet high, it was cut down in Victoria, Australia, in the 19th century.

Leaves

Leaves contain many cells, each with a unique purpose.

Stomata are minute breathing pores on the underbelly of the leaf. They take in air and release moisture.

Two **guard cells** protect the **stoma**. They expand and contract in order to adjust the amount of water the tree releases.

The cells on the upper side of the leaf are called **chloroplasts**. They contain **chlorophyll** and act as solar panels, using the sun's energy to convert carbon dioxide and water into food in the form of sugars and starches. This process is called **photosynthesis** and means "putting together with light." Photosynthesis also produces the **oxygen** that helps to keep the air clean.

Leaf litter is the dead and rotting leaves and twigs that collect beneath a tree. **Insects** use it for food and refuge. In turn, they help with its decomposition.

Roots

Roots are a tree's anchor and help to keep it standing upright. A root system consists of a heavy, wood-like primary root for support and fine webs of hair-like secondary roots called feeders. These turn into primary roots and are replaced as the tree grows. A tree's root system needs fertile soil in order to absorb enough oxygen, water and nutrients.

Tree trunks consist mostly of dead wood, but deep inside is a vital life-support system that carries water and minerals from the roots up to the branches and leaves through a unique plumbing system of small tubes called **xylem**.

Bark offers protection from harsh elements and gnawing animals, as well as from birds and insects that might bore and drill the tree's surface. Bark grows and stretches; its seasonal rings and cracks are as individual as a fingerprint.

A tree's outward growth occurs in the **cambium layer**. Most mature trees grow wider by an inch a year. The cambium produces a **ring** each year, which you can count to get a tree's age. The circumference or distance around a tree is called the **girth**.

Every year

Germination

In order to grow, a tree needs the right combination of **sunlight, oxygen** and **temperature**. Seeds start sprouting with the coming of spring. They take in water and feed on shell-stored nutrients. When the seed cracks its coat, minuscule roots stretch into the earth to hold the plant firm and to suck up more moisture.

Germination of seedling

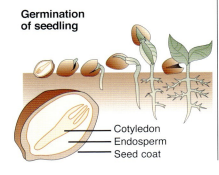

Pollination

Flower pollination is important to a tree's reproductive cycle. Once a blossom has matured, the anthers of its stamen open to release pollen grains. Anemophilous trees are pollinated by the wind. Others, called entomophilous trees, rely on small animals and insects. Fertilization is a result of pollen touching the flower's stigma, making it possible for the male and female cells to join.

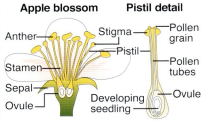

Autumn

In fall, as daylight decreases, leaves on deciduous trees change their color. The chlorophyll manufacturing process, which uses sunlight to make carbohydrates, shuts down, revealing leaves in glorious autumn shades. Temperature, light and water supply determine their color intensity, so for brightly colored leaves the best weather is clear, dry and cool. Leaves fall or are blown off because a special layer of cork cells grows between the leaf and the tree, leaving a protective scar. This process allows the tree to save its energy over the winter.

Food for thought

The fruit of a tree is its seeds. The type and shape of a seedcase will determine whether a seed is dispersed by mammals, birds, wind or water. Often seeds, such as walnuts and pecans, provide food for people as well as small animals and birds. When planted, or left on the ground in the right conditions, seeds will germinate and a new tree will grow.

TROUT

What are trout?
Trout are freshwater fish belonging to the salmon family, **Salmonidae**. They usually live in clear, cool streams and lakes, but many species are **anadromous**, meaning they ascend rivers from the sea to breed. Trout are native to North America, northern Asia and Europe. Several species were introduced to Australia and New Zealand in the 19th century by amateur fishing enthusiasts, where they have displaced several native species.

Classification
There are five types of fish in the large **Salmonidae** family (whitefishes, graylings, trout, salmon and char). Trout are members of the sub-family **Salmoninae**:

Oncorhynchus (Pacific salmon and trout) includes 10 species worldwide.

Salmon (Atlantic salmon and Brown Trout) includes two species in North America.

Salvelinus (fish called Char) includes five species in North America.

Migratory fish
Salmon are migratory and return to their **natal streams** to breed when mature. Dams built by man prevent the fish from moving upriver. Declining wild populations have led to the development of **fishways**, or **fish ladders**. These structures are placed on or around man-made barriers to aid migration. Most fishways enable fish to pass around the barrier by swimming and leaping up a series of relatively low steps into the waters on the other side. For successful migration, the water's velocity has to be great enough to attract fish to the ladder, but not strong enough to wash fish back downstream or to tire them to the point where they can't continue their journey. There are five types of fish ladders:

Rock ramp fishways
Pool and weir
Vertical-slot fish passages
Denil fishways
Fish elevators

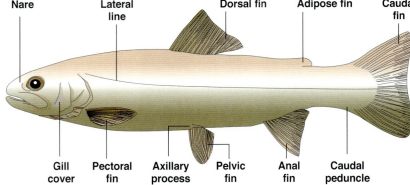

Life cycle of rainbow trout
Water temperature determines the time most trout and salmon breed. It also determines how long it takes for the fertilized eggs to hatch.

A sperm (milt) penetrates the egg through the micropyle, leaving the tail behind.

A secreted enzyme helps the hatching trout break through the eggshell.

Rainbow-trout fry develop purple or blue "parr" marks.

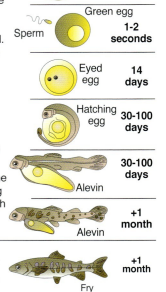

History of trout
It is thought that Salmonidaes earliest ancestors appeared about 100 million years ago. By the end of the **Miocene epoch** (24 million to 5 million years ago), major branches of Salmonidae were established in the fossil record.

Trout anatomy
The fins of trout are entirely without spines. All trout have an **adipose** (fatty) fin along the back, near the tail. Many isolated populations have become morphologically different. Many distinct populations show no significant genetic differences, so what may appear to be a large number of trout species is actually considered to be a smaller number by most **ichthyologists** (scientists who study fish). Trout of the eastern United States are a good example of this.

Fun fact An image of a trout will be struck onto the Washington state quarter.

The brook, aurora and silver trout display very different physical characteristics and coloration, but, genetically, they are one species – Salvelinus fontinalis. Trout color and patterning provide camouflage. Coloration changes as a fish migrates to new habitats. Trout newly returned from the sea appear silvery, while another genetically similar fish that has been living in a stream or lake may bear pronounced markings or bright color. Generally, wild fish appear to have more vivid colors and patterns than those raised on farms.

Holyoke fish elevator
On the Connecticut River

Fish trap allows counting and movement over dam

Fast moving water attracts fish

Hoist lifts the elevator to the opening into the trap

Crowding area draws fish into elevator

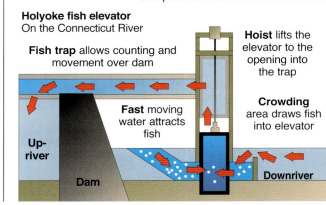

Genus oncorhynchus

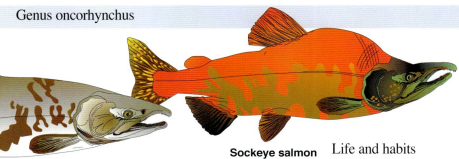

Pink or humpback salmon 18 to 24 inches long; the most abundant Pacific salmon species

Chum salmon 24 to 31 inches long; a very abundant Pacific salmon species

Sockeye salmon 21 to 26 inches long; the most important commercial salmon species in North America

NOTE: All examples are male; spawning colors

Genus salmo

Atlantic salmon 30 to 36 inches long; it is unlikely this once-abundant species will return to former numbers.

Brown trout 10 to 12 inches long; a European species introduced to North America in 1880.

Important food fish
Trout are sought recreationally by **sport fishermen**. They are often raised on farms to stock waters that have been overfished. They can be caught with a regular rod and reel, but **fly fishing** was developed primarily for trout and has extended to other fish species. Trout are capable of "learning," and in catch-and-release fisheries, they become harder to catch each time they are landed.

Genus salvelinus

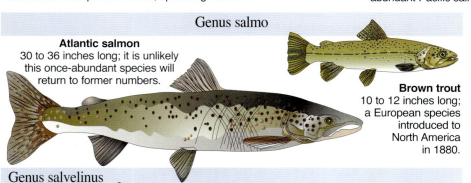

Arctic char (Taranet's char) 12 to 18 inches long; the most complex of the Salmonidsto classify

Bull trout 8 to 10 inches long in streams; 12 to 18 inches in lakes. The bull trout is a predator of other fish.

Brook trout 12 to 28 inches long; this species has adapted to warmer waters; it is the least specialized form of char.

Life and habits
Trout are **opportunistic feeders** and will eat aquatic invertebrates and insects. In lakes, **zooplankton** is a large part of the trout diet. Large lake-dwelling trout will become **piscivorous** (fish eating), preying upon small fish.

Trout dwell in cold water, and their body temperature is the same as the water around them. Their growth rate is determined by water temperature and continues until death. They can live 25 years or more, but the average life span is six or seven years.

All trout, salmon and char begin and end their lives in fresh water. Most of them reproduce in cold, moving water by creating excavations called **redds**.

Atlantic salmon can spawn more than once; Pacific salmon die after spawning.

Turtle basics
Turtles and tortoises are **reptiles,** and are related to lizards, crocodiles and snakes.

All of them have a **skin, scute** or **scale** covered **shell.**

They are **cold-blooded,** meaning their body temperature changes as the air temperature of their environment changes.

Even if they spend most of their lives in the water, they return to the land to nest and lay **eggs.**

Where they fit in
Turtles and tortoises are members of the animal order called **chelonia.** In 300 million years they have changed little.

They are descendants of primitive "stem" reptiles called Cotylosaurs (now extinct).

There are 250 to 300 species.

Tortoises are commonly land-dwelling, while turtles or terrapins are aquatic.

Traits
Turtles and tortoises are divided into two groups based on the way the turtle withdraws the head.

Pleurodira are the side-neck turtles. They fold the head to the side as it is drawn into the shell, and are found in South America, Africa and Australia.

Cryptodira are the hidden-neck turtles. They fold the neck into an S-shaped curve and have eight bones in the neck.

Anatomy
The shell of a turtle is the feature that has allowed it to survive for millions of years. It is a specialized structure that is fused to the turtle's bones. The shell is composed of two parts – the carapace, or upper shell, and the plastron, or bottom shell.

The spine is not flexible, meaning the only body parts a turtle can move are its legs, neck and tail.

Turtle behavior
Being ectothermic (cold-blooded), most turtles and tortoises must spend part of the day basking in the sun to raise their body temperature and activity level. When it is cold, they become sluggish, and in winter, they go into torpor, a dormant state of inactivity much like hibernation.

Females usually use the same spot every year to lay eggs.

TURTLES and TORTOISES

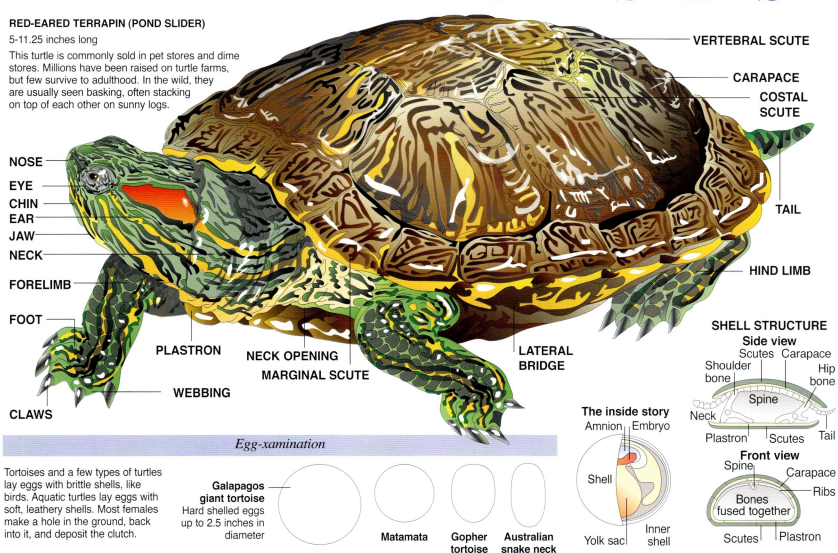

RED-EARED TERRAPIN (POND SLIDER)
5-11.25 inches long

This turtle is commonly sold in pet stores and dime stores. Millions have been raised on turtle farms, but few survive to adulthood. In the wild, they are usually seen basking, often stacking on top of each other on sunny logs.

Egg-xamination
Tortoises and a few types of turtles lay eggs with brittle shells, like birds. Aquatic turtles lay eggs with soft, leathery shells. Most females make a hole in the ground, back into it, and deposit the clutch.

Galapagos giant tortoise — Hard shelled eggs up to 2.5 inches in diameter

Matamata · Gopher tortoise · Australian snake neck

Freshwater turtles

MATAMATA
15 inches long

This South American turtle is the strangest-looking turtle on Earth. Along the head and neck of the Matamata are fleshy knobs that sway in the current. Its shell is often algae-covered, and the turtle lies in wait for prey at the muddy river bottom. To catch fish, it opens wide, sucking water and fish into its mouth.

SPINY SOFT-SHELL
Males 5-9 inches long
Females 6-18 inches long

Easy to recognize because its shell is covered with soft, leathery skin, not scales or scutes. It has a long snout that is used like a snorkel to breath while remaining submerged.

Land-dwelling turtles

BOX TURTLE
4-8.5 inches long

The box turtle has a hinged plastron that allows it to completely withdraw its head, feet and tail into a tight fitting package that cannot be pried open by even the most clever predator. Youngsters hatch in fall and hibernate all winter, growing to about 4 inches long. If they survive, they may live to be 100 years old.

DESERT TORTOISE
9-14.5 inches long

This tortoise eats grasses, and feeds during the early morning and late afternoon to avoid the blistering heat of midday. During this time they hide in burrows excavated in the soil which can reach up to 30 feet in length. During winter, many may group together in a single burrow, becoming active again in the early spring.

Marine turtles

LEATHERBACK
50-84 inches long

These giants hold all records for sea turtles. They are the largest, heaviest, fastest and longest-living marine reptiles. Their bodies are smooth, streamlined and flexible, and they can swim up to 100 meters in 10 seconds.

LOGGERHEAD
31-48 inches long

A night-nester from May until August, though coastal area development has destroyed many nesting sites. In the past, this species could reach 1,000 pounds, but these giants are gone now that marine turtle populations are critically endangered.

Underfoot

Exploring the world's most expansive ecosystem

A new realm to consider

Go outside. Look down. Really look down. In fact, squat down and consider what you're standing on.

There may be over a billion living things under your left foot. Who knows how many more billion are under your right foot. And that isn't including the more obvious insects, plants, toads, birds, worms and slugs you may observe near your feet right away.

Every landmass on Earth is covered with some kind of soil. The uppermost layers of the soils of the Earth are habitats for a large community of living things.

Unseen world

Soil is a complex, living environment. Five factors contribute to the mineral, organic and moisture content of soil, and determine what type of life it can support: **microbe action, weather, topography, parent material and time scale.**

Scientists have classified the world's soils into 12 groups which, as a whole, form the world's largest ecosystem.

Consider this:

- Each gram of soil can contain 1,000,000,000 microbes or more. (Yes, that's a billion.)
- There are 10,000 known species of soil microbes, exhibiting more biodiversity than the entire Mammalia class.
- You could fit 28 billion soil microbes in the space of just one pygmy shrew, one of the world's smallest mammals. Here's a pygmy shrew at actual size:

Pygmy shrew

Know the lingo

- The scientists who study soil are called **pedologists.**
- An area of an individual kind of soil is called a **polypedon.** Polypedons can be very large, like a prairie, or as small as a square meter.
- **Mineral soils** are those that contain less than 20 percent organic matter.
- **Organic soils** are those that contain more than 20 percent organic matter.
- Particles in the soil are brought together by soil organisms. This process is called **aggregation.**

TYPES OF SOILS

Soils are constantly being formed and destroyed. Some rocks are softer and more easily pulverized by weather or decomposition. As rocks erode, their mineral content determines the kind of soil they eventually will become.

The size of the mineral particles of an eroding rock also contributes to soil **texture.** Densely packed microscopic particles, such as **clay,** do not drain well.

Sands are the largest soil particles. Their grains can be both seen and felt.

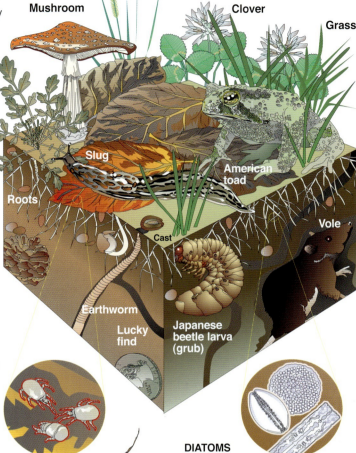

SOIL'S BEST FRIEND

Earthworms constantly burrow through the uppermost layers of soil. They pull plant debris into their burrows to eat and soften the soil by moving through it. Fertile droppings, called casts, are the byproduct of this activity.

SOIL MITES

Members of the **Acari** order. They are eight-legged animals that feed on leaf litter. Scientists estimate that there are 500,000 kinds of mites.

DIATOMS

Part of marine and freshwater algae. Their shells are made of silica and form two halves that fit together like a lidded box. When they divide, each offspring takes half of the shell and then grows the other half. Round diatoms cannot move; elongated ones can. When fossilized, they are called diatomaceous earth.

CENTIPEDE

Its name means "100 feet," but most have only 36 to 40 feet.

Activity corner

Make a Tullgren funnel

What you need:

- Quart jar with wide mouth
- Funnel that fits in the jar mouth
- Sieve, mesh or piece of screen that fits in the funnel
- A strong lamp
- A soil sample (compost piles provide the most fun)

How to do it:

1. Assemble the funnel as shown.
2. Turn on the light.
3. Leave undisturbed for several hours.
4. Check the jar for your minute zoo by pouring the contents onto a white dish. Work quickly so you don't damage your discoveries.

Record your observations.

HOW IT WORKS

The Tullgren funnel uses light to isolate small invertebrates and insects from a soil sample. Usually, soil-borne creatures flee from sunlight, preferring to live in damp darkness.

The sieve prevents soil from falling into the jar, but allows the tiny animals to escape the light.

Be a responsible scientist and return your sample and its inhabitants to the area where you found them.

FOR FURTHER STUDY

- Try another kind of soil — how does it differ?
- Try another sample from the same place in a different season.

FIELD GUIDE

- Identifying soil creatures can be difficult. A hand lens can help.
- Classify your critters by number of legs:

6 legs: Insect

8 legs: Spider or mite

More than 8 legs: Isopod, millipede or centipede

Jumpers: Springtail

Wrigglers: Worms

Slime trailers: Mollusks

A closer look at some factors that influence soil formation

Microbe action

Soil biologists study the living creatures in the soil. Some are so tiny they can be seen only with a powerful microscope. These tiny creatures, called microbes, are the most abundant soil organism. Bacteria, protists and some fungi are microbes. They must be surrounded by water to live.

Soil bacteria play a vital role in the Earth's health. They are largely decomposers, helping to recycle dead plants and animals into nitrogen and carbon, the building blocks of life.

Protists are simple organisms such as amoebas, diatoms or ciliates.

Slime molds are a funguslike group of protists. They reproduce by forming spores.

Time scale

Fine soils take a long time to form. There may be billions of microbes at work doing decomposition, but it still takes about 500 years for them to form an inch of topsoil.

Soil formation begins when rain, snow, ice, freezing temperatures and environmental forces erode rock. The material that results is called **parent material,** which breaks down further into mineral particles.

Soil organisms begin to populate the parent material. Plantlike lichens (the **symbiotic** relationship of a fungus and algae) produce acids that **decompose** rock. When soil organisms die, their bodies collect with the mineral particles.

Soil horizons appear as the soil develops. The uppermost, or **A Horizon,** contains the most organic material. It is also known as **topsoil.** The deepest layer, or **C Horizon,** is sometimes called **subsoil.**

Soil development continues over time. Well-developed soils can support a diverse layer of vegetation. Some soils may include a middle layer, or **B Horizon,** that is rich in minerals that have been washed downward from the topsoil with drainage water.

Weather

Temperature and moisture dictate how quickly the microbes can work. Generally, heat and moisture cause microbes to move fast, reproduce in abundance, and consume organic material quickly. That's why a compost pile heats up and breaks down faster in the summer. Rock and stone depend on water and wind to pulverize them into fine particles. Plants help hold the newly formed soil with their roots, and worms, small invertebrates and insects then begin their work.

VENOMOUS animals

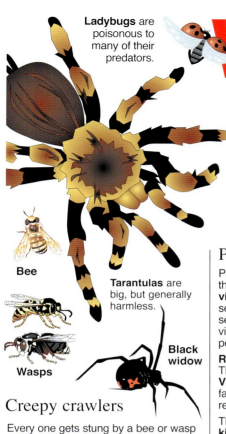

Ladybugs are poisonous to many of their predators.

Tarantulas are big, but generally harmless.

Bee

Wasps

Black widow

There are many poisonous creatures in nature, all with varying degrees of toxicity. Most are not deadly to people. Their poisons are used to discourage attacks and to aid in hunting. Some animal bites and stings can be life-threatening. If you are stung or bitten by a venomous animal, always seek medical treatment. There are anti-venom serums available that can save your life.

Creepy crawlers

Every one gets stung by a bee or wasp eventually and unless you are **allergic** it is more a painful inconvenience than anything else. But some bites are more dangerous than others...

Brazilian butterfly caterpillar

Many insects advertise that they are poisonous with bright colors. Many harmless creatures mimic the dangerous ones.

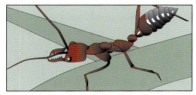

The Australian **bulldog ant** has a poisonous stinger.

All spiders are venomous, but only a few are dangerous to people. Just half an inch long, the black widow spider is one of the most poisonous of all North American spiders. Tarantulas are the largest spider. Their bite is painful, but not deadly.

Scorpions are relatives of the spider. They range in size from a quarter inch to 8 inches — smaller scorpions are often more lethal. About 30 species live in the U.S and of these only one or two are venomous. A poisonous sting causes severe pain, vomiting and sweating in humans, and if left untreated can result in death.

The scorpion's stinger is located at the tip of its tail.

Scorpion

Poisonous snakes

Poisonous snakes can be divided into three groups: **rear-fanged, elapids** and **vipers**. Snakes can't hear and they don't see very well. But they do have a keen sense of smell and are sensitive to vibration. Snakes almost never attack people unless threatened or surprised.

Rattlesnakes belong to the viper family. They are famous for their rattling tails. **Vipers** strike very quickly. Their long fangs move forward for the bite, then retreat, folding into the roof of the mouth.

The largest venomous snake is the **king cobra** from India. It can grow up to 18 feet long and its poison is powerful enough to kill a person in 15 minutes. It has been estimated that cobras kill 10,000 people a year in India. Cobras and mambas belong to the elapid group.

There are 30 species of rattlesnakes living in the North America.

Diamondback rattlers are more poisonous than other rattlesnakes.

Rattlesnake

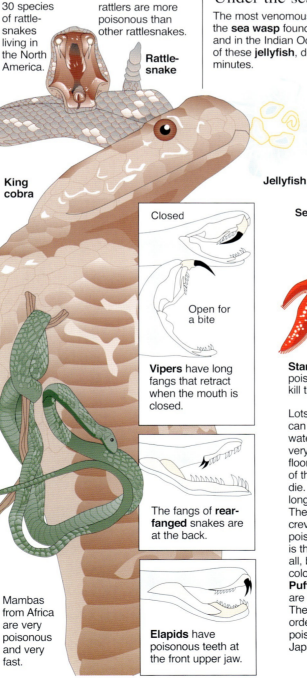

King cobra

Closed

Open for a bite

Vipers have long fangs that retract when the mouth is closed.

The fangs of **rear-fanged** snakes are at the back.

Elapids have poisonous teeth at the front upper jaw.

Mambas from Africa are very poisonous and very fast.

The **lion fish** has poisonous spines.

Sand dollar

Under the sea

The most venomous of sea creatures is the **sea wasp** found near the Phillipines and in the Indian Ocean. If stung by one of these **jellyfish**, death can occur in minutes.

Sea anemones, sea cucumbers, sand dollars, some starfish and a variety of coral are toxic to varying degrees.

Jellyfish

Sea urchin

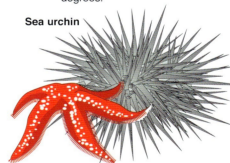

Starfish or sea stars use a poisonous digestive juice to kill their prey.

Lots of poisonous fish can be found in tropical waters. **Stonefish** look very much like the ocean floor and more than half of those who are stung die. **Moray eels** have long, snakelike bodies. They hide in rocks and crevices and many are poisonous. The **lionfish** is the most poisonous of all, but because of its colors it is easy to avoid. **Pufferfish or blowfish** are called **fugu** in Japan. The very foolish or brave order this sometimes poisonous specialty in Japanese restaurants.

Gila monster

Leaping lizards

The only poisonous reptile found in North America is the **gila** (pronounced heela) **monster**. These shy lizards live in the Southwestern United States and Mexico. They use their venomous bite to paralyze prey. The poison causes weakness and dizziness in humans, and very rarely, death.

The **fire salamander's** bright colors warn of its poisonous skin.

The poison of the **poison-dart or arrow frogs** is sometimes used to make deadly arrows.

There are more than 50 colorful species of poison-dart frogs in South and Central America.

Toad

Many frogs and salamanders warn predators of their poison with bright colors, but others, just as dangerous, have neutral or camouflage colors. Many common toads also have poisonous skin. The poison from one species of poison-arrow frog found in South America is toxic enough to kill 20 people.

The one and only

The male **duckbill platypus** from Australia is one of the few mammals in the world that are poisonous. Hollow spines on the ankle of the rear legs are connected to a venom gland. The sting causes extreme swelling, followed by general weakness that can last for a month.

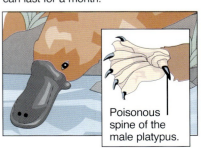

Poisonous spine of the male platypus.

Scavengers of the sky
VULTURES

Vultures are large birds of prey that are often perceived as ugly, dirty symbols of death and destruction. But a vulture in flight is graceful and beautiful, often confused with the noble hawk. Vultures are largely misunderstood birds that play a vital role in keeping the environment clean.

What's the difference?

There are two groups or families of vulture. **New World vultures** are found in North and South America. **Old World vultures** are native to Europe, Africa and Asia. Both groups are carrion (decaying animal flesh) eaters and for many years scientists believed that all vultures were raptors (large birds of prey in the order Falconiformes).

In the 1990s, DNA tests indicated that New World vultures were actually related to storks and ibises (this is still debated in some scientific communities). New World vultures are now recognized as Ciconiiformes, in the family Cathartidae. Old World vultures are more closely related to hawks and eagles, and belong to the Accipitidae family.

The California condor is critically endangered. In an effort to save the species, it is being bred in captivity and released into the wild. The condor has a nesting period of five months — the longest of any bird. It can grow up to 55 in. (139.7 cm) long with a wing span up to 9 ft. (2.74 m).

California condor
Gymnogyps californianus

Old and new

There are seven species of New World Vultures. New World vultures have a special nostril hole in their beak. Most of these birds have a well-developed sense of smell. They also have a small, elevated hind toe, but their feet and legs are weak and unsuitable for capturing prey. New World vultures are mostly silent because they do not have a voice box (syrinx), but they can hiss and grunt. They do not build nests, preferring to lay eggs on the ground or in rock and tree cavities.

There are 15 species of Old World vultures: African White-Backed, Asian White-Backed, Bearded (Lammergeier), Cape Griffon, Cinereous (Asian Black), Egyptian, Eurasian Griffon, Himalayan Griffon, Hooded, Lappet-Faced, Long Billed, Palm Nut, Red-Headed (Pondicherry), Ruppells Griffon, White-Headed.

Many Old World vultures build stick nests. Most have very keen eyesight and can spot a carcass up to 4 miles away.

Interesting facts

- Most vultures are bald or have very few feathers on their heads. This helps keep the bird clean and disease free when feeding on rotten carcasses.
- Vultures regurgitate (vomit) to feed their young.
- Some species will gather in roosts that number in the hundreds, or even thousands.
- Vultures usually have one mate a year. Both male and female share parenting responsibilities.

King vulture
Sarcorhamphus papa

The king vulture measures up to 32 in. (81.3 cm) and has a wingspan up to 5 ft. (1.52 m).

Red-headed vulture
Sarcogyps calvus

This large bird is becoming more and more rare. It can still be found in the western Himalayas and in central India, but it is rarely seen in Singapore and Indonesia.

Egyptian vulture
Neophron percnopterus

This scavenger grows up to 27 in. (68.6 cm) long and has a wingspan up to 5.5 ft. (1.68 m).

Black vulture
Coragyps atratus

The black vulture is sometimes called a carrion crow. This bird is common throughout the southern United States and has adapted to city and town life. The black vulture cannot smell as well as the turkey vulture, and will often let other vultures find food and then dominate the feeding site.

Eurasian griffon
Gyps fulvus

This powerful bird launches itself off high cliffs and can soar for several hours.

Turkey vulture
Cathartes aura

The turkey vulture's range extends across most of the United States into Central and South America. It can be up to 25 in. (63.5 cm) long, with a wingspan of 5 to 6 feet (1.52 to 1.82 cm).

Lappet-faced vulture
Torgos tracheliotus

Up to 45 in. (114.3 cm) long
Wingspan up to 9 feet (2.74 m)

Beating a bad rap

The modern (Western) stereotype of vultures depicts them as harbingers of death and destruction. They are considered repulsive, and the word vulture is sometimes used in a derogatory manner to describe a person who's selfish and greedy. But vultures have not always been so maligned.

In ancient Egypt, the vulture was associated with Mut or Nekhbet (the mother and queen of the gods).

In Greek and Assyrian mythology, the vulture is a descendant of the griffon, guardian of the mysteries of life and death.

In many Native American cultures the vulture is an important tribal symbol that represents the cleansing of the spirit and the strength to accept difficulty.

In southern Africa, because the Nubian Vulture is always observed in pairs, it is associated with protection and love.

What's for dinner?

Vultures are carrion eaters, which means they eat dead things. Decaying and rotting carcasses are their favorite food (some even eat the bones). But Old World vultures have been known to attack newborn and wounded animals. Scientists estimate that vultures can digest food with 100 times the microbial toxins (botulins) that a human could tolerate.

NOTE: Illustrations are not drawn to scale.

Weeds & Wildflowers

Woodland wildflowers

Woodland flowers usually emerge in early spring, before trees leaf out and shade the forest floor. Many die back after flowering, storing energy in large underground roots or rhizomes.

Jack-in-the-pulpit
This plant has an unusual "flower" called a **club**, which is surrounded by a hood-like bract called a **spathe**. In dark woods the spathe is purple. The plant grows to almost 2 feet tall, and the its clustered, berry-like fruit turn bright orange in the fall.

Dutchman's breeches
This spring plant is named for the shape of the flower.

Columbine
This plant grows along open woodland areas and into fields. It seeds in undisturbed areas, and is pollinated by moths and butterflies.

Trillium
Some trilliums have become endangered due to overcollecting from wild populations. The plant needs rich soil in mature forests to grow. There are several species; most are found in forests east of the Rockies. The trillium is the national flower of Canada.

Mesquite
Native peoples of the Southwestern desert used mesquite for food, shelter, weapons, tools, fiber and fuel. Today, cattle ranchers consider it a pest on pasture, although cattle spread undigested mesquite seed in their manure.

Weed and wildflower basics

Weeds are plants that grow where they are unwanted. Any type of plant may be considered a weed, but weed plants are generally thought to be those that have no use. Some weeds are destructive. They affect crops by competing for sunlight, nutrients and water. Weeds may also shelter insect pests or diseases that can harm crops. In the United States, more than $8 billion is spent by farmers each year to control destructive weeds.

Some weeds can be beneficial. In most natural places, it is rare to see bare soil. In undisturbed wild places, dormant seeds will sprout and grow, quickly filling any bare patches of soil. The plants protect the soil from erosion. They may also serve as shelter or food for animals or insects. Many flowering weeds, or **wildflowers**, have been cultivated and improved by man to be used in gardens. Some of the most popular varieties of garden plants had humble beginnings as weeds in a field. Plant breeders collect seeds or roots from wildflowers in order to grow and **cross-breed** them with similar plants. To improve the flower or growth of the original plant, breeders pollinate flowers using scientific methods. Using the science of **genetics**, it may take many years to create a **hybrid** plant with the desired traits. You may recognize traits of some wildflowers and their hybridized offspring in flower gardens.

Types of weeds

ANNUALS
Annual weeds sprout from seed, grow, flower, set seed, and die completely in each growing season.

BIENNIALS
Weeds that sprout from seed, and grow leaves in the first season. They blossom, set seed and die completely the next season.

PERENNIALS
Weeds that sprout from seed and grow from sturdy roots that do not die in the winter. New growth returns each season.

Parts of a flower

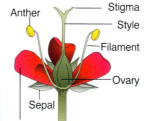

Perfect Flower: Anther, Stigma, Style, Filament, Ovary, Sepal, Petal, Stem

Composite Flower: Ray flower, Bract, Disk flower, Achene, Ray flower, Stem

Desert wildflowers

Desert lupine
All flowers of the pea family (which lupines belong to) have one petal on top and two on the bottom. Often called Coulter's lupine, this plant is a favorite among bees and relies on several species, including bumblebees and honeybees, to pollinate it.

Indian paintbrush
The bright red bracts of this parasitic plant hide inconspicuously in the flowers above them. They lack a well-developed root system and rely on a host plant for water and nutrients. The seedlings cannot grow until they find a host.

Wetland wildflowers

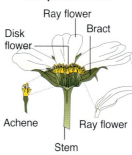

Arrowhead
This aquatic plant (left) spreads in shallow bogs, waterways and along the edges of ponds. The entire plant sprouts from underwater roots that take hold in the soft muddy bottom of wetlands.

Purple loosestrife
Although admired as a garden specimen this plant has escaped into many of North America's native wetland areas. It is an aggressive self-seeder, and can quickly overtake the natural vegetation of a wetland, choking out all other plant growth. It is originally from Europe.

Blue flag
This iris grows with its roots (rhizomes) sometimes completely submerged in water. Bright yellow "beards" can be seen at the top of each dangling petal.

Meadow and field wildflowers

Tall buttercup
This flower was introduced to North America from Europe. Its bright yellow flowers are abundant everywhere, but especially in wet meadows. The plant can grow 2 to 3 feet high.

Common thistle
This spiky, rugged plant thrives in pastures and on disturbed open land. Its nectar is so sweet that bumblebees can become intoxicated after collecting it. The thistle is the national flower of Scotland.

Chicory
This flower is common along road sides and in pastures. Early farmers brought the plant to North America.

Ragweed
This nuisance plant (below) produces massive amounts of pollen that many people are allergic to. It is an annual and grows 1 to 3 feet tall.

WHALES

Whales are mammals that have adapted perfectly to life underwater. Scientists call them **cetaceans** and they have identified 79 different species, including porpoises and dolphins. Many face extinction because of commercial fishing and pollution. There are two types of whales: **baleen** and **toothed**. We celebrate them for their great size and haunting songs, as well as for their intelligence and mystery.

Baleen whales
suborder Mystceti

Baleen whales are big – even the smallest reaches 17 feet when fully grown. There are 10 species: blue whales, gray whales, right whales, minke whales and humpbacks. Except for the minke whale, most are endangered.

Minke whale *Balaenoptera acutorostrata*

Baleen whales are toothless and use baleen plates and fringes to filter their food. These whales eat mostly **krill** (tiny, shrimplike crustaceans) and small fish. They filter these sea creatures with the sievelike **baleen** at the front of their mouths and then force the water back into the ocean.

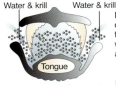

In summer, most baleen whales prefer the cold waters of the Arctic and Antarctic oceans. A large one will eat more than 4 tons of **krill** daily. In winter they migrate and seek warmer waters.

Right whales
family Balaenidae

Right whales were hunted by commercial whalers for more than a century and are now very rare. Whalers called them "right" whales because they were just the right size for catching.

Bowhead whale *Balaena mysticetus*

Rorqual whales
family Balaenopteridae

There are six species of rorqual whales and, except for the humpback, they have a similar shape, differing only in size and color. Female rorquals are usually bigger than the males. These whales have multigrooved throats and about 300 baleen plates on each side of their jaw.

Humpback whales sing highly complex songs. Their songs can last for hours and are unique to individual whale populations. Often the songs change from one year to another.

Humpback whale
Megaptera novaeangliae

Gray whales
family Eschrichtidae

Gray whales have only 2 or 4 throat grooves, instead of hundreds, like the right and rorqual whales.

Gray whale *Eschrichtius robustus*

Splish splash

Breaching occurs when a whale propels its entire body head first out of the water and then falls back, with a loud thump and a lot of spray. Killer whales often breach in order to stun their prey. They herd fish to the surface and use their bodies and tails to pound them to death.

Some scientists believe that whales also use breaching to communicate with one another.

Size and anatomy

Whales can grow to an enormous size because their bodies are supported by water. Sometimes whales become stranded on land because of illness or disorientation. Unless it is quickly returned to the sea, the sheer weight of its own body can crush a whale's internal organs. The whales below are shown to scale, illustrating their comparative sizes.

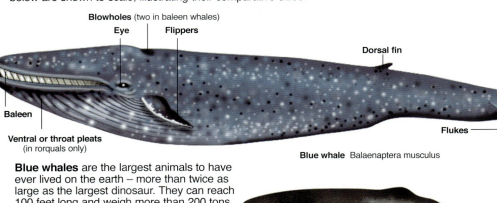
Blue whale *Balaenaptera musculus*

Blue whales are the largest animals to have ever lived on the earth – more than twice as large as the largest dinosaur. They can reach 100 feet long and weigh more than 200 tons. An elephant could stand comfortably on the tongue of an adult blue whale.

Sei whale *Balaenaptera borealis*

Human *Homo sapiens*

White (beluga) whale *Delphinapterous leucas*

Harbor porpoise *Phocoena phocoena*

Sperm whale *Physeter catodon*

Killer whale *Orcinus orca*

Beluga whales are called "sea canaries" because of their intricate singing. They live in the cold waters of the subarctic and Arctic.

Killer whales are the largest of the dolphins. They are highly skilled hunters that feed on fish and squid. They sometimes prey on seals and birds as well. However, they have never been known to attack humans.

How they breathe

Although whales breathe less often than other mammals, they still need air to live. They breathe through a **blowhole** or nostril on the top of their head. Baleen whales have two blowholes; toothed whales have just one. When a whale breathes, it surfaces, spouts a spray of moist, stale air, takes in a fresh supply of clean air, closes its blowhole and dives beneath the surface. The **spray** of each whale species has a unique shape.

Minke whale | Right whale | Sperm whale

A whale of a problem

Years of commercial whaling and pollution have caused a serious decline in present whale populations.

All whales listed on this chart are endangered.

Populations (in thousands):

Whale	Original*	1997	Threats
Sperm	240	197	Hunting**
Blue	226	13	Hunting**
Fin	543	123	Pollution
Humpback	146	4	Fishing
Right	120	3	Nets, pollution
Sei	254	51	Hunting**
Gray	20	11	Fishing nets
Bowhead	20	2	Oil, gas drilling

* Estimates for 150 years ago **Illegal

Diving depths

Maximum diving depths and underwater times for various whales:

Whale	Depth	Time
Porpoise	984 ft.	6 min.
Bottlenose	1,476 ft.	120 min.
Finback	1,148 ft.	20 min.
Sperm	6,562 ft.	75-90 min.

Toothed whales
suborder Odontoceti

The 69 species of toothed whales are divided into five families. These include dolphins, porpoises and sperm whales. **Toothed whales** have very sharp teeth and their main diet is fish and squid. Toothed whales often live in mixed groups called **pods**.

Beaked whales
family Ziphiidae

There are 18 known species of beaked or bottlenose whales. Some of these rare cetaceans have never been seen alive and are identified only when their bodies wash up on shore.

White whales
family Monodontidae

Narwhals and beluga both belong to this family of toothed whales. The male narwhal's slender spiral tusk is really an elongated tooth.

Narwhal *Monodon monoceros*

Dolphins
family Delphinidae

There are 32 species of dolphins, making this cetacean family the most extensive and diverse.

Common dolphin *Delphinus delphis*

Striped dolphin *Stenella coeruleoalba*

Sperm whales
family Physeter catodon

Sperm whales are the largest of the toothed whales. Their bulging skull protects an organ made up of weblike pipes containing waxy yellow oil called **spermaceti**. Scientists think this organ helps with echolocation and controlling buoyancy.

Babies and young

In general, whales only have one baby at a time. An infant whale is called a **calf** and its mother is a **cow**. She has two nipples that deliver a fatty kind of milk. At birth, a blue whale calf is as big as an elephant. It drinks about 175 pints of milk a day.

Communication

Whales do not use vocal cords to produce their famous, haunting songs. Like bats, most whales use a process called **echolocation** to help them locate food and obstacles. This involves sending out high-pitched clicking sounds that bounce off objects and send back an echo. Whales use this technique to determine the exact position of their prey.

Along for the ride

Parasites such as **barnacles** and **whale lice** attach themselves to the skin of whales. Whales rub against objects such as ships in order to get rid of them.

Whale lice

Barnacles

Whaling

Whale back when
Most historians believe that in prehistoric times, coastal people from all over the world probably killed and ate beached or stranded whales. The Norwegians are thought to be the first to hunt whales at sea. Four-thousand-year-old rock carvings in **Norway** depict whale-hunting scenes.

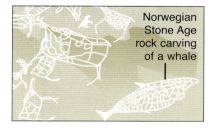
Norwegian Stone Age rock carving of a whale

The Basques
The Basque people of southern France and northern Spain hunted whales in the Bay of Biscay in the 10th century. These early whalers used small boats and worked close to shore. They speared whales with harpoons attached to ropes until the animals eventually died, and then towed them to shore. By 1200, a commercial market for whales was established, and larger ships carried the smaller boats farther out to sea. Whalers carved up the dead whales in the water and then lifted the whale blubber (fat) and baleen (long, bony plates in a whale's mouth) up to the larger ship.

Basque whalers hunted a particular kind of whale. This whale was preferred because it was the right size, slow moving, had large amounts of baleen and floated when killed. It became known as the "right whale."

Right whale

Whaling's heyday
By the 17th century, many nations competed for rich whale-hunting grounds. For the next 200 years, whalers expanded their operations and made huge profits. Dutch and English whalers preyed on bowhead whales around the islands of Svalbard (north of Norway). Within about 100 years, they killed all the whales in this region and began to hunt elsewhere in the Arctic.

North America
North American colonists hunted whales off the Atlantic coast during the 1600s. At first, they favored right whales, but during the 18th and 19th centuries, **sperm whales** became the whale of choice. Whalers collected the pale yellow sperm oil from the head and blubber to make lamp oil and lubricants. Spermaceti, a waxy oil found in the sperm whale's head, was used to make candles. **Ambergris** came from the whale's lower intestines. Ambergris was used in perfumes and was worth its weight in gold.

Whaling expanded to the Pacific Ocean, and between 1820 and 1850, the American sperm-whaling industry thrived on both coasts. The industry had a fleet of more than 730 ships and employed more than 70,000 people. About 10,000 whales were killed each year. By the end of the 19th century, petroleum replaced spermaceti and sperm oil, and the whaling industry took a dive.

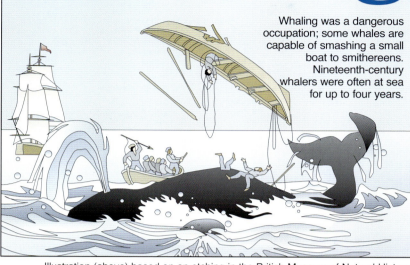

Whaling was a dangerous occupation; some whales are capable of smashing a small boat to smithereens. Nineteenth-century whalers were often at sea for up to four years.

Illustration (above) based on an etching in the British Museum of Natural History

Sperm oil

The demand for whales in the 19th century was as overwhelming as the number of products created from them. Bones and baleen were used to make fashionable **corsets**, umbrella ribs, canes, brushes and knickknacks. **Blubber** was refined into candles, lamp oil, margarine, soap, cosmetics, medicine and motor lubricants. Whale skin was used to make shoes, boot laces, saddles and suitcases.

Sperm whale

Whales were food for the Inuits, American Indians, Japanese and natives of the North Atlantic and North Pacific.

Early whalers used a variety of tools in their work — harpoons for catching, lances for killing and knives for carving. Sharp cleats or spurs were worn over boots to prevent slipping while on a whale's back.

Harpoon, made of soft iron

Lance, used for the kill

Blubber knife, for cutting layers of fat

Flensing spade, for striping blubber

Modern whaling
Whaling techniques changed very little for about 700 years. But in the mid-1800s, commercial whaling began to use modern inventions to assist in the hunt.

1852 — The bomb-lance, an explosive harpoon, was invented. This deadly harpoon allowed the whalers to keep a safer distance from the whale.

1857 — Steam engines were incorporated into whaling ships. This increased the speed and safety of the ships. But traditional catchers, or rowing boats, were still used.

1863 — The first steam catcher was built by Svend Foyn, a Norwegian sea captain. It was an 82-foot (25m) schooner that combined open rowing and the steam engine. The speed and maneuverability of these boats increased the danger to whales.

1865 — The darting gun was a highly accurate harpoon that exploded when embedded in the whale.

1868 — The mounted harpoon gun was another invention of Svend Foyn. It fired from a cannon-like device onboard a whaling ship. (A modern form of this gun is still used by whalers today.)

1925 — The factory ship was home to a crew of about 400 men and a fleet of about 12 catcher boats. As the name suggests, it was a floating processing plant, which allowed the whalers to stay out at sea for longer. These vessels used aircraft, and later sonar, to find and track the whales.

Whaling cleats/spurs

Due to these modern techniques, more whales were killed between 1900 and 1940 than had been killed in the previous 400 years.

Conservation & conflict
The excessive killing during the 1800s and early 1900s severely damaged whale populations around the world. The International Whaling Commission (IWC) was established in 1946 to regulate the whaling industry and to protect whales from over-hunting.

In 1982, the IWC voted to ban commercial whale hunting worldwide. By 1988, most nations had complied with the ban, but in the 1990s, Norway and Japan resumed whale hunting, shielded by exemptions. The IWC allows whaling for scientific purposes and allows native peoples who have traditionally hunted whales for food to continue their hunts under specific guidelines. Norway says that whaling is a vital part of their culture, and Japan claims it kills whales for scientific reasons (but sells the meat commercially).

International Whaling Commission logo

Population estimates
Scientists use **aerial** surveys to track and count whales in order to estimate populations.

Species	Original level	Present level
Blue	228,000	11,700
Bowhead	30,000	7,800
Bryde's	90,000	43,000
Fin	548,000	110,000
Gray	20,000	18,000
Humpback	115,000	10,000
Minke	490,000	880,000
Right	100,000	3,200
Sei	256,000	54,000
Sperm	2,400,000	1,950,000

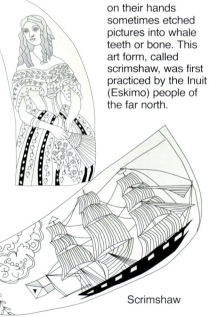

Whalers with time on their hands sometimes etched pictures into whale teeth or bone. This art form, called scrimshaw, was first practiced by the Inuit (Eskimo) people of the far north.

Scrimshaw

The modern harpoon gun is usually mounted on the deck of a ship and has a cannon-like launcher. It has a deadly spear attached to a rope so that the injured whale cannot get away.

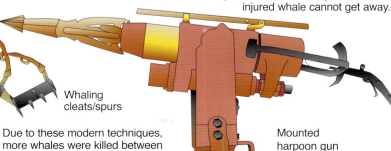

Mounted harpoon gun

Gray wolf
Canis lupus
tundrarum

WOLVES

A wolf resembles a German shepherd, but it has a bigger head, bigger feet and a long, bushy tail.

The gray wolf

The gray wolf is also known as the **timber** wolf or the **tundra** wolf. There are several subspecies of gray wolves in North America: the arctic wolf, the Mexican wolf, the eastern wolf, the Great lakes/western U.S wolf and the Alaskan or Canadian wolf.

There are two other wolf species: The red wolf (found in the southeastern U.S.) and the Abyssinian or Ethiopian wolf (found only in **Ethiopia**).

Wolves will trot at about 5 mph (7 km/h) and sprint at speeds up to 45 mph (70 km/h). A wolf's territory depends on food availability.

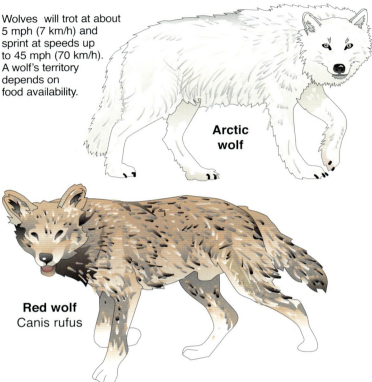
Arctic wolf

Present-day wolf range

Great ancestors

Wolves are descended from a carnivorous weasel-like animal called the **miacis**. The miacis had five toes and could probably climb. Dogs, cats, bears, raccoons, civets, weasels and skunks are also descended from this animal.

Miacis
(Paleocene period: 65 million to 55 million years ago)

The next ancestor in the wolf's evolution was **cynodictis**. The cynodictis resembled the civet of today (a living fossil), but had some doglike qualities.

Cynodictis
(Eocene period: 55 million to 38 million years ago)

About 10 million years ago, a creature evolved called the **tomarctus**. The tomarctus looked very much like the wolf of today and is the direct ancestor of all members of the dog family.

Tomarctus
Miocene period
(25 million to 5 million years ago)

Reduced range

Gray wolves can be found throughout the northern hemisphere (generally north of 15 degrees north latitude). Wolves were once one of the most plentiful mammals on Earth, but are now listed as endangered. **Man** is the wolves' main enemy. Habitat destruction and hunting have decimated wolf populations. They have been reintroduced in many regions and in some areas are making a respectable comeback.

In February 2005 a U.S. federal judge struck down a 2003 ruling that downgraded wolf populations from endangered to threatened and allowed ranchers to shoot them if caught attacking livestock.

Dismal numbers

Estimated worldwide wolf populations:
- 150,000 gray wolves
- 500–700 Abyssinian wolves
- 250 red wolves

Mexican wolf

Abyssinian wolf
Canis simensis

Red wolf
Canis rufus

The red wolf

The **red wolf** once lived throughout the southeastern United States from Pennsylvania to Florida and as far west as Texas. By the mid-1970s, the red wolf populations were so small that the animal was in danger of extinction. Between 1973 and 1980 all known wild red wolves were captured and kept in captivity in an effort to save them. Today, about 100 red wolves can be found in the wild (mostly in North Carolina).

The Abyssinian wolf

The **Abyssinian** wolf is also known as the Ethiopian wolf, simien jackal, red jackal and simien fox. These wolves are found only in Ethiopia and live primarily on rodents. They will take larger prey if it is injured, very young or very old. Ethiopian wolf populations have suffered serious blows in the past 20 years. A **rabies** epidemic in the early 1990s and another in 2003 killed off more than two-thirds of the population. With the combination of habitat destruction and hunting, this wolf is seriously endangered and is likely to become extinct.

Canis lupus

The scientific or Latin name for the gray wolf is Canis lupus which means "the dog who is a wolf." In Europe, the animal's name is spelled with an "e" (i.e., grey wolf). In North America it is spelled with an "a" (i.e., gray wolf). Traditionally, scientific Latin names always begin with a capital letter and are underlined or italicized.

Misunderstood

Wolves are often blamed for loss of livestock and the spread of rabies. Wolves have also been accused of taking babies and young children as prey. But wolves rarely kill people and when they do it is usually because they have gone mad from rabies.

Territories range in size from about 62 miles (100 km) to 1,243 miles (2,000 sq. km).

All in the family

Wolves are social animals that like to live and hunt in **packs**. A pack is usually made up of a family of wolves (parents and offspring) and rarely numbers more than 10 wolves. Within a pack there is a distinct social **hierarchy** and every wolf knows its place.

Hunting

Wolves are primarily **carnivores,** eating mostly meat. They hunt in packs and will take down large prey, but they also eat smaller animals. Wolves also scavenge carcasses and will eat insects, nuts and berries. A wolf can go without food for an entire week, but when food is plentiful it can gorge itself on a meal of up to 22 pounds (10 kg).

Folklore

The wolf has played a role in the stories and folklore of many cultures. Western fables like "Peter and the Wolf" and "Little Red Riding Hood" portray the wolf as a frightening creature. China has a nasty wolf called Lon Po Po. But many Native American cultures revered the wolf as a symbol of bravery and loyalty.

According to myth, the founders of Rome, Romulus and Remus (twins) were raised by a she-wolf.

A Nordic myth tells of a wolf named **Skoll** that chases the sun goddess Sol and a wolf called Hati that chases the moon.

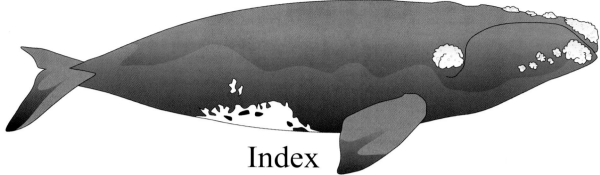

Index

A

aardvark 2
acacia trees 29, 32
accipitidae family 86
Acipenser brevirostrum 26
acorn 29
adapids 38
Africa 1, 3, 7, 14, 25, 32, 33, 35, 37, 39, 45, 46, 52, 54-58, 60, 62, 63, 65, 69, 85, 86
Africa, Saharan 38
Age of Dinosaurs 53
Age of Mammals 53
aggregation 84
aggregations (of squirrels) 77
agouti, Brazilian 64
Ailuropoda melanoleuca 50
Ailurus fulgens 50
Ajaia ajaja 27
Alaska 34, 66, 74
Alasmidonta heterodon 26
Alcyonaria 65
alder 78
Aleutian Islands 74
algae 2, 84
Alliance for Zero Extinction 7
Alligator mississippiensis 14, 26
alligators 26, 27, 63, 64, 75
allosaurus 18
allotheria 53
allspice 29
almond blossom 29
aloe 29
Alopias vulpinus 73
alpaca 10
Alvin 47
alyssum 29
amaranth 29
amaryllis 29
Amazon River 21, 60, 63
Amazon water lily 63
ambergris 89
ambrosia 29
Ambystoma californiense 26
ambystomatidae 67
American bittern 78
American Central Flyway 74
American Pacific Flyway 74
Ammonis comua 54
ammonites 17, 54
amphibians 7, 30, 54, 67, 78
Anaplura 8
anatomist 16
Andes Mountains 28, 64, 69
anemones 48
　green 72
anglerfish 48
Anodorhynchus hyacinthinus 51
ant colony 1
Antarctic 28
Antarctic Circle 52
Antarctica 36, 37, 45, 46, 52, 77
anteaters 2, 33
　silky 2
Antechinus 40
antelopes 33, 39
anthozoans 65
anthropoids 56, 57, 61
antlers 66
ants 1, 2, 8, 60, 61
　leaf-cutter or parasol 63
apatosaurus 18
apes 55, 56
aplacophora 71
Appalachian Mountains 74
apple blossom 29
Ara ararauna 61
Arabia 10
Arabian desert 10
arachnid family 76
arachnids 69
　spiders 69, mites 69, ticks 69, harvestmen 69
aralinga solstitialis 60
Aratinga pertinax 51
arbor vitae 29
arbutus 29
Arcea herodias 27
archaeopteryx 18
Archipélago de Colón. See Galapagos Islands
archosaurs 16
　crocodiles 16, flying reptiles 16, thecodonts 16
Arctic 74, 79
Arctic circle 66
Arctic Ocean 6, 45, 46, 52, 66, 70, 80
Argema mimosae 61
Argentina 33, 64, 74
Arizona 3
armadillos 2
arrowhead 87
Arroyo toad 26
Artiodactyls 33
Asia 1, 3, 4, 6, 10, 36, 39, 45, 46, 53-58, 60, 61, 64, 65, 76, 79, 80, 82, 86
Asia, South 38
Asia, Southeast 38
Assyrian mythology 86
aster 29
ateles Geoffroyi 62
atelidae 57
Atlantic Coast 72, 74, 79
Atlantic flyingfish 45
Atlantic Flyway 74
Atlantic football fish 46
Atlantic loggerhead 26
Atlantic Ocean 27, 45, 46, 54, 68
atolls, coral 65
Atta cephalotes 63
Auckland Islands 52
Australasia 61
Australia 7, 28, 33, 37, 40, 45, 46, 52, 56, 61, 65, 77, 79, 82, 85
Australian bulldog ant 85
aveneae 33
avocados 62
azalea 29
Azores 68
Aztecs 49

B

baboons 55, 57
Babylonia 22
baby's breath 29
bachelor's buttons 29
bacteria 7, 63, 84
balaenaptera borealis 88
balaenaptera musculus 88
balaenidae family 88
balaenopteridae family 88
bald cypress trees 27
bald eagle 26
balenoptera acutorostrata 88
Bali 80
bamboo 4, 33, 50
bananas 62
bandicoots bilbies 40
banjo fish 54
barley 33
barnacles 72, 88
　gooseneck 72, rock 72
basidiomycota 42
basil 29
Basques 89
Bast or Bastet, Egyptian goddess of love and fertility 12
bats 3, 26, 44, 60, 61, 62, 69
　fisher 3, flying fox 3, Franquet's epauleted 62, fruit 3, hammer-headed 3, hoary 3, horseshoe 3, kitti's bag-nosed, leaf-nosed 3, megabats 3, microbats 3, North American 3, Ozark big eared 26, Old World 3, red 3, roost 3, silt-faced or hollow-faced 3
bats, vampire 3, 60
　hairy-legged 3, white-winged 3
bay leaf 29
Bay of Biscay 89
Bay of Fundy, Canada 74
beaches 1, 74
bears 1, 4, 12, 75, 80, 90
　American black 4
　　blue or glacier 4, island white 4, Kermode's 4
　ant bear (giant anteater) 2, Asiatic black,
　　Himalayan or moon 4
　big brown 4
　　Alaskan 4, grizzly 4
　giant panda 4
　polar 4, 70
　　ice bear, sea bear, white bear or walking bear 4
　sloth 4
　　honey bear 4, Indian 4
　spectacled 4
　sun 4
　　Malayan 4
beaver lodge 1
beavers 1, 64, 77
bees 8, 85
　honey 8, bumblebees 87
beetles 5, 8, 61, 84
　carrion 5, checkered 5, click 5, Colorado potato 5, cucumber 5, dung 5, Eastern hercules 5, fire 5, fireflies 5, 8, 44, frog 5, 63, giant stag 5, golden tortoise 5, ground 5, Japanese 5, 8, 84, June-bugs 5, ladybeetle 5, ladybug 4, 5, 8, leaf 5, lightning bugs 5, 8, long-horned 5, Northeastern beach tiger 26, predacious diving 5, scarabs 4, 5, soldier 5, Southern pine 5, tiger 5, tumblebugs 5, water scavenger 8
begonia 29
Beijing Zoo 50
belemnites 54
bentgrass 33
Bermuda Triangle 68
Big Cypress, Florida 27
bighorn sheep 26
biodiversity 7
biologists 62
bioluminescence 47, 48
biomes 26, 33, 51
birch trees 66
bird of paradise 29
birds 1, 3, 7, 51
　flightless 28
　　cassowaries 28, emus 28, kakapo 28, kiwi 28, ostriches 28, penguins 28, ratites 28, rheas 28, tinamous 28
bivalves 71
black swallowers 48
black-footed ferret 26
blubber knife 89
blue flag 87
bluebell 29
bluegrass 33
　meadow 33
bluejoint grass 33
bobcats 59
Boca Raton, Florida 27
bogs 78
Bolivia 4
bomb-lance 89
Borneo 4, 55, 61, 63, 80
botanists 9, 13, 62
Bounty Islands 52
Bouvet 52
brachiation 58
Brachypelma smithi 63
Bradipodicola hahneli
Bradypus tridactylus
Brazil 7, 33, 60, 62
Brazilian butterfly caterpillar 85
British Colombia 9
British imperialism 36
British Museum of Natural History 89
broadleaf trees, oak, maple, eucalyptus, palm 81
brome 33
brontosaurus 18
brontotherium 53
bryozoans 68
Bubo virginianus 44
budgerigars 51
buffalo 33, 39
Bulo microscaphus californicus 26
bulrushes 78
Burma 4
burrowers 1
burrows 1
bushbabies. See galagos
Buto hemiophrys baxteri 26
buttercup 29
buttercup, tall 87
butterflies 8, 60
　malachite 63, monarch 41

C

cacao seed 62
Cacatua galerita 51
cacatuidae family 51
Cactaceae 9
cactuses (cacti) 9, 15, 29

Christmas 9, columnar 9, globular 9, horse crippler 9, leaf 9, opuntia 31, pincushion or thimble 9, prickly pear 9, saguaro 1, 9, segmented 9
caduceus 75
caiman 63
caiman crocodilus 63
calendula 29
California condor 26, 86
California freshwater shrimp 26
California smelt (grunion) 41
callithricidae, marmosets, tamarins 57
callithrix jacchus 62
Cambodia 80
camellia 29
camels 10, 33
    Arabian 10, Bactrian 10, dromedaries 10
Camelus bactrianus 10
Camelus dromedarius 10
camouflage 75
Canada 7, 59, 64, 66, 74, 87
Canada geese 49
Canada lynx 26
cancer 62
Candlemas Day 34
Canis lupus 26
Canis rufus 90
canyons 1
capuchins, brown 57
capybaras (water pig or water hog) 64
Carabidae 5
caravels 68
carcharodon carcharias 73
Caretta caretta 26
Caribbean 74
caribou 66
carnation 29
carnivores 4
carnivorous plants 11
    active trappers 11, American pitcher plants 11, 78, bladderworts 11, butterworts 11, marsh pitcher 11, passive trappers 11, phial pitcher 11, sundews 11, trumpet pitcher 11, Venus' flytrap 11, waterwheels 11, West Australian pitcher plants 11
cartilage 73
Caryophyllales 9
Caspian Sea 80
catamount 6
Catharanthus roseus 62
cathartes aura 86
cathartidae 86
cats 12, 44, 80, 90
    big 6, Birman 12, Burmese 12, Devon Rex 12, dinictis 12, hoplophoneus 12, Maine Coon 12, Persian 12, Russian Blue 12, saber-toothed tiger 12, Scottish Fold 12, Siamese 12, Somali 12, Turkish Angora 12
cattails 29, 78
cattle 33
cebidae 57
cedar 29
celaceans 21
Celorhinus maximus 73
Cenozoic era 36
centipedes 8, 84
Central America 1, 9, 14, 22, 28, 40, 57, 60, 62, 63, 74, 86
cephalopods 54, 71
Cephalotus 11
cercopithecinae 57
cercopithecines 57
Cereus 9
cervidae family 66
cetaceans 35, 88
chameaileonidae 61
chameleons 61
chamomile 29
chapparals 9
char, Arctic (Taranet's char) 82
charaxes bernardus 60
Charles Darwin Research Station 31
Chatham Island 52
cheetah 6, 80
Chelonia mydas 27
chemosynthesis 48

chichona plant 62
chicle 62
chicory 87
Chile 74
chimaeras 54
chimpanzees 55
Chimu 31
China 7, 10, 21, 22, 33, 36, 50, 60, 61, 67, 80, 90
chinchilla 64
Chinook salmon 26
chipmunks 77
Chiroptera order
chitons 71
chocolate 62
chokeberry 78
Choloepus didactylus 60
chorates 7
chrysanthemum 29
Chrysomelidae 5
cicada killers 8
cicadas 8
Cicindela dorsalis dorsalis 26
ciconiiformes order 86
cinereous 86
citrus fruit 62
civets 12, 90
Cladium jamaicense 27
clams 70, 71
clay 84
Clean Air Act of 1970 23
Clean Water Act 23
climbing plants, lianas, bush ropes, strangler figs, monkey ladder vine 61
clover 29, 84
cnidaria 65
cobra 75
Coccinellidae 5
cockatiels 51
cockatoos 51
    sulphur-crested 51
coconuts 62
cocoons 1
coelacanth 54
Coelophysis 17
coffee 62
Colbert, Edwin 16, 17
Coleoptera order 5, 8
coleopterists 5
Colima culture 20
colobinae 57
colobus abyssinicus 60
Colombia 4, 7, 64
colubus, red 57
columbine 29, 87
Common Cause 23
Comoro Islands 38
conchology 71
conifers 7
    pine, fir 81
Connecticut River 82
constriction 75
conures 60
Cope, Edward Drinker 16
coragyps atratus 86
coral 46, 71, 72
    boulder 65, brain 65, crown-of-thorns 65, depressed brain 65, fire 65, flower 65, fungus 65, imperforate 65, ivory bush 65, large-cupped fungus 65, lettuce 65, orange 65, perforate 65, reef-forming 65, rose 65, spiny candelabrum 65, staghorn 65, star 65, stony 65, tan lettuce-leaf 65, tube 65
coral reefs 65
coralline algae 65
coriander 29
corn 33
cornflower 29
Corynorhinus townsendiingens 26
coscoroba coscoroba 79
Costa Rica 61
cougar 6
Coulter's lupine. See desert lupine
coyotes 1, 59
crabs 72
    fiddler 72, hermit 72, horseshoe 72, mole 72, 74, purse 74, rock 72, Sally Lightfoot 31, sand 72
Cretaceous period 19, 53, 54, 55
crocodiles 14, 27, 54, 63, 75
Crocodilia 14
crocodilians
    alligators 14, American alligator 14, American crocodile 14, caimans 14, dwarf crocodile 14, gharials 14, Nile crocodile 14, spectacled caiman 14
Crocodilius niloticus 14
Crocodylus acutus 14
crocus 29
Crozet Islands
crusafontia 53
crustaceans 7, 8, 72
cryptobranchoidea 67
Cuba 7
curare 62
currents 45, 46, 68
    Gulf Stream 68, North Equatorial 68, North Atlantic 68, Canary 68
cuttlefish 54
cycad trees 18, 81
cyclamen 29
Cyclopes didactylus 2
Cygnus atratus 79
Cygnus buccinator 79
Cygnus columbianus 79
Cygnus cygnus 79
Cygnus melanocoryphus 79
Cygnus olor 79
cynodictis 20, 90
cyrptodira 83
Cystophora cristata 70

D
daffodil 29
dahlia 29
daisy 29
dandelion 29
darting gun 89
Darwin, Charles 31
Dasypus novemcinctus 2
Dasyuromorphia, Australasian carnivorous marsupials 40
Daubentonia madagacarien 60
Daubentonilidea, aye-ayes 56
de Berlanga, Fray Tomas 31
deer 33
    mouse 33, white-tailed 33
deinonychus 19
Delaware 34
Delaware Bay 74
delnopis spinosus 76
delphinapterous leucas 88
delphinidae family 88
delphinium 29
Delphinus delphis 21
delphinus delphis 88
Dendrobates 30
Dendroica kirtlandii 26
dens 1
desert 1, 9, 15
desert locations 15
    Arabian Peninsula, Arctic, Atacama, Chihuahuan, Colorado Plateau, Gibson, Gobi, Great Basin, Great Sandy, Great Victoria, Iranian, Mojave, Simpson, Sonoran, Stony, Sturt, Taklamaklan, Tropic of Cancer, Tropic of Capricorn, Turkestan
desert lupine 87
desert lynx 15
desert tortoise 26
desert, Southwestern 87
deserts, coastal 15
deserts, cold winter 15
deserts, polar 15
deserts, subtropical 15
Desmodus rolundus 60
diatoms 84
dicamptodontidae 67
Dicotyledonae 9
Didelphimorphia 40
Didelphis virginiana 44
dinosaurs 14, 16, 53, 54, 75
    ornithischians
        ankylosaurus 16, pachycephalosaurus 16, parasaurolophus 16, stegosaurus 16, triceratops 16, 19
    saurischians
        allosaurus 16, brachlosaurus 16, ceratosaurus 16, dromaeosaurus 16, herrerasaurus 16, plateosaurus 16, tyrannosaurus rex 16, 19
dinotherium 25
Dionaea 11
Diprotodontia 40
Diptera 8
dogfish 47, 54
Dogger epoch 18
dogs 12, 20, 34, 80, 90
    bloodhound 20, border collie 20, bull terrier 20, chihuahua 20, collie 20, dalmatian 20, English bulldog 20, English cocker spaniel 20, English springer spaniel 20, German shepherd 90, herding 20, hounds 20, Irish setter 20, Irish wolfhound 20, Mexican pottery dog 20, pomeranian 20, saluki 20, skye terrier 20, sporting 20, St. Bernard 20, terriers 20, toy 20, utility (nonsporting) 20, working 20
dogwood 29
dolphinfish 45
dolphins 3, 21, 88
    Amazon 63, Atlantic bottle-nosed 45, Baiji 21, Bhulan 21, Hector's 21
dolphins, marine 21
    bottle-nosed 21, common 21, Indo-Pacific humpbacked 21, killer whale or orca 21, long-finned pilot 21, Risso's 21, striped 21
dolphins, river 20
    Boto 21, Franciscana 21, whitefin 21, striped 88, Susu 21
dragon, Chi Lung Wang 22
dragonflies 8
dragons 22
    Fafnir 22, Goin, Grabak, Gravitnir and Grafvolud (Norway) 22, Hotu-Puku 22, Jormungandr 22, Lernean Hydra 22, leviathan 22, Mo'o or Moko 22, Tiamat 22, Vitra 22, wyrms 22
drey (nest) 1, 77
Drosera 11
dune formation 15
    barchan 15, longitudinal 15, parabolic 15, self 15, star 15, transverse 15
dunes 74
Dutchman's breeches 87
dwarf seahorses 45
dwarf wedge mussel 26
Dytiscidae 4, 5

E
eagle ray 46
eagles 34, 49, 60, 75, 86
    golden 59
Earth Day 23
earthquakes 75
earthworms 2, 84
echidnas 2
Echinocactus 9
echinoderms 65
echolocation 3, 21, 44, 88
ecosystems 7, 84
Ecuador 4, 7, 31, 62, 64
Edentata group 2
eels 68
    freshwater, yellow, brown 68, gulper 48, moray 85
eggs 1, 24
    alligator 24, birds' 4, chicken 24, fish 24, frog 24, goose 24, hummingbird 24, insect 24, ostrich 24, oyster 24, snapping turtle 24
Egypt 86
Egypt, ancient 42
eland 33, 39
Elateridae 5
elephant grass 33
elephants 25
    African 25, African bush 25, African

forest 25, Asian 25, musth 25
endangered species 26
Endangered Species Act 23, 26
end-Permian event 54
entomologists 5
Environmental Protection Agency 23
Eocene period 20, 36, 53, 54, 55, 90
Eos bomea 51
eotheria 53
epiphytes (air plants) 61
    orchids, staghorn fern, pitcher plants 61
Epomops franqueti 62
equator 60
equus 53
Erignathus barbatus 70
erosion 63
eschrichtius robustus 88
Eskimos 89
estuaries 1, 74
Ethiopia 90
eucalyptus 29, 37, 81
eudocimus ruber 63
euparkeria 17
Eurasia 33, 37
Europe 1, 18, 19, 39, 53, 54, 64, 66, 76, 79, 82, 86, 87
Europe, western 17
Eurypterida 69
eusmilus 53
Everglades National Park 27
evergreens 60
evolution theories 16
evolutionists 16
exoskeletons 69, 71, 76
extinction 26

F
Falco peregrinus anatum 26
falconiformes order 86
falcons 49
    American peregrine 26
Falkland Islands 52
Far East 6
Federal Duck Stamp 74
Federal Occupational Health and Safety Act 23
felidae 6, 44, 80
felinae 80
Felis concolor coryi 27
fennel 29
fens 78
fern 29
fescue 33
festuceae 33
Ficus walkinsiana 61
finches 31
    cactus eater, 31, insect eater 31, seed eater 31, vegetation eater 31
fir 29
fish 3, 4, 54, 68
fish ladders 82
fishways 82
flax 29
fleas 35
flensing spade 89
flies 8, 35
Flinders Island 40
Florida 90
Florida Everglades 27
Florida gar 27
Florida Keys, Florida 27
Florida panther 27
fly fishing 82
foraminiferans 65
forests, cloud 60
forests, equatorial evergreen 60
forests, tropical moist 60
forget-me-not 29
forsythia 29
Fort Lauderdale, Florida 27
Fort Myers, Florida 27
fossils 54
foxes 1, 59
    red 34
foxglove 29
foxtail barley 33
Foyn, Svend 89
France 89
frogs 3, 30, 62
California red-legged 26, flying 63, golden dart 30, Goliath 30, Javan flying frog 30, leopard 30, 78, paradoxical 30, poison-dart or arrow 30, 85, red-legged 30
fruit 4
fuchsia 29
fugu. *See* pufferfish
fungi 7, 42, 63, 84

G
Galagonidae 62
galagos (bushbabies) 55, 62
Galapagos Islands 31, 52
Gallic Epoch 19
Gambusia holbrooki 27
Ganges River 21
gardenia 29
Gardner, John 23
garfish 45
garúa 31
Gashun Gobi 9
gastropods 71
Gavialis gangeticus 14
gazelles 33, 39
geckos 62
General Sherman tree 81
Genghis Khan 36
geologists 16
geranium 29
Germany 17, 22
Ghana 62
Ghost Ranch 16, 17
giant anaconda 75
giant isopods 48
gibbons 55, 61
    white-handed 58
gila monster 85
ginkgo 18, 81
ginkgo or maidenhead 81
giraffes 32, 33, 39
gladiolus 29
Glaucornys 44
gliders 40
Globicephala melaena 21
Glossopsitta porphyrocephala 51
Gobi desert 9
Gondwana 37
Gopherus agassizii 26
gorillas 55
Gould, Stephen Jay 16
Grampus griseus 21
grasses 29, 84
    cereal 33, grazing 33, ornamental 33, sugar cane 33, turfgrasses 33, woody 33
grasshoppers 8
grasslands 33, 39
    prairies 33, savannas 33, steppes 33
grayling 82
Great Barrier Reef 65
Great Britain 79
Great Plains 33
Greece 49
Greek mythology 86
Greek traders 12
Greenland 36, 66, 70
Greenland halibut 47
griffon 86
groundhogs 1, 64
guanaco 10
guano 3
Guatamela 7
guenons 57
guitar fish 54
Gulf Coast 72
Gulf of Mexico 27, 41, 68, 74
Gymnogyps californianus 26, 86
gyps fulvus 86

H
Haliaeetus leucocephalus 26
hamsters 64
    common 64, golden (Syrian) 64
hares 59
    Arctic 59, European 59, snowshoe or varying 59
harpoon 89
harpoon gun, mounted 89
hartebeeste 39
Hawaiian honeycreeper 26
hawks 3, 34, 49, 59, 75, 86
    Cooper's 3
hawksbill 45
hawksbill seaturtle 46
heath shrubs 78
heather 29
hedgehogs 75
herons 72
    great blue 27, 72
herpetologists 67
herrings 45
Heterandria formosa 27
hibernation 3, 4
hibiscus 29
Himalayan Mountains 69, 86
Hippocrates 42
hippopotamus 33, 35
    pygmy 35, river 35
HMS Beagle 31
holly 29
hollyhock 29
Holocene epoch 36, 53
Holyoke fish elevator 82
hominoids 58
    great apes, orangutans, gorillas, chimpanzees, bonobos 58
    lesser apes, gibbons, siamangs 58
homo sapiens 73
Honduras 7
honey 4
honeysuckle 29
hornets 8
horses 36, 53
    African wild ass 36, asses 36, Clydesdale 36, colt 36, dam 36, evolution of Eohippus (Dawn Horse) 36, Equus 36, merychippus 36, Mesohippus 36, pilohippus 36 filly 3, foal 36, mare 36, purebred 36, shetland pony 36, stallion 36, vlatka 36, zebras 36
humans 55, 59, 73
hummingbirds 60, 61
hyacinth 29
hybodus 54
hydrangea 29
hydroids 68
hydrozoans 65
hylobates 61
hynoblidae 67
hyracotherium 53

I
ibises 86
    scarlet (stork) 63
ichthyologists 46
ichthyosaurs 54
Iguana iguana 61
iguanas, green 61
iguanas, marine 31
impala 39
India 7, 14, 22, 33, 57, 60, 69, 80, 85
Indian Ocean 45, 46
Indian paintbrush 87
Indochina 4
Indonesia 3, 7, 86
Indonesian islands 80
Indo-Pacific region 71
Indridae, indris, avahis, sifakas 56
Indus River 21
inia geoffrensis 63
insects 1, 2, 3, 4, 7, 8, 62, 63, 84
    aquatic 78
International Code of Botanical Nomenclature 9
International Whaling Commission 89
invertebrates 54, 68
Ireland 75
iridium 53
iris 29, 87
Islas Juan Frenandez 52
isopod 84
Israel 22
Italy 17
ivy 29

J
jack-in-the-pulpit 87
jackrabbits 59
    antelope 15
jaguars 6, 62-64
Japan 67, 71, 89
jasmine 29
jawfish 1
    "well digger" 1
jonquil 29
Jurassic period 53, 54

K
kafir 33
Kalahari Desert 41
kangaroo rats 15
kangaroos 40
Kayapo Indians 62
Kennedy, John F. 23
Kerguelen Islands 52
king cobra 75, 85
Kirtland's warbler 26
koalas 37, 40
krill 88
KT event 53
Kung bushmen 41

L
La Diable 20
La Plata River 21
ladybugs. *See* beetles
lagomorphs 59
Laika 20
Lake Okeechobee, Florida 27
Lake Victoria 7
lakeshores 74
lammergeier 86
Lampyridae 5
lance 89
land plants 7
langur, entellus 57
langur, hanuman 57
lanternfish 47, 48
Laos 80
larkspur 29
larvae 1
lasiodora 76
Lassie 20
Late Triassic epoch 17
Laurasia 37
laurel 29
lavender 29
least killfish 27
lemmings 41
lemon 29
lemon balm 29
lemur catia 62
Lemuridae 56
lemurs 38, 56, 62
    aye-aye 38, 56, 60, blue-eyed 38, brown 38, common brown 38, dwarf 56, eastern lesser bamboo 38, golden-crowned sifaka 38, gray mouse 38, indris 56, Malagasy names of 38, Megalaciapis 38, pygmy mouse 55, ring-tailed 38, 55, 62, Sanford's 38, sifakas 56, true 56
Lenni Lenape people 34
Leontopithicus rosalia 61
leopards 6, 62
    clouded (mint leopard) 61, snow 6
Lepidoptera 8
Lepisosteus platyrhincus 27
leporidae family 59
Les Trois Freres cave 49
leukemia 62
Li Li (panda) 50
Lias epoch 18
lice 8
lichens (reindeer moss) 66
Liguus fasciatus 27
liguus tree snail 27
lilac 29
lily 29
lily of the valley 29
limestone 65
linophryne 48
lionfish 45, 85
lions 6, 39
Lipotes vexillifer 21

litoria infrafrenata 61
Little Red Riding Hood 90
lizards 3, 14, 61, 67, 69, 75
    leaping 62
llamas 10
Loepardus pardalis 26
Lon Po Po 90
lories 51
lorikeets 51
    purple-crowned 51, rainbow 51, scaly-breasted 51
lorises 55
    arboreal 56, angwantibos 56, galagos 56, nocturnal 56, omnivorous 56, pottos 56, slow 60
lorliidae family 51
lory, red 51
lovebirds, rosy-faced 51
Loxodonta Africana 25
lualara 75
Lycosa carolinensis 76
Lynx canadensis 26

M
macaques, Japanese 55, 57
macaws 51
    blue-and-yellow 61, hyacinth 51, scarlet 60
macropoma 54
Macropus, red kangaroo 40
Madagascar 7, 38, 52, 56, 60, 61, 62
magnolia 29
Magnoliophyta 9
mahogany 62
malacology 71
malaria 62
Malay Peninsula 4
Malaysia 3, 60, 63, 80
Malm epoch 18
mambas 75
mammals 7, 54, 80
    egg-laying or monotreme 53
Mammilaria 9
mandrills 57
mangabeys 57
mangrove forests 60
mangroves 1, 27
Mantell, Gideon 16
maple trees 81
marigold 29
marjoram 29
Marks, Johnny 66
marmosets 62
    pygmy 57
marmoteers 34
marmotologists 34
marmotophiles 34
marmots (groundhogs, woodchucks) 34, 77
    hoary 34, Olympic 34, yellow-bellied 34
marshes 78
marsupials 37, 40
    kangaroos 40, koalas 40, marsupial "moles" 40, Tasmanian devils 40, wombats 40
mastodon 25
Mbuti tribe 62
McDonald Islands 52
megachiroptera 3
megaloceros 53
Megaplera novaeangliae 88
megatherium 53
Melopsittacus undulatus 51
Mesozoic era 16-19, 53, 54
    Cretaceous period 16, 19, Early Cretaceous 19, Late Cretaceous 19, Middle Cretaceous 19
    Jurassic period 16, 17, 18, Early Jurassic 18, Late Jurassic 18
    Permian period 16, 17
    Triassic period 16, 17, Middle Triassic epoch 17
mesquite 87
metamorphosis 5, 30, 67
Metatheria 40
Mexico 2, 7, 14, 28, 57, 63, 64, 69, 74, 85
miacis 12, 20, 80, 90
Miami, Florida 27

mice 44, 49, 69, 77
    deer 64, grasshopper 64, house 64
microbes 84
Microbiothera, Monito del monte 40
Microchiroptera 3
Middle East 10, 12, 39, 69
migration 41, 66
    human 41
migratory birds 41
    Arctic tern 41, falcons 41, flycatchers 41, hawks 41, herons 41, owls 41, ruby-throated hummingbird 41, swallows 41, warblers 41
millet 33
millipedes 7, 84
mimosa 29
Ming Ming (panda) 50
minks 59
mint 29
Miocene epoch 36, 40, 53, 55, 90
Mississippi River 69, 74
mistletoe 29
Mitchell's marsh satyr 26
moeritherium 25
Mollusca 71
mollusks 7, 46, 65, 71, 84
    clams 7, 46, 47, conch 46, cuttlefish 7, limpets 7, 46, moon 46, mussels 7, 46, octopuses 7, 47, oysters 7, 46, 47, scallops 46, slugs 7, snails 7, 46, 47, squids 7, top 46
molting 76
Mongolia 80
monkeys 55, 56, 57, 60, 61
    blackhanded spider 55, 57, Diana 57, golden lion tamarin 61, guereza 60, New World 55, 57, night 57, Old World 55, 57, patas 57, proboscis 57, red howler 57, spider 62, squirrel 57
monkshood 29
monodon monoceros 88
moray eel 45
mosquitoes 3, 8, 44
mosquitofish 27
moss 29
moths 3, 8, 44
    African moon 61, Cecropia 44
mountain lion 6
mud daubers 1
mudflats 74
mushrooms 42, 63, 66, 84
    chanterelle 42, morel 42, oyster 42, portobello 42
    nonpoisonous
        aspen scaber stalk 42, common mycena 42, edible boletus 42, field 42, Mary russula 42, parasol 42, shaggy mane 42, shitake 42, table 42
    poisonous
        destroying angel 42, emetic russula 42, fetid russula 42, fly agaric 42, fly amanita 42, green-spored 42, jack-o'-lantern 42, toadstools 42
mussels, blue 72
Mustela nigripes 26
Myanmar 80
mycologist 42
mycorrhizae 77
Mymecophaga tridactyla 2
myrtle 29
mythical creatures 43
    unicorn, mermaid, griffon, dragons, basilik

N
Namib Desert 15
nanook. See bears, polar
Naples, Florida 27
narcissus 29
nasturtium 29
Native Americans 71
native people 62
nautilius 54
nautiloids 71
nectar 3
Nelson, Gaylord 23
nematodes 7

Neocomian epoch 19
Neonympha mitchellii mitchellii 26
Neophron percnopterus 86
neopilina 71
neoteny 67
Nepal 57
Nepenthes 11
nests 1
New Guinea 28
New Mexico 16, 17
New South Wales, Australia 37
New Zealand 7, 21, 22, 28, 52, 75, 82
newts 67
    California 67, Eastern 67
Nicrophomae 5
night creatures 44
    bats 44, cats 44, Cecropia moths 44, crickets 44, fireflies 44, flying squirrels 44, great horned owl 44, mice 44, mosquitoes 44, moths 44, opossums 44, raccoon 44, slugs and snails 44, spring peepers 44
Nile perch 7
Nile River 63
nine-banded armadillo 2
nitrogen 11
Norse mythology 22, 90
North Africa 10
North America 2, 9, 17, 18, 19, 27, 33, 34, 37, 45, 46, 49, 53-55, 64-66, 71, 74, 76, 77, 78, 79, 82, 85, 86, 87, 88
North Atlantic Ocean 54, 70
North Carolina 90
North Korea 80
North Pacific 70
North Pole 66, 70
northern hemisphere 70, 75, 79, 90
Northern Territory, Australia 37
Norway 89
Norwegians 89
Notoryctemorphia 40
nursing colony (bats) 3
Nycticebus coucang 60
Nymphicus hollandicus 51

O
oak trees 1, 81
oarfish 47, 48
oats 33
oceanographers 46
oceans 45
    abyssopelagic zone 48, bathypelagic zone (dark) 47, epipelagic zone (sunlit) 45, hadalpelagic zone 48, mesopelagic zone (twilight) 46
ocelot 26
octopuses 54, 71
Odobenidae 70
Odobenus rosmarus 70
Odonata 8
Odontaspis taurus 73
Oijik (Wejak) or Wojack (woodchucks). See marmots
oleander 29
Oligocene epoch 36, 53, 55
omomyids 57
Oncorhynchus tshawytscha 26
opah 46
opossums 3, 37, 40, 44
    "shrew" opossums 40
Opuntia 9
orange 29
orangutan 61
orchid 29
Orcinus orca 21
Oreomystis mana 26
Origin of Species, The 31
Orion 69
ornithologists 28, 74
Ornithoptera alexandrae 60
Orthoptera 8
oryzeae 33
Otariidae 70
ovenbird 1
oviraptor 19
Ovis canadensis 26
Owen, Richard 16
owls 3, 49, 59, 69, 75
    burrowing 33, elf 1, 49, great horned 44, 49, saw-whet 49, short-eared 49, snowy 49
oxpecker bird 35
oystercatcher 31
oysters 71

P
paca 64
Pacific coast 79
Pacific dogwood 7
Pacific Ocean 45, 46, 48
    Izu-Ogasawara Trench 48, Kermadec Trench 48, Mariana Trench 48, Philippine Trench 48, Tonga Trench 48
Pakistan 21
palaeomastodon 25
Paleocene period 12, 53, 55, 90
palm leaves 29
palm trees 81
Pampas 33
Panama 31, 64
panda, giant 50
panda, red (lesser) 50
Pangaea 37
Pangea 16, 54
pangoins 2
paniceae 33
pansy 29
panther 6
    Florida 27
Panthera leo 39
Panthera nebulosa 61
Panthera onca 63
pantherinae 80
papaya 62
paper wasps 1
Papua, New Guinea 60
Paraguay 64
parakeets 51, 62
    brown-throated 51, mustached 51
Paramelemorphia 40
Paris 32
parrots 51, 61
    African gray 51
partina 33
Patagonia 9
Paucituberculata 40
peat 78
peccary 33
pedologists 84
Pelecanus onocrotalus 27
penguins 52
    Adelle 52, African (Jackass) 52, Chinstrap 52, Emperor 52, Erect-crested 52, Flordland 52, Galapagos 52, Gentoo 52, Great Auk 52, King 52, Little Blue 52, Macaroni 52, Magellanic 52, Peruvian (Humboldt) 52, Rockhopper 52, Royal 52, Snares Island 52, Yellow-eyed 52
Pennsylvania 34, 90
peony 29
peppermint 29
perennibranchiates 57
periwinkle 62
    rosy 62
Permian period 16, 17, 54
permineralization 54
Peru 4, 7, 31
pesticides 3
Peter and the Wolf 90
petrification 54
petunia 29
Pharaohs 36, 42
Phascolarctos, koala 40
Phidippus variegatus 76
Philippines 7, 80
phlox 29
Phoca fasciata 70
Phoca groenlandica 70
Phoca hispida 70
Phocidae 70
Phocoena phocoena 88
Phoenician traders 12
photopores 47
photosynthesis 9, 54, 61, 81
physeter catodon family 88
phytoplankton 45, 72, 78
Piccard, Auguste 48
pigeon, North American passenger 7

pigs 33
pikas 59
Pilocene epoch 36, 40, 55
pine 1, 29
pineapples 62
Pinguicula 11
pinnipeds 70
piranha 63
pitcher plant 78
placentals 40
placerias 17
placochelys 54
plague 64
plankton 45, 54, 68, 72
plants, nonvascular 13
    algae 13, mosses 13
plants, vascular 13
    ferns 13, gymnosperms 13
Platanista minor 21
plateosaurus 17
platybelodon 53
Platycerium bifurcatum 61
platypus, duckbill 85
Pleistocene epoch 53, 55
plerosaurs 54
plesiadapiforms 55
plesiosaurs 54
plethodontidae 67
pleurodira 83
Plinius the Elder 54
Pliocene epoch 53
pohutukawa 7
pollen 3, 87
pollination 3
Polynesians 22
polypedon 84
polyplacophores 71
pondweeds 78
Pongogypmaeus 61
Pontoporia blainvillei 21
Pony Express 36
poppy 29
porcupines, North American 64
porpoises 21, 88
    harbor 88
Portugal 53
Portuguese 68
Portuguese man-of-war 45
potter wasp 1
pottos 55, 60
prairie dogs 1, 77
prehensile tail 2
primates 38, 55
    anthropoids 38
        baboons 38, chimpanzees 38, gibbons 38, gorillas 38, humans 38, langurs 38, macaques 38, mandrills 38, Old World monkeys 38, orangutans 38
    prosimians 38
        bushbabies 38, galagos 38, lemurs 38, lorises 38, pottos 38, tarsiers 38
primatologists 38, 55
primrose 29
Prince Edward Islands 52
Proboscigera aterrimus 51
Procyonidae family 44
pronghorn 33
prosimians 55-57, 61
proteidae 67
protists 84
    amoebas, diatoms, ciliates, slime molds 84
protoceratops 19
protoctists 7
prototheria 53
Przhevalsky, Nikolai 10
psittacidae family 51
Psittacula alexandri 51
Psittacus erithacus 51
pteranodon 19
pufferfish or blowfish 85
puma 6
Punxsutawney Phil 34
pupae 1, 8
purgatorius 55
purple loosestrife 87
pycnodus 54
python 75

Q
Queen Alexandria's birdwing 60
Queen Anne's lace 29
Queensland, Australia 37
Quetzalcoati 22
quinine 62

R
rabbits 59
    cottontail 59, domestic dutch 59, European 59, French lop-eared 59, jackrabbits 59
        antelope 59, black-tailed 59
raccoons 1, 3, 12, 44, 50, 75, 78, 90
rafflesia 63
rafflesia arnoldi 63
ragweed 87
rainforests 2, 7, 60-63
    canopy 2, 61, emergent layer 60, floor 63, understory 62
Rana aurora draytonii 26
Rangifer tarandus 66
raptors 49, 86
ratfish 47, 48
rats 75, 77
    black (roof or ship rats) 64, brown (sewer rats) 64, desert kangaroo 64, naked mole 64
rattlesnakes 75, 85
    diamondback 85
rays 54, 73
Recovery Act 23
red cedar 78
redds 82
redfish (ocean perch) 46
red-osier dogwood 78
redwoods 81
reed 33
reefs, bank or barrier 65
reefs, fringing 65
reindeer 66
Remus 90
reptiles 7, 14, 17, 18, 54, 75, 83
    flying reptiles 17, 18
        pterosaurs 17, eudimorphodon 17
    marine 54
Resource Conservation Act 23
Rhacophorus reinwardii 63
Rhamphasios toco 60
Rhincodon typus 73
Rhinolophis ferrumequinum 44
Rhizophora mangle 27
rhyacotritonidae 67
rice 33
    wild 78
Rin Tin Tin 20
roaches 8
Rocky Mountains 19, 74
rodents 3, 64, 77
    beavers, chipmunks, gerbils, gophers, guinea pigs, hamsters, marmots, porcupines, lemmings, mice, muskrats, prairie dogs, rats, squirrels, voles 64
Rome 90
Romulus 90
Roosevelt, Theodore 4
roots, buttress 63
rose 29
roseate spoonbill 27
rosewood 62
roughhead grenadier 47
roughie 46
Rudolph, the Red Nosed Reindeer 66
ruminata 33
rushes 78
Russia 59, 80
rye 33

S
sage 29
Sagra buqueti 63
saguaro cactus 1
Sahara Desert 10, 14, 15, 25
salamanders 67
    Asiatic 67, California tiger 26, Congo eels 67, dwarf siren 67, fire 85, hellbender 67, lungless 67, marbled 67, mudpuppy 67, Pacific giant 67, red 67, tiger 67, 78, torrent 67, waterdogs 67
Salamandidrae family 67
salamandroidea 67
salmon 41, 82
    Atlantic 82, humpback 82, Pacific 82, pink 82, sockeye 82
salmonidae 82
salt marshes 74
Sami (Lapps) 66
San Francisco Bay 74
sand 84
sand dollars (sea biscuits) 72
sand hoppers 72
sandalwood 62
sandbug 72
sandbur 33
sandworms 72
saprotrophs 42
sarcogyps calvus 86
Sarcophilus 40
sarcorhamphus papa 86
Sargasso Sea 68
sargassum fish 68
    pipefish 68, triggerfish 68
sargassum, nudibranch 68
sargassum, pelagic 68
Sarracenia 11
Saudi Arabia 10
Saur or Suening 20
Savanna 32
sawfish 54
sawgrass 27
Scandinavia 66
scaphopods (tusk shells) 71
Scarabaeidae 5
scorpions 69, 85
    Emperor 69, south African 69, stripe-tailed 69, yellow fat-tail 69
scorpions, anatomy of 69
scrimshaw 89
scutellosaurus 18
scyliorhinus canicula 73
Scythian epoch 17
Scythians 36
sea anemones 65, 72
sea cow. See West Indian manatee
sea cucumber 48, 72
sea feathers 65
sea horses 72
sea lions 70
    Californian 70, steller 70
sea stars. See starfish
sea urchins 1, 72
seals 4, 70
    bearded 70, Caribbean monk 70, eared 70, earless 70, Guadalupe fur 70, harbor 70, harp 70, Hawaaian monk 70, hooded or bladdernose 70, North Pacific fur 70, ribbon 70, ringed 70, true 70
seashells 71
    black hammer shell 71, black murex 71, blackened frog 71, chambered nautilus 71, green turbo 71, Hebrew cone 71, humpback cowrie 71, lettered cone 71, Marlin's spike auger 71, Pacific triton 71, pecten albican 71, pen shell 71, Perry's triton 71, spider conch 71, sundial 71, thorny oyster 71, tiger cowrie 71, true heart cockle 71, Venus' comb murex 71
seashore, lower beach 72
seashore, middle beach 72
seashore, upper beach 72
Seattle 23
seaweed (algae) 46, 72
    agarum 46, 72, alaria 46, codium 46, 72, mermaid's hair 46, 72, sargassum 46, 72, sea lettuce 46, 72
sedge grasses 27, 66, 78
Senonian epoch 19
Sequoia National Park 81
sequoias 81
Serrasalmus niger 63
Shag Island 52
sharks 46, 54, 70, 73
    basking 73, blue 73, goblin 73, great white 73, Greenland 46, hammer-head 46, 73, horn 73, mega-mouth 73, salmon 73, sand tiger 73, sandy dogfish 73, shortfin mako 73, thresher 73, tiger 73, whale 73, white 46
Shorebird Sister Schools program 74
shorebirds 74
    American avocet 74, avocet 74, American oystercatcher 74, golden plover 74, lesser yellowlegs 74, piper plover 74, plover 74, phalaropes 74, red knot 74, sandpipers 74, semipalmated sandpiper 74, short-billed dowitchers 74, spotted sandpiper 74, stilts, 74, snipes 74, tumstones 74, Wilson's phalaropes 74,
shortnose batfish 48
shortnose sturgeon 26
shrews 69
    pygmy 84
shrimp (prawns) 47
shrub-carr 78
shrubs 66
Siberia 6
sifaka, diadem 56
Silk Road 10
Silphinae 5
Silurian period 54
silver hatchetfish 48
Singapore 86
Siproeta stelenes biplagiata 63
sirenoidea 67
skates 47, 54, 73
skipjack tuna 45
skunks 3, 12, 49, 75, 90
sloth moth 2
sloths 2, 61
    three-toed 2, two-toed 60
slugs 44, 71, 84
snails 4, 44, 71
snakes 2, 3, 14, 61, 62, 75, 85
    desert 75, garter 75, mamba 85, water 75
    poisionous
        vipers 75, 85, elapids 75, 85, rear-fanged 75, 85
snapdragon 29
snipe eel 47
soil mites 84
soils 84
    mineral 84, organic 84
soldier crabs 1
sorghum 33
Sousa chinensis 21
South Africa 17, 42
South Amazon basin 14
South America 1, 2, 4, 9, 14, 28, 31, 33, 37, 40, 45, 46, 52, 55, 57, 60-65, 67, 69, 74, 79, 83, 85, 86
South Georgia 52
South Korea 80
South Pole 52, 70
Southeast Asia 56, 61, 62, 63
southern hemisphere 4, 28, 52, 70, 79
spadefoot toad 15
spagnum mosses 78
Spain 57, 89
spathobathis 54
spearmint 29
spermaceti 46, 88
spermathecae 67
spider webs 76
    bowl and dolly 76, dome 76, orb 76, tangled 76, triangle 76
spiderflower 29
spiderlings 76
spiders 1, 2, 7, 8, 76, 84
    black widow 76, 85, brown recluse 76, fisher 76, garden 1, 76, hunting 76, jumping 76, ladybug 76, lynx 76, ogre-faced stick 76, tarantula 76, tarantula, Mexican red-knee 76, trapdoor 1, 7, varied widow 76, water spider 1, 76, wolf 76
sponges 65
springtails 84
squids 47, 48, 54, 71
squirrels 1, 44, 64, 77

Albert's 77, Eastern gray 64, Eastern gray 64, 77, flying 44, 64, 77, fox 77, ground 77, red 77, tree 64, 77, Western gray 77
Sri Lanka 57
Stanella coeruleoalba 21
starfish 48, 72, 85
    Eastern 72
stegosaurus 18
Steiff, Margarete 4
Stenella coeruleoalba 88
stickleback 1
stonefish 85
storks 86
strawberry 29
stromatolites 54
Strychnos toxifera 62
succulents 9
sudan grass 33
sugar cane 62
suiformes 33
Sumatra 4, 55, 61, 63, 80
sunflower 29
Suriname 74
Susa, city of 36
Svalbard 89
swamps 78
swans 79
    black 79, black-necked 79, coscoroba 79, mute (European) 79, trumpeter 79, tundra 79, whooper 79
Sweden 66
sweet basil 29
sweet pea 29
Sweet William 29
swordfish 47
Syncaris pacifica 26

T
tadpoles 4, 30
tapir, Malayan 63
Tapirus indicus 63
tarantulas 63, 69, 76, 85
    red-kneed 63
tarsiers 55, 56, 62
Tarsius tarsius 62
Tartars 36
Tasmania 40, 52
Tasmanian devil 40
tawny rajah 60
taxonomic classification 38, 80
taxonomy 55
teak 62
teddy bears 4
termites 2
terrapins 83
Tethys seaway 54
Texas 90
Thailand 3, 4, 80
therapsid 53
theria, marsupials 53
theria, placentals 53
thistle, common 87
thrinaxodon 53

thyme 29
Tibet 57
ticks 35, 69
tides 45, 46
tigers 6, 80
    Balinese 80, Bengal 80, Caspian 80, Indochinese 80, Javan 80, Siberian 6, 80, South China 80, Sumatran, 80
timothy 33
toads 30, 85
    American 30, 84, Arroyo 30, spadefoot 30, Wyoming 26, 30
toco toucan 60
Tohono O'odham Indians 9
Tolypeutes matacus
tomarctus 20, 90
torgos tracheliotus 86
tortoises 83
    Australian snake neck 83, Galapagos giant 83, gopher 83, Matamata 83, Pinta Island 31
transpiration 60
tree fern 81
tree frogs 61
    white-lipped 61
tree shrews 56
    feather-tailed 56
trees 81
    broadleaf 81, coniferous 81, decidious 81
trees, germination 81
trees, needle leaf (conifers) 81
trees, pollination 81
trees, tropical and sub-tropical 81
Triassic period 53, 54
triceratops 19
Trichechus manatus 27
Trichoglossus chlorolepidotus 51
Trichoglossus haematodus 51
Triest I submersible 48
trillium 87
trilophodon 25
tripod fish 48
Tristan de Cunha 52
Tropic of Cancer 60
Tropic of Capricorn 60
tropical hornbill 1
trout 82
    brook 82, brown 82, bull 82, rainbow 82
tsunamis 45
Tuareg tribesmen 15
tulip 29
Tullgren tunnel 84
tuna 47
tundra plants 66
Turkestan Desert 15
    Kara-Kum 15, Kyzul-Kum 15
Tursiops truncatus 21
turtles 14, 41, 54, 68, 75, 78, 83
    freshwater 83
        Matamata, spiny soft-shell 83
    green 27, 41

    land-dwelling 83
        box 83, desert 83
    marine 83
        leatherback 41, 83, loggerhead 83, red-eared terrapin (pond-slider) 83
tylopoda 33
typhus 64
tyrannosaurus rex 19

U
ultrasounds 3
UNESCO 31
ungulates 66
United Arab Emirates 10
United States 7, 14, 26, 59, 64, 69, 74, 85, 86, 87, 90
uplands 78
urchin 48
Utricularia 11

V
Vancouver Island 34
Venezuela 4, 7, 14, 64
venom 75
vent worms 48
vertebrates 53, 73
vibration 75, 76
Victoria Amazonica 63
Victoria, Australia 37, 81
Vietnam 80
violet 29
viper 75
viperfish 48
viruses 7
voles 49, 84
Vombatus 40
vulture, turkey 33
vultures 33, 86
    black 86, king 86, New World 86, nubian 86, turkey 33, 86
    Old World 86
        African white-backed 86, Asian black 86, Asian white-backed 86, bearded 86, Cape griffon 86, Egyptian 86, Eurasian griffon 86, Himalayan griffon 86, hooded, 86, lappet-faced 86, long billed 86, palm nut 86, red-headed (Pondicherry) 86, Ruppells griffon 86, white-headed 86

W
wallabies 40
walruses 4, 70
Waorani Indians 62
warthog 33
wasps 1, 8, 85
water lily 29
waterfowl 78
waves 45
weasels 12, 59, 75, 90
weaverbird 1
weeds 87

annuals 87, biennials 87, perennials 87
weedy seadragons 45
weevils 4, 5
welwitschia 15
West Indes 68
West Indian manatee 27
West Palm Beach, Florida 27
wetlands 74, 76
whale lice 88
whales 21, 41, 45-47, 70, 88, 89
    baleen 88, beaked 88, blue 88, 89, bottlenose 47, bowhead 88, Bryde's 89, finback 47, 88, gray 41, 88, 89, humpback 88, 89, killer (orca) 45, 70, 88, minke 88, 89, porpoises 47, right 88, 89, rorqual 88, sei 88, 89, sperm 46, 47 88, 89, toothed 88, white (beluga) 88, white (narwhal) 88
whaling 89
wheat 33
whitefish 82
white pelican 27
wildebeests 39, 41
wildflowers 87
    meadow and field 87, woodland 87
willow trees 66, 78
wistaria 29
witchcraft 12
wolves 1, 34, 90
    Abyssinian or Ethiopian 90, Arctic 90, gray 26, 90, Mexican 90, red 90, timber or tundra 90
wombat, coarse-haired 40
woodchucks. *See* marmots
woodpecker 1
woolly mammoth 25
World Heritage site 31
worms 63, 84
    annelid 65

X
Xenarthra order 2

Y
Yangtze River 21
yarrow 29
yellow jacket 8
yellowfin tuna 45
Yggdrasil (the "Tree of Life") 22

Z
Zaire 62
Zalophus californianus 70
zebras 39, 41
zinnia 29
ziphiidae family 88
zoantharia 65
zoologists 5, 28
zooplankton 78, 82
Zygocactus 9

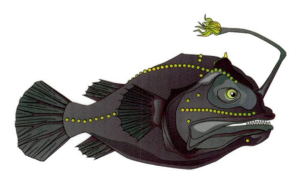